My Search For
B. Traven

By *Jonah Raskin*

The Mythology of Imperialism

Out of the Whale

Underground

Puerto Rico: The Flame of Resistance (co-author)

My Search For
B. Traven

JONAH RASKIN

Methuen, New York

Library of Congress Cataloging in Publication Data

Raskin, Jonah
  My search for B. Traven.

  1. Traven, B.—Biography. 2. Raskin, Jonah,
1942–   —Biography. 3. Authors, Mexican—
20th century—Biography. 4. Authors, American—
20th century. I. Title.
PT3919.T7Z85   813'.52' [B]   80-15834
ISBN 0-416-00741-4
ISBN 0-416-00751-1 (pbk.)

Manufactured in the United States of America by
Fairfield Graphics, Fairfield, Pennsylvania.

First Edition.

Published in the United States of America by
Methuen, Inc.
733 Third Avenue
New York, N.Y. 10017

To the memory of Sam and Max

ACKNOWLEDGMENTS

I want to thank Heddy Yampolsky and Marie Louise Grischkansky for their translations from German to English. Heddy Yampolsky translated Rolf Recknagel's *B. Traven: Beiträge zur Biografie*, B. Traven's *Land des Frühlings*, *Trozas*, *Aslan Norval*, and all issues of *Der Ziegelbrenner*. Marie Louise Grischkansky translated *An das Fraulein von S.* My brother Adam Raskin translated from Spanish to English.

I am grateful to the following people for sharing their memories of Traven: Rudolfo Usigli, Gertrude Duby, Vitorino Trinidad, Dr. Federico Marin, Federico Canessi, Bodil Christensen, Dr. José G. Perralta, Bill Miller, Heddy Yampolsky, Marianne Yampolsky, and Judy Stone. Rosa Elena Luján made Traven's papers available to me and described her life and experiences with her husband.

Paul Chevigny of the New York Civil Liberties Union helped me obtain Traven's CIA, FBI, and State Department files under the Freedom of Information Act. H. G. Pearson and T. L. Rush of the British Home Office in London searched their files on Ret Marut and discovered valuable information.

Over the past years I have been able to present my developing ideas about Traven in print. The following editors opened their pages to me: Allen Young of *The Washington Free Press* and Liberation News Service; Robert Friedman of *University Review;* Greg Mitchell and Peter Knobler of *Crawdaddy;* Michael Nill and Jan Edwards of *Liberation;* Ron Reimers of *Praxis;* and Professor Michael Wilding, editor of the Australian literary anthology *The Radical Reader.*

I have benefitted from discussions and correspondence with Cedric and Mary Belfridge, Max and Ann Geismar, Humberto Quinones, Abbie Hoffman, Herbert Klein, Emily Putter, Michael Strong, Eric Foner.

Adam Raskin, Angela Massimo, and Gus Reichbach, my attorney and literary agent, gave crucial aid step by step in the search for Traven. Danny Moses believed in me and my work when no one else seemed to. And, finally, I want to thank Fred Jordan for his enthusiasm and conviction.

PREFACE

In the early sixties a down-and-out professor of creative writing handed me a paperback copy of *The Treasure of the Sierra Madre* with Humphrey Bogart's picture on the cover, and a rare hardback edition of *The Rebellion of the Hanged,* and told me that B. Traven was "a great proletarian novelist." I took the books home, but I wouldn't touch them because I was totally committed to Henry James and the cultural and aesthetic values he embodied. I wrote a thesis on James and followed my master to Europe. I turned my back on America and bowed down before the gods of the Old World.

And then, in July 1965, I found myself in Paris one evening with not much to do. Walking the streets of the Left Bank, I saw Bogart's photo tacked to a theater billboard and a notice announcing the showing of the film *The Treasure of the Sierra Madre.* I paid the five francs and went inside thinking that if the French liked it, it couldn't be bad.

The film was fantastic. It was bitter and ironic and funny and sentimental all at the same time—the Traven trademarks, I was to learn. Later that night I roamed the Paris streets until I found an open bookstore, and was both amazed and surprised to find *The Treasure of the Sierra Madre* in a cheap paperback edition. I read the novel first in French, and since then in

English about half a dozen times—until I could almost recite it line for line.

At the end of the summer I went back to London and didn't think more about B. Traven. It wasn't until 1967 when I returned to the States and started to write for the "underground press" that I remembered him. I was a Professor of English and American Literature at the State University of New York, Stony Brook, and a close friend was an editor of a radical newspaper. He suggested that I write a literary column introducing hippies, students, the counter culture at large, to novels, poetry, plays. I accepted the job and began turning out weekly pieces, but I made the mistake of celebrating two women novelists, Christina Stead and Doris Lessing. The women on the staff of the paper told me male critics couldn't write about women novelists, that they didn't understand female creativity. I grumbled for a few days and then I wrote an essay about B. Traven and *The Treasure of the Sierra Madre*. Nobody complained about that.

At that time I still didn't know there was a *mystery* about B. Traven. I didn't care about his biography. I just knew that I admired his work, his sense of how all things were turned inside out and upside down, and his craftsmanship too. The books seemed to be innocently told, seemed to be formless, but they were beautifully structured. They were a joy, an inspiration to read.

Then, in the early seventies, I read Traven with a vengeance, and became a kind of walking prophet for B. Traven, telling everyone he was the ancestor of both Che Guevara and Carlos Castaneda because he had gone to live with the Indians in the 1920s, and then had defended guerrilla warfare. I devoured the Hill & Wang editions of his novels, underlining, taking notes, looking for patterns and themes. I wrote an essay entitled "B. Traven: Writer from the Jungle," and published it in *University Review*, along with an old black and white photo of Traven wearing a white shirt, bow tie, and looking very dignified. Still, I wasn't concerned with the riddle of his identity. I didn't mention the word "mystery" once in the article.

From Lawrence Hill I obtained the name and address of B. Traven's widow, Rosa Elena Lujan, sent her the article, and in a few weeks received a warm response. "Traven's life was so fabulous that it always seems or does 'interfere' with his work no matter how hard he always tried to avoid this," Senora Lujan wrote. And then she added, "I appreciate you do not mention 'the mystery' about his life. You understand Traven when you say he was 'a man who suicided the colonialist in himself, and was reborn among the colonized.' Also when you say, 'He was a sailor who wrote, not a writer who sailed.' "

Maybe it was because I didn't mention the mystery that Rosa Elena Lujan liked me. Maybe it was something else. But she did like me as I found out when I went to Mexico City in July 1974. I liked her too; she was very beautiful and very cordial and she was devoted to B. Traven. We agreed that we'd write a biography of B. Traven. I went back to the States, drafted a proposal and found that Lawrence Hill was willing to publish the book.

It took about six months to tie up loose ends, but finally, in January 1975, I went to Mexico. For ten months I listened to Rosa Elena's stories, read Traven's manuscripts, diaries, notebooks, letters, interviewed his friends, visited the places he visited, tried to look at Mexico through his eyes. I went to the jungles of Chiapas, talked to the lumberjacks (the descendants of the men Traven described in *The Rebellion of the Hanged*), and to Vitorino Trinidad, an eighty-five-year-old man who had been Traven's guide in 1926.

I identified with Traven. At first this was a conscious process or choice, a kind of intellectual game. Later, it took on the power of dream and the subconscious. Traven took hold of my imagination. He invaded me. Now I was surrounded by mystery.

I gathered a lot of material about him, but it became apparent that Rosa Elena and I would never write a biography of B. Traven. Rosa Elena fabricated stories about her husband. She was not only a part of the mystery—the leading lady, one might say—but an author of the drama as well. Rosa Elena had not met Traven until he was in his late sixties; he had not been open or honest about his extraordinary life. That was, of course, a source of embarrassment to Rosa Elena. She was unwilling to admit that she did not possess the "truth" about her own "late husband," as she called him. To make up for the lack of information she concocted tales and compounded the mystery. Mystery bred mystery.

In addition, Rosa Elena was a woman of leisure. She had her social obligations and was not prepared nor trained to spend the long hours of hard work necessary to write a book. Though we were supposed to share the tasks equally, I ended up carrying the burden. This I found out while writing the essay "Remembering Traven" and preparing the galleys for *The Kidnapped Saint,* a collection of Traven's stories published by Lawrence Hill in 1975.

The more I dug into Traven's past, the more I understood that Traven did not want a biography. Rather, he craved anonymity. He had constructed his life in such a way as to make it impossible to write a biography. He had burned papers, dropped false clues, told lies. In our age of celebrities, Traven's behavior was bizarre. I found it so, and yet it was also refreshing. I admired the B. Traven who rejected fame, who didn't want to appear on television, or see his name in lights. Most of us writers today are greedy for literary attention, but B. Traven wanted to be left alone. It wasn't an act or a gimmick, it was a genuine rejection of the fame industry that manufactured personalities and then dumped them a week, a month, or a year later, when a new personality came off the assembly line.

In the autumn of 1975 I said goodbye to Rosa Elena and came home to the States. For two years I wrestled with myself. I had boxes of notes and I had a mind packed with images and memories. Traven still haunted me. And so did Rosa Elena, her family, all the people I met in Mexico. I decided to record my experiences, to describe what I had learned, and what was still unknown about Traven. Here is my journey, my search. It is not literary criticism in the conventional sense, but I intend it to introduce you to B. Traven's novels, from *The Death Ship* (1926) through *The Bridge in the Jungle* (1928) to *Macario* (1949). I want to show how life and art, criticism and creation, merge; how Traven, and Mexico, are a part of my being. For me Traven is alive. I hope that I have been able to convey that feeling in these pages.

PART ONE

"The vague, the mysterious meant more to me than a possibly prosaic explanation."

"If I had never tried bluffing at some critical occasions in my existence on earth I would have lost my life long, long ago."

"The only real defense civilized man has against anybody who bothers him is to lie."

—B. Traven, the first two quotations from
The Cotton Pickers (1925), the last from
The Death Ship (1926)

1

I signed the register: name, address, occupation, nationality. The clerk handed me a cast-iron key and mumbled my room number. I couldn't understand him, but when I asked him to repeat what he had said he just pointed to the stairs. I dropped the key into my coat pocket, picked up my suitcase, and walked up the dark stairway.

There was no light in the corridor and only the thinnest stream of light from the street lamp. I struck a match and looked at the first door. There were no numbers on it or above it, but the word "IXTAL"—possibly a lodger's name. Other doors were identified by initials or pictures torn from old magazines.

Someone coughed. I lit another match and held it above my head. An Indian woman was mopping the tile floor. She coughed again and pointed to a shadow on the wall.

"*Aqui, senor,*" she said.

"*Gracias,*" I answered.

"*Las llaves son viejas,*" the Indian woman explained. She rose from the floor, pushed the door gently, and flicked the switch. A dim bulb above the bed cast shadows into the corners. Now I could see that the keyhole was plugged with a piece of wood, that it could neither be locked nor unlocked. It could only be swung back and forth on two heavy, cast-iron hinges.

In the center of the room was a cot with a thin, moldy green blanket, and a mosquito net stabbed with holes. A chest leaned against the stucco wall, its legs ready to collapse at a moment's notice. The room was precisely what I wanted, what B. Traven would have taken. There were no tourists, no room service, no hot water, no wall-to-wall carpeting in the hotel. It was for Mexicans, old men and old women, travelers from the countryside on business in the capital.

Remember the Oso Negro, the hotel B. Traven describes in *The Treasure of the Sierra Madre:*

> The Hotel Oso Negro would not have been much of a hotel back home. Even here, in the republic, where good hotels are rare, it would not be classed among the decent ones. Just a kind of cheap lodging house, it was.
>
> The hotel never closed, and the clerks had a busy time. There was not a half-hour day or night when there was not at least one patron to be called because he had to go to work. Few tourists stopped in this hotel, and if they did, it was mostly by mistake and they went back home telling the world what a dirty country the republic was.

It had taken many hours of careful searching, but I had finally found a hotel that came close to matching Traven's description. It was the Hotel del Bosque, the "Hotel of the Woods." The paint on the sign had peeled and all you could read was Hotel   que.

It was dusk. I propped the bench against the door to ensure a modicum of privacy, and stretched out on the hard cot. Two thin mattresses were covered with a mangy blanket; there were no sheets and no pillow cases.

Through the wall I heard the crackle of a radio. My next-door neighbor was stamping his feet in time to the music. The tune was familiar but the words sounded strange. I put my ear to the cool, stucco wall and listened carefully. It was rock 'n' roll, the Rolling Stones' "Paint It Black," but it was sung in Spanish; and in this Latin rendition turned from an angry, bitter song to a gentle ballad, almost a lullaby.

I tore off a few sheets of *Excelsior,* stuffed them into my pocket, and walked to the end of the hall. The Indian woman was still on her hands and knees mopping the tile floor. With the corridor in darkness I had no way of knowing whether it was clean or not. She seemed able to detect dirt blindfolded. There were two doors: one for the toilet, the other for the shower. The shower cost fifty centavos extra and with the water rationing could only be used for an hour in the morning and an hour again in the evening. There was no window and no electric light so I left the door open. The toilet was an ancient contraption; there was no seat and, as I had expected, no toilet paper. That was a luxury. The floor was covered with a thin layer of foul water, and the battered straw basket was overflowing with soiled newspapers. I pulled the chain; the waters roared and the level of slime rose a fraction of an inch.

Back in the room I locked my suitcase, shoved it under the bed, and plodded down the dark stairs. In the lobby two men were drinking Carta Blanca and watching *Kojak.* I recognized the program; it was six months old by United States standards but the hottest new show in Mexico. There was also a small cafe in the hotel, and though a woman stood behind the counter ready to serve supper, the stools were empty—evidently a judgment on her cooking. I decided to try my luck at one of the restaurants along the street.

"Hay comida china en el barrio?" I asked. The desk clerk seemed annoyed by my question. He tilted his head to one side, deliberated a moment, and answered, "No, there's no chink food here. You'll have to go to the center of town."

Outside there were only a few street lamps. Mounds of dark earth, pyramid-shaped, had cracked the pavement, and huge blocks of cement arranged in layers, like a cake, threatened to collapse against the Hotel Que. There were deep pools of dark water and the sound of buzzing mosquitoes. I leapt across the stream that flowed down the embankment, then trudged through the mud. A few blocks away a bright light glowed. I headed toward it, and as I got closer smelled charcoal-broiled beef.

A wooden platform had been carelessly thrown down in the midst of the mud. Two cooks, wearing white hats and aprons drenched in grease and spattered with fat, flipped steaks over an open fire. Overhead was a large green and white umbrella, propped up by four thick wooden posts. Under the umbrella, colored bulbs, strung together like Christmas decorations, offered meager light. About a dozen men were eating—mostly workers from the construction project underway. The highway was cutting across the city and the old neighborhood was being torn down.

One diner looked up from the table. He had a gold-plated buck tooth, and a cigarette tucked behind an ear. I paused a moment deliberating whether or not to eat here when the cook made up my mind for me. He handed me a menu and offered me a seat. The menu was handwritten on brown paper so wrinkled and stained that I couldn't read it, though I could see the prices. Everything was either five or six pesos and I figured I was 20–25 pesos hungry.

In a few minutes the food was ready. I wasn't given a knife or fork, but a handful of toothpicks and paper napkins. On the plate were four small steaks. By North American standards they weren't steaks at all. Each one was about the size of my palm and about as thick as my thickest fingernail—maybe two ounces of beef.

The steaks looked exactly alike. I was hungry but I didn't want to bite into them yet. I stared at them unable to figure out the difference between them. Why did one steak cost a peso more than another? I called the cook and told him that he had made a mistake. He looked deeply offended. If I had complained to the head chef at an exclusive French restaurant in New York he wouldn't have been more indignant than that Mexican chef staring at my plate. Couldn't I see? Two of the steaks had a thin strip of fat; they were six pesos each. The other two steaks had no fat and they were five pesos.

6

"You have to pay for fat," he said. "Isn't it the same in the States? Everyplace fat is more. I know you Americans eat steaks as big as your eyes, and we have big eyes too—but, *senor,* we can't afford to satisfy them."

I picked up a lean steak, placed it carefully inside a warm tortilla, added a *cebolla* blackened by the fire, a little salt and *salsa,* and took a bite. Delicious! The best steak I have ever eaten. The cook watched the expression on my face, dismissed me with a "humph," and returned to the charcoal broiler. My four "steaks," *cebollas,* and beer cost 25 pesos 50 centavos—a little over $2.00.

I walked back to the hotel, once again leaping across the puddles, and scaling the mounds of dirt. In the lobby the television was still on, though no one was watching. I made my way upstairs in pitch darkness, my feet guiding me.

I wanted to read in bed, but the light was so dim that the only way I could see the words on the page was if I stood on the mattress directly under the bulb. Imagine standing *up* in bed to read a book.

I wrapped myself—with my clothes on for warmth—in the moldy blanket and thought of Traven's arrival in Mexico City fifty years earlier. I wondered where he had lived, and how the city had looked then, shortly after the end of the revolution. I wondered why Traven had never, except for two short stories, written about Mexico City and its inhabitants. He lived here and yet he chose not to write about it. Traven's Mexico City was a mystery.

Traven's New York I could see. He described it enthusiastically in *The Death Ship:* the Hudson River spilling into the Atlantic Ocean, the island of Manhattan, the elegant "sheiks" of the 1920s, promenading down Broadway with their "sumptuous babes dressed up like chorus-line queens"; the workers in Union Square waving red flags and dreaming of paradise in a far-off place called Russia; the brutal boxers and the wild crowds of Madison Square Garden, cheering as though this was the modern Roman Colosseum; Ellis Island and the deportation of sinister, criminal types.

7

Traven's New York was firmly lodged in my imagination. So was his Tampico; he had described it in *The Cotton Pickers* and *The Treasure of the Sierra Madre*. I saw the docks, the port, the oil tankers, the hotels that threatened to collapse into the harbor, the crowded noisy Chinese restaurants, the bars, whorehouses, and gambling dens—all tainted with the smell of oil. I saw the seedy characters of the streets, panhandling, picking pockets, throwing dice, looking for a free meal or a job, and always keeping an eye out for the policeman's club.

But Traven's Mexico City I couldn't see. I could only *imagine* how it might have been: in the city underworld—cops and criminals chasing each other down crooked alleys; in the cold dark churches—candles flickering and incense burning; or in the working class barrios—ragged children, filth, and garbage rotting in the streets. Traven was silent about Mexico City. He had not revealed its secrets as he had revealed the secrets of the jungle.

I couldn't get very far imagining Traven's Mexico City. Nor could I fall asleep. I was clawed by bedbugs, *pulgas,* bitten by mosquitoes. They were embedded in the blankets and the mattress, and they attacked from the air. I put on my socks and shoes and went outside for a walk.

The night was quiet. Outside the hotel it was dark, but on the horizon I could see the light and the heat generated by the more prosperous sections of the city. I descended the hill listening to the trees sway in the wind. At the bottom I saw a large, rectangular area enclosed by a high chain fence with barbed wire at the top. A column of smoke rose from the very bottom of the pit and climbed slowly toward the black sky. The fire was dying out; there was still red embers at the center, but at the edges only cold, gray ash.

Then I saw a hand reach out from the shadows and toss three or four twigs on the hottest coals. They caught fire and illuminated the hand, a wool blanket, and the man's sullen face. He had black eyes, thick hair, and curly sideburns. I didn't think he had heard or seen me, but in a teasing tone of voice he suddenly asked, "Come to take my things, have you?

8

A thief?" Then he chuckled and invited me to join him by the fire. He extended his hands over the flames and rubbed them together. I noticed that despite all the mud his trousers and shirt were absolutely clean. He lifted a blackened pot and offered me *frijoles negros,* the remains of his supper. They didn't look appetizing and neither did the drink he poured into a tin cup.

"It'll make me sick," I said. "The water has germs." The Indian explained that he drank as much of the water as often as he wanted and had never been sick. He couldn't understand why my stomach, my intestines could be so different from his. After all, we were both humans. Why couldn't we both drink the same water?

He was a ditchdigger from a small town in Chiapas, fifteen hundred miles away. He had been working here on this job for six months, had even built himself a shack. Inside, a pile of newspapers reached the ceiling. There was an empty Coca-Cola bottle, a kerosene lamp with a rag for a wick, and a large bag of white rice some of which had spilled on the floor. To live in the shack he had to pay an official ten pesos a week because the materials for the building, the scraps of wood and metal, were government property.

"Why don't you live in the hotel?" I asked.

"Only the big foremen live there," he said. Most of his words were Spanish, but occasionally he used an Indian word or expression I didn't understand. "And even if I had the money I wouldn't take a hotel room. My family is going to join me here. This will be our home. A hotel can never be a home." He took a sip from the cup, rinsed his mouth, and spat the water into the fire.

"Why have you come here?" he asked.

"To write a book about a man named B. Traven," I said. "Ever hear of him?"

"No."

"You should read his books."

"Can't read. My boys can, but I never learned. Does he live up there too?"

9

"Who?" I asked.

"This Traven."

"No, no, he's dead," I said.

"Then how will you learn about him?"

"I'm going to read his books, papers, letters, talk to his friends, family, his wife."

"He must have been a very important man," the ditchdigger said. "to have so many books and papers. I don't have a single one. Tell me, where does his wife live?"

"Near Chapultepec Park," I said, pointing to the light from the south.

"Oh, yes, it's very nice there," he said. "Much nicer than it is here. They have fine hotels in the Zona. Say, *senor,* could you lend me a few pesos just for a week? I can pay you back when I get my wages."

I gave him a five-peso note, then walked up the hill. By comparison with the ditchdigger's shack the Hotel Que now seemed the very height of elegance.

2

Before the sun rose the sound of the machines woke me. I opened the mahogany shutters and peered down the hill. Bull-dozers shoved the earth into mounds, trucks carted it away, and a crew of men with picks and shovels raced behind trying desperately to keep pace. My shoulders were covered with mosquito bites, and the bedbugs had inflicted bright, red marks on my belly. I was still tired but too nervous to sleep any more. I put on a clean white shirt and cotton trousers, brushed my hair, collected my notebooks and pens.

I walked down the Paseo de la Reforma, the broad tree-lined avenue that was built in imitation of the Champs-Elysees and for that reason was disliked by B. Traven. Anything modeled after European styles and fashions he detested. Mexico ought to preserve its own native traditions, he argued, and not import or copy foreign ways.

The sidewalks sparkled, the window panes glittered. Offices and banks were ready for business. I looked at the photographs in the movie houses: *The Exorcist* and *The Great Gatsby* were the main attractions. Next door, the book store displayed the latest Harold Robbins novel. At the intersection of Revolucion I had coffee and a *bollo*. I bought a lottery ticket from a young barefoot girl, and settled in my chair to read *El Dia*, the liberal pro-government newspaper. The headlines announced new discoveries of oil in Tabasco and Chiapas, and the editorial writers speculated that the Mexican economy would improve, that relations with the United States would enter a new era of cooperation.

Now, Reforma was congested with traffic, and the sidewalks were crowded with people on their way to work. I strolled leisurely until I reached the corner of Rio Mississippi and Rio Lerma. In this neighborhood all the streets were named after the rivers of the world. In the adjoining neighborhood the streets were named after famous scientists, philosophers, and writers. My favorite intersection was "Tolstoi y Leibnitz" because, ironically, it boasted the best pizza parlor in Mexico City.

The corner of Lerma and Mississippi had once been elegant, and there were still old dignified houses, but it was becoming shabby, commercial, noisy. I stood in the shade and took in the scene. A *tienda*, a small grocery and liquor store, was situated at the intersection. Next to it, a beauty salon with rows of hair dryers, and then Numero 61: the house where Traven had lived the last twelve years of his life with Rosa Elena Lujan. Traven liked the neighborhood, and especially the name Rio Mississippi. He had chosen it above Rio Amazonas, Rio Rhin, Rio Danubio. Traven's house was a three-story building; the drab green paint was peeling, and the windows were streaked with soot. Across the street, a three-masted clipper ship had been transported from the ocean and turned into a bar and discotheque. I was quite sure that Traven wouldn't have approved.

In the center of the Rio Mississippi workmen were digging up the earth and removing the tall palm trees. Mississippi was a two-way street, with a narrow strip of grass that ran down the center. The grass was also being removed. The street was soon to be one-way. The birds had been dislodged from their old homes in the palm trees and were now perched on the ship's masts and on the top balcony of Traven's house.

On the sidewalk in front of the *tienda* was a newspaper kiosk and a juice stand. A young girl sliced and squeezed oranges by

hand, and threw the rinds into a wooden crate in the gutter.
There was a long line of customers; some took the orange juice
straight, others asked for raw eggs to be added. Under the
awning of the *tienda* an old white-haired woman sold roses,
and next to her a young man operated a knife and scissor
sharpener that was attached to a bicycle. All he had to do was
pedal and the grindstone spun round and round.

I rang the bell. Soon a voice behind the door asked, "*Quien
es?*" The mail slot opened and two dark eyes peered up at me.
The lock was unlocked and a small green door in the larger
green gate opened, and a short, round woman in a white
apron bowed slightly and said, "*Pase usted, senor.*" I stepped
over the metal bar at the bottom, bent my head, and entered
the cool courtyard. There was a stone patio and two black
steps leading to a carved wooden door.

The woman escorted me into the library and disappeared.
It was cool and quiet. There were books on three walls, from
the ceiling halfway down to the carpeted floor, two comfortable arm chairs, a table with a black telephone, and a
Mexico City telephone directory bound in a leather case. I
opened the cover and noted the name "Hal Croves" scrawled
across a sheet of paper. I looked under Hal Croves but there
was no listing, and then under B. Traven, but there was no B.
Traven in the telephone directory either.

There was a sketch of Traven on the wall. I had seen a
photograph of him as a much younger man, wearing a hat
tilted playfully to the side, a bow tie, white shirt, and dark
jacket. The sketch on the library wall was probably done
thirty-five or forty years later. Here Traven wore no hat; his
face was thinner, gaunter. I could see the rage round the
nostrils and I could almost hear him breathe, his lungs expand, then expel the air suddenly. His eyes were intent; he
was watching something, or someone, catching every detail of
activity.

On one wall below the bookcases were three black and
white drawings of peasants and soldiers armed with rifles and
machetes. They were illustrations for Traven's novel *The Re-*

13

bellion of the Hanged. The center sketch—it was reminiscent of Goya's "Disasters of War" series—portrayed a blindfolded man, his hands and feet bound, hanging from a mahogany tree.

On the opposite wall were Aztec artifacts of serpents and dogs, and a bronze cast of a pair of hands—*his* hands, I assumed. They had turned green; the fingers were long and thin, the knuckles bony, and the veins thick. They looked like the hands of a man accustomed to toil.

Two small dogs entered the library. The shaggy terrier rubbed his neck along the back of my calves; the poodle sniffed me cautiously, turned up its nose, and curled up in the corner. I liked the terrier. He sat on his hind legs and watched me take Traven's books from the shelf, turn the pages, inspect the bindings, check the quality of the paper.

All Traven's books were here—including the rare *Land in Springtime* and *Letters to Fraulein von S.*—and in almost every edition. There were books in English, German, Spanish, Dutch, Norwegian, Russian, Hungarian, Arabic, French, Japanese, and a few languages I had never even seen before. There were the beautiful Axel Holmstrom editions published in Stockholm, and there were cheap paperback editions from Hong Kong, Paris, and London.

On most title pages he was identified as B. Traven, but in some editions he was Ben Traven, Benno Traven, Bruno Traven, Benito Traven, depending on the whim or inclination of the publisher. The titles varied, too, depending on the language, date, and place of publication. *The Rebellion of the Hanged* was entitled *Modesta*, after the book's heroine, in a Scandanavian edition. *The Cotton Pickers* was *The Vagabond* in one edition and *The Wobbly* in another. *March to the Monteria* was *March into the Empire of Mahogany* in a German edition (a better title, I think); and *Midnight Call* became *Bandit Doctor* (also, I think, a title that comes closer to Traven's own intentions).

The shelves contained rare editions that collectors would have paid hundreds, perhaps thousands of dollars to obtain:

14

the Gutenberg Book Guild editions published in Berlin in the 1920s, the British editions published by Jonathan Cape, the Alfred Knopf editions issued in the 1930s, and the Mexican editions translated by Esperanza López Mateos, sister of the former President of Mexico Adolfo López Mateos. Some of the books claimed to be translated from the German, but other editions of the same books gave no indication that they were translated from German or any other language. One rumor I heard in New York publishing circles was that Traven translated his own manuscripts, but sent them to his publishers with the explanation that they were translated by "Eric Sutton." Attempts had been made to locate Mr. Sutton but he was nowhere to be found.

A few editions had no copyright and were stamped "Pirated Edition." Traven had written comments in a few books. On the title page of the 1933 Gutenberg Book Guild edition of *Government* I read, "Every word in this book is directed against dictatorship. It was seized and burned by the storm troopers under order of Goebbels." On the next shelf were the Gutenberg editions of Traven's books that were published in Zurich, Switzerland, after the Nazis raided the Berlin offices. The Gutenberg Book Guild was a socialist publishing house and a workers' book club. The Nazis destroyed the press, arrested the editors, burned the books.

I thumbed through a ragged paperback entitled *Stories by the Man Nobody Knows*, a clever title for a collection of Traven short stories, but one which must have irritated the author. On the last page of the last story—"The Story of a Bomb," a tragicomic tale about Indian miners and a bizarre dynamite explosion—Traven had drawn a pen through half a dozen sentences. Below them he noted, "I never wrote these words. They were added by an editor without my permission."

Depending on which dust jacket I read, there was a different version of B. Traven's life. The Robert Hale British edition of *March to Caobaland* noted:

In a short biography of B. Traven recently published

it was stated that the "B." does not stand for Bruno, Ben, Benno, Berick, Bendrich. . .Of the 30-odd photographs published during the last twenty years in American, Mexican, and European magazines not one is authentic. B. Traven was born in 1900 of American-born parents of Norwegian descent. He lives on his ranch in Chiapas, Mexico. He never receives visitors.

I had the sneaking suspicion that Traven himself was the author of those lines, and that his intention was to throw literary detectives off the track, and to generate more mystery. I pulled the Penguin edition of the same book from the shelf and read on the flyleaf:

For more than forty years the identity of B. Traven was the subject of international conjecture and legend. He had a readership of millions; the film of his best-selling novel *The Treasure of the Sierra Madre* won an Academy Award; yet he shunned publicity with the vehemence with which most writers pursue it. Wild speculation held him to be at various times a fugitive Austrian archduke, a leper, or an arctic explorer. In 1967 an American journalist claimed that she had spoken to Traven, now a frail and deaf man living in Mexico. This mysterious writer died in Mexico City in 1969 at the age of 79.

The American Hill & Wang edition claimed:

B. Traven's will, written on March 4, 1969, three weeks before his death in Mexico City, states that Traven Torsvan Croves was his real name, that he was born in Chicago, Illinois, on May 3, 1890, the son of Burton Torsvan and Dorothy Croves, and that he had used as noms de plume B. Traven and Hal Croves. . .By the 1960s, Traven, a septuagenarian living quietly in Mexico City, could look back on a writing career that had seen his books published in over thirty countries and read by millions. But when he died in 1969 he was still an obscure figure in the country of his birth.

Each dust jacket offered a different story. The number and variety of conflicting reports was unbelievable—and infuriating, since it was my job to disentangle the web of confusion, to write the biography of a man who defended his right to lie, who admitted his preference for the mysterious over the precise, and who confessed that he had been a big bluffer all his life. I don't know why, but I was confident that I could solve the mystery. I would clear everything up in a few weeks, perhaps a month, and return to New York.

3

Rosa Elena entered the library talking as fast as she was walking. I didn't catch the beginning of her sentence but I heard "...seriously ill...no one else...but I'm glad to see that you've already started to work." She seized the copy of *Stories by the Man Nobody Knows* and thumbed through the pages. "You see how they mutilated Traven's work," she said. "He always brought his books to a swift conclusion, but some publisher added these lines because he thought they explained the ending. Well, Traven didn't want everything *explained* like that." The poodle emerged from behind the chair and the terrier curled up at my feet.

"These are the Skipper's dogs," Rosa Elena said. (Sometimes she referred to him as "the Skipper," sometimes as B. Traven, or as "my husband," or "BT," or Croves.)

Rosa Elena looked casual, informal. She was wearing black slacks, fluffy green slippers, and a white cashmere sweater. Her hair was short and black, combed straight back so that it highlighted her forehead. Her complexion was dark; she looked more Indian than Spanish, and a lot younger than I had expected her to be.

"Gigi is very sophisticated," Rosa Elena said, petting the poodle. "And Tabasco—you know one of our states is named

Tabasco and the Skipper thought. . ." She broke off her sentence and instructed the plump woman to set down the silver tray. *"Gracias,* Petra," she said. The woman tried to curtsy, but obviously didn't have much training and botched it. Rosa Elena poured coffee into two miniature cups, and as she held the silver sugar and cream containers added, "The Skipper took his black. I have a sweet tooth but suit yourself."

Rosa Elena Lujan and I had been corresponding with one another for about a year, discussing the possibility of writing a biography of B. Traven. Finally, in January 1975 she had written: "Come to Mexico immediately. We'll begin writing. Money is no problem. There are royalties from Traven's novels and I will share what I have with you." I cabled a reply, "Will arrive tomorrow," then packed a suitcase and a crate of my copies of Traven's books, books that I had already carted three thousand miles, from New York to San Francisco.

Next, I needed a visa, but to obtain a visa I needed a passport or a birth certificate. Unfortunately, I had neither, not on hand. So I tried to obtain what the consulate said was the next best thing—a notorized statement in which I said that I was born in the United States, that I was an American citizen, and that I had never been a citizen of any other country. I typed up an original and a carbon and walked down Mission Street, going from notary to notary. There wasn't a shortage of them—and yet I was refused in every single place! One woman shouted, "I don't *know* you're an American citizen, or that you were born here. The fact that you speak good English doesn't prove a goddamn thing! Dozens of illegal aliens walk in here off the street every day, dressing and talking like you. So how do I know who you really are and where you really come from, honey?"

"But I want to go *to* Mexico," I explained. "I'm not trying to enter the country illegally, I'm trying to leave it legally."

"Surely you're planning to come back," she said.

"Yes, of course," I said.

"Well, then, it's out of the question. If you were leaving and never returning I'd notarize your statement like that, but since you say you're coming *back* I just can't. Might lose my license!"

Finally, I went to a lawyer on Nob Hill and explained my predicament. Fortunately, he had read Judy Stone's articles about B. Traven that had appeared in *Ramparts* in the late sixties, and he also remembered the plot of *The Death Ship*. The Nob Hill lawyer (he had made his money defending marijuana merchants) found my tale amusing. He asked his secretary to notarize my statement free of charge and wished me the best of luck.

In the library on the Rio Mississippi, Rosa Elena showed me the notes she had prepared for the introduction she was writing to a new collection of Traven's stories entitled *The Kidnapped Saint*. The notes were good. They described their life together; very tantalizing.

"We'll work together," Rosa Elena said, beaming. "It's the best way to learn about my husband. I will tell you everything, *everything*, more than enough to write four or five books. You will know *all* the secrets—and, remember, there have been others before you, that no good Heidemann from *Stern*, William Weber Johnson from *The Los Angeles Times*, and Judy Stone from that Hearst paper in San Francisco. You know, Traven never liked Hearst."

"Didn't like Hearst, eh?" I mumbled. "Maybe I should start taking notes?"

"I couldn't trust Heidemann with my eyes open," Rosa Elena continued, oblivious of my interruption. "He made up the most rotten stories about the Skipper to boost the circulation of *Stern*. Honestly! And he took a manuscript of Traven's that rightfully belongs to me. Outrageous! Remind me to take care of that little matter. We must get it back! As for Johnson, he insisted on the facts, and as you very well know 'the facts' can't reveal the *real* life of a man as unusual as Traven." Now, for the first time, I noticed that Rosa Elena pronounced Traven as though it were a Spanish name: she rolled the *r*, the *a* was hard, and the *v* became a *b*. *Trrahben* she called him.

"Judy Stone had the best chance to write the biography

20

when she interviewed Croves in '66, but Judy didn't know the right questions to ask. Finally, Croves turned off his hearing aid and let Judy go on yapping to herself. Of course, she wrote her articles anyway, reporters always do, and naturally they were one-sided. It's really too bad! I tried to help her, and Croves did enjoy *Ramparts*. It appealed to his radical, muckraking spirit but. . .he didn't even want to read the issue with Judy's article in it."

Even as Rosa Elena spoke I wondered what I was going to do. I couldn't be a sensationalist like Heidemann; I couldn't make up stories; nor could I insist on the facts as Johnson had. And how would I know not to ask the wrong questions, as Judy Stone had done?

"I have read your book about Kipling and Conrad," Rosa Elena continued. She certainly knew how to flatter me and I smiled appreciatively.

"As for Conrad, my husband didn't like his sea stories. He would tell me that the real heroes of the sea weren't the captains who appear in Conrad's books, but the working men who shovel the coal and scrub the decks."

While Rosa Elena was talking I was scratching. The *pulgas* must have jumped to Tabasco and nestled in his fur too, because he was scratching with his paw.

"Where are you staying?" Rosa Elena asked suddenly, with more than casual interest. I think some of the *pulgas* had landed on her as well.

"Over on Melchor Ocampo," I said.

"But there are no tourist hotels in that section," she said.

"I know. That's the idea. I wanted to stay in the kind of place that, er, your late husband B. Traven writes about in *The Cotton Pickers* and *The Treasure of the Sierra Madre*."

"Well, just because he wrote about them doesn't exactly mean that he did those precise things, or that you have to do them either," Rosa Elena said, scratching the back of her neck.

"But I thought that the books were autobiographical," I said.

"Yes, of course they are. Traven never ever made up stories. He most certainly lived in hotels like the Oso Negro, where you slept on a cot in a cold courtyard for fifty centavos a night, but he didn't like those hotels, and as soon as he had the money from writing stories he got out of Tampico, went to Chiapas, lived in Acapulco. He was in and out of Mexico City all the time, but he preferred the countryside. He wanted to be close to the land, to the earth. Chiapas and Guerrero were his real homes. You know my husband's ashes were spread in Ocosingo by airplane. You'll have to go there and talk to Vitorino Trinidad, Traven's guide in *la selva*. The last eight years of his life Traven and I lived here, and as you can see this is no rundown hotel. He liked to live well and that's no crime.

"For the time being you can sleep in Malu's room. But you must shower and change your clothes immediately, or there will be *pulgas* all over the house."

Upstairs I showered in steaming hot water, then changed into a white silk shirt and gray cotton trousers with wide cuffs that had been Traven's.

Rosa Elena gave me a tour of the first, or, as the Mexicans call it, the "ground floor"(our second floor becoming their first floor). The living room was quite different from the library. There was a beautiful Chinese silk tapestry on the wall, a painted wood carving of a church saint, and an oil painting of Rosa Elena, perhaps thirty years younger, wearing a black satin evening gown that revealed her soft, round shoulders and curving bosom.

"That was painted when I lived with my first husband Carlos Montes de Oca," she said. "He was a real playboy, liked to drink, gamble, and party. We had some good times, but it was such a boring, empty life."

On the walls in the dining room three small Diego Rivera sketches were hung. I walked across the room, and a woman literally followed in my footsteps. As I later learned, her name was Herme, and she was the housemaid. Herme was compulsive about cleanliness, so much so that she soon made my life miserable. She loathed dirt, loathed everyone who brought

22

dirt into the house. Now she scowled at me as though I had thoroughly soiled the room.

"How could Traven live with her?" I asked.

"Oh, Herme didn't work for us while the Skipper was alive," Rosa Elena said.

"But you had servants, didn't you?"

"Yes, of course. The Skipper liked having servants. You will, too, because they give you more time for writing."

Behind the glass doors was a sheltered patio, then a small, well-tended lawn, a few plants, and an immense bust of Traven mounted on a cement block. The yard was too small for him. Here he was confined; he needed a large open plaza, or a clearing in the jungle, not a backyard garden.

"The Skipper spent a lot of time here," Rosa Elena said. "He played with Gigi, Tabasco, and Caroline, his pet monkey —that is, until she fell in love with our neighbor and ran away with him." Rosa Elena led me into the kitchen. Petra was singeing chicken wings and legs on the gas burner, peeling the thick yellow skin, and pulling out the feathers the butcher had missed.

We sat down in the breakfast room. Old issues of *Excelsior* were piled in front of the windows, and fat flies buzzed against the panes. The tablecloth was checked. There was a portrait of a mother and child on the wall.

"I want you to know everything about Traven," Rosa Elena said. "I have no secrets from you." She put on a pair of broken eyeglasses and offered me a chocolate. "I was not the first woman in his life, not by a long shot, but I'm not the jealous type and so I'll tell you all about the others. In Germany before the war he lived with Elfriede Zielke. I've seen her picture; she had a beautiful face and body but Traven told me she wasn't very bright. They had a daughter and she is living in East Germany today. When we went to Berlin in '59 my husband refused to see her. You see, he denied that he had a daughter, didn't ever want children. No—no children for him! He had had such very bad experiences with his own parents that he didn't want to bring a child into this world.

"Then, after Elfriede came Irene Mermet. Sometimes she called herself 'Alda.' Like him, she had many aliases. Irene was also an actress and one of those European anarchist types. She wasn't very attractive, but she had a very good mind. When Traven met her she had no family, and she was in trouble with the police for debts. I think he liked her because she was an orphan and an artist like himself. Anyway, they lived together during the war. Then in '24 they came to Mexico, but Irene didn't like it here, couldn't adjust to our ways, so she returned to Germany and went to university. That was better for her, I think.

"And then there was Esperanza. Esperanza was a Communist, in the Party, and Traven fought with her like cat and dog because he didn't like those political ideas. But he respected her, thought she was a great woman. They were very close and Esperanza would have liked to marry him, but Traven refused. He didn't want to marry, and frankly she wasn't his type. Esperanza, well, she went to the other side when he rejected her; she became a lesbian, but she married Roberto Figueroa, just to stop people from gossiping about her. She had no sex with him because he was on the other side too. I hope you're not that type."

"No, no, not me," I said.

"Well, I'm glad to hear that. Esperanza went on year after year, tormented. And she was in physical pain from a mountain climbing accident. She lived on aspirin and then on much heavier drugs too, and finally she committed suicide. That was shortly before I went to work for Croves."

"Did he blame himself for her death?" I asked.

"I don't think so, and yet long after I met him, he was still sad about Esperanza. Then we decided to live together and get married. Believe me, none of the other women were as close to him as I was. None of them knew what I know about Traven."

4

In the afternoon I paid my bill and moved from the shabby Hotel Que to Malu's elegant room. Her single bed had a brass frame and a gold slipcover, and no *pulgas*. Against the opposite wall was a chest of drawers and a scalloped mirror. I could lie in bed, my head propped up by pillows, and look at the reflection of my face. On my right, beige curtains extended the length of the room; behind the curtains was a wall of glass and a glass door that led onto the balcony. On my left was a closet with sliding doors, six or seven drawers built into the wall, a long rack of dresses, blouses, skirts and, on the floor, two dozen pair of shoes—high-heeled shoes, shoes with pointy toes and black bows—all brightly polished.

The stairway from the first floor arrived in the center room of the second floor. There were more bookshelves, a record player, and a collection of rock 'n' roll albums—Bill Haley and the Comets, Fats Domino, Ray Charles. There were two comfortable couches and a Singer sewing machine. Two days a week an eccentric old woman sat at the machine, or on one of the sofas, mending torn shirts or adjusting hems and waistlines. She was a remarkable seamstress, but an unpleasant person. She had a peculiar habit of staring and laughing without explanation. Rosa Elena complained about her, as she complained about Herme's compulsive cleanliness, but tolerated them both. "After all, we can't do without them," she said.

Rosa Elena's office was also on the second floor and was always locked. The key to the door was on a large key ring with at least a dozen other keys that unlocked other doors, file cabinets, wood chests, and trunks. Rose Elena rarely let the key ring out of her sight. Usually she clutched it in her hand. While she was eating she placed it on the table beside her plate. Still, this preoccupation with keys and locks didn't prevent things from being taken. There was always something missing—a sheet, vase, book—and never an adequate explanation of where they had gone. Periodically Rosa Elena would scold Petra and Herme; for a few days nothing would be missing. Then the disappearances would start again.

The office desk was littered with files, unanswered letters months old, newspaper clippings, and shopping lists. Under this pile was an electric typewriter. The shelves in the office held rare editions of magazines like *Vorwärts, Simplicissimus,* and *Westermann's Monatshefte,* where many of Traven's stories originally appeared in the mid-twenties. Here too were files of the reviews of Traven's books—fifty years of critical notices. On the wall was a charcoal sketch of Traven; his nose was exaggerated, and had the effect of making him look comic.

Across from my bedroom, in the back of the house, a red brick patio overlooked the garden and the statue of Traven. Federico Canessi, the sculptor, had designed the figure so that the eyes watched you, followed you, whether you were above him looking down, or on the ground floor looking directly into his face.

Rosa Elena and I worked mornings and afternoons on the second-floor patio. She had made pages of notes about Traven, and we worked on them together to expand them into the essay that would introduce the new volume of stories, *The Kidnapped Saint.* In our initial conversations in the library and in the breakfast room, Rosa Elena had been open and frank about the women in Traven's life. But working on the introduction she was guarded about Irene Mermet, Elfriede Zielke,

Esperanza López Mateos. She stressed Traven as a family man. The house on the Rio Mississippi was a ship. Traven was "the Skipper," Rosa Elena first mate, Chele the second, Malu the third.

"He loved my two daughters as much as if they were his own," Rosa Elena said. "We took them everywhere we went, had no secrets from them, were an intimate loving family. Traven played games with Chele and Malu. He introduced them to Shakespeare's plays, encouraged them to dress up in old silk and satin rags and recite Lady Macbeth's and Portia's soliloquies."

Rosa Elena insisted that the Indians of Chiapas loved Traven, treated him as a brother, gave him their arrowheads, bows, and pipes as a token of their respect. "And he loved them," she said. "He lived as simply, as starkly as they, slept on the cold, hard ground, wrapped only in his serape, ate beans and rice for breakfast, learned their languages, respected their customs and beliefs."

While talking about the Chamula Indians, Rosa Elena mentioned that she and Traven had eaten magic mushrooms. "It was a very sensual experience," she said. "You'll have to try it. It's very powerful. Of course, drugs weren't new to him. When he was a sailor he traveled to China and smoked opium. Then, in Chiapas, he smoked marijuana with the Indians. But he could concentrate so hard, draw his thoughts together in one spot, that he could imagine anything and make it happen too, without the use of drugs."

"We would play mental telepathy games. The Skipper would be here at work. I would be in town shopping. If he wanted me to bring something special home he would concentrate on that thing. The thought would hit me and I would buy it. It never failed to work. I remember the first time it happened. When I got home he said, 'I'm dying for that brandy.' I hadn't unpacked yet. 'How did you know that I bought brandy?' I asked. 'It was a spur of the moment thing.' Well, the Skipper explained how he communicated the idea of the brandy to me. He had seen the Indians of Chiapas predict the coming of a person or event. Through intense mental effort they could force something that was lost to reappear, exactly where it was supposed to be."

Rosa Elena insisted on including Traven's belief, as she put it, "that the individual story isn't important until it flows into the collective life. Traven shared this belief with the Wobblies and the anarchists, men like Joe Hill. They all felt that there was no personal story worth telling. Traven never wrote only about himself, but about all working people. He had fantastic adventures but he didn't describe them unless he felt they were shared by others."

To celebrate the completion of our project we went to a Chinese restaurant in the Zona Rosa. Rosa Elena recognized a friend sitting alone at a table in the back. His name was Bill Miller and he rose to greet us. Miller was tall and powerfully built. He was a North American and spoke English with a New York accent. We sat down at his table and ordered tequilas and munched on Chinese noodles. Miller had a financial proposal. He had invented, he said, a machine that turned black and white film into color. "Listen, Chelena, now we'll be able to make *The Treasure of the Sierra Madre* into a technicolor spectacular. Think of the bright colors, the lush jungle scenery, the bloody assault on the train! You've seen Bogart in *The African Queen*. He's a million times better in color. We'll improve *Treasure*—and make a pile of money for ourselves too."

"That's a very nice idea, Bill, but I like *Treasure* in black and white, and so did the Skipper. Besides, just now I haven't any money to invest in your crazy schemes." Rosa Elena sipped her tequila and, without taking her eyes from Miller, told me, "Bill and the Skipper were good friends. They used to get drunk together and tell funny stories. Bill fought in Spain against Franco; when he went back to Hollywood the studios told him he had no job. So he came to Mexico. Every week now he has a new scheme to make money. Last week he insisted that we write a screenplay based on Traven's *The Night Visitor*. Next week it will be something else."

28

"Traven would have gone for this idea big," Miller said. "It's ripe, honey, I'm telling you." Miller finished his tequila and ordered another round for all of us.

"When did you meet Traven?" I asked.

" '38," Miller said. "Traven welcomed the veterans of the International Brigades who settled in Mexico, offered to help us financially too. Big-hearted guy! Very generous! We got to know each other. He was a disciplined, thorough bastard, wrote every day. That's the way you've got to work—hard! Traven told me he learned the meaning of hard work harvesting wheat in Nebraska. That was the most back-breaking labor of all, worse than shoveling coal on a death ship."

"Here's to back-breaking labor," Rosa Elena said, clinking her glass against mine and winking at me. "You see the kind of work Bill does best."

Bill Miller wasn't one bit insulted. He called the waiter and ordered food and beer for the three of us—won ton soup, egg rolls, sweet-and-sour pork, beef and broccoli, and shrimp fried rice.

While we were eating Miller and Rosa Elena recollected a series of bizarre incidents about cremations. "A friend of Traven's died in Monterrey," Miller said. "He was cremated and the ashes were shipped by train to Mexico City. We went to the station to pick them up, but unloading the freight car the stupid porter broke the urn and the ashes scattered in the wind. What the hell! I looked at Traven and he looked at me. In the street I found an old jar. We filled it with sand—and sand is what we delivered to the widow, pure Mexican sand."

"The Skipper didn't want his ashes kept in a jar," Rosa Elena said. "He used to tell me he would crawl into the jungle, die alone in peace, and let the animals devour his corpse. You know, Bill, he had a European friend who died in Mexico. After the cremation he mailed the ashes across the Atlantic. The family thought that the ashes were some kind of powdered Mexican soup mixture. The Skipper received a letter saying they had enjoyed the soup very much and wanted to know what it was called. My husband was crazy. He wrote

29

back to say that it was an ancient Aztec recipe invented by Montezuma's chef. It was typical German stupidity, the Skipper said, eating the ashes of their own relative."

I didn't know whether Miller and Rosa Elena were pulling my leg or not. The stories seemed real and yet they were unbelievable at the same time. I had had too many tequilas and beers so that it didn't matter any more. With all the stories, laughter, food, and drink, it wasn't until four that we finished lunch. When the waiter brought the check Miller said he was low on funds and had an important meeting he couldn't afford to miss. "I should have known," Rosa Elena said, picking up the tab. Miller shook my hand earnestly and kissed Rosa Elena on the lips. "Think about that investment idea," he said.

We walked back to the Rio Mississippi and got into the car —a white Mustang—because Rosa Elena wanted to visit her sister. "It's a hot rod for teenagers," Rosa Elena said. "I don't like it. Like my husband, I prefer to walk. You know, he covered Mexico on foot. It's the only way to see a country, he said."

The sister's home was in the most luxurious neighborhood in Mexico City. "We're very different people," Rosa Elena said. "You can't imagine how upset she was when I divorced Carlos and married Traven. It was the first divorce in the family. To this day my sister hates Benito Juárez and wants Díaz to be back in power. Imagine that! My own sister thinks that dictatorship is best for the people. Long, long ago when I explained that I had supported Lázaro Cárdenas for President she told me, 'He's a communist. He'll take away everything we own.' And when the government nationalized the oil, as Traven always wanted to happen, she was terrified that our hacienda would go next. 'After the revolution we'll have to sleep in the same room as our servants,' she said. Just the thought of being close to her maid at night made her sick to her stomach. Now, can you understand what it meant for me to marry Traven? He represented everything my family opposed!"

While Rosa Elena visited the sister in her bedroom, I waited in the living room. It was like being at Versailles. The furniture was Louis Quatorze; I had the feeling that the crowned heads of Europe had gathered here two hundred years ago.

I had wanted to meet this older sister but Rosa´Elena said that would be impossible. "She was a very beautiful woman and now her face is dry and wrinkled. She doesn't allow men to look at her any more. Of course she's not ugly, but she was so used to men kneeling at her feet and worshiping her face that she can't stand them looking at her now, not even for a moment."

5

The parrots had the brightest plumage I had ever seen. There were three of them in three bamboo cages, hanging in the patio of Dr. Federico Marin's house. The feathers were yellow, green, orange, blue—the colors of the jungle in bloom. Dr. Marin, or "Fedde" as Rosa Elena called him (and he called her "Chelena," affectionately), held out his hand and fed the parrots seed. *"Hola que tal?"* he asked each bird.

Dr. Marin was a large, heavy man, though not fat. His hair was sparse and carefully combed. He wore an elegant blue house coat, pleated trousers, and brown slippers. Rosa Elena explained that he was recovering from a slight heart attack. "He was with his girl friend and it was too much for him," she said in a motherly tone of voice. "He's old now, but he tries to act like he's still a strong, young bull. She's here too, *la rubia.*" Rosa Elena brought my eyes to rest on a young woman, thirty or thirty-five years old, very tall and thin with long blonde hair. She wore a turquoise dress, a string of pearls, and large tear-shaped earrings that sparkled in the reflected sunlight.

Dr. Marin moved slowly, deliberately, as though nursing a deep wound. The blonde in the turquoise dress talked excitedly. She tossed her head back so that you could see her white neck, and, at the same time, flicked her hair to the side with a bounce of her right hand. Dr. Marin watched her and let out a little cry of pleasure.

Dr. Marin was a retired gynecologist. However, from time to time he examined his old patients, and new ones too, especially if they were as attractive as *la rubia*. His house was behind Rosa Elena's, but you couldn't see it from there because an ivy-covered wall blocked the view. Dr. Marin was a widower.

"After Traven's death he proposed to me," Rosa Elena whispered. "Fedde is a very sweet man, and I love him dearly, but I knew that it wouldn't work out. I told him it was too soon, that I wanted to wait awhile. I didn't want to hurt his feelings. He understood completely. Now we're very good friends. You see, my husbands Carlos and Traven were both 'packages,' as we say in Mexico; they were real characters, each in his own way. Another 'package' like Fedde I didn't need."

"Do you think that you'll ever marry again?" I asked. "After all, you're still young and very attractive."

"Oh, well, thank you very much," Rosa Elena said, fluttering her eyelashes. "If I ever *do* marry again, the man will have to love Traven and his writings as much as I."

Dr. Marin's living room had the unmistakable stamp of a bachelor intellectual who had collected books, art, music, and fine wines his whole life. The sofas and the chairs were shabby, but maintained a hint of their former elegance. There were soft pillows with gold tassels, Indian blankets carefully folded and ready to be used in the evening chill. An old radio in a tall, wood case stood on wrought-iron feet, and 1930s dance music—played by a big band—vibrated from the speaker. Several of the books Dr. Marin had authored were displayed on top of the radio. One was about gynecology, another about coffee, tea, wine, and herbs, with illustrations of the beans, leaves, and bushes that bore the various potent fruits.

Dr. Marin came from an unusual family. His sister Lupe had been married to Diego Rivera. A copy of Diego's portrait of Lupe hung in Dr. Marin's living room. Both Lupe and her brother had the same soft brown complexion and look of sadness mixed with joy. The expression on Lupe's face was extraordinary. She seemed to be deeply sad, perhaps in pain, and yet there was also a feeling of ecstasy in her face. She looked like she was giving birth, not to a child, but to a new emotion. Her green eyes were tearful, yet there were no tears.

Dr. Marin introduced me to his guests: Rudolfo Usigli, the playwright and former Mexican Ambassador to Lebanon and then Norway. *"Mucho gusto,"* Usigli whispered, his lips barely moving. He had a salt-and-pepper mustache and he held an ivory cigarette holder between his stained teeth. The moment one cigarette was finished he removed it with his finger tips, produced a silver case and lighter, fitted in another cigarette, and immediately began smoking again.

Standing behind Usigli was a businessman who was flirting with a woman from *Excelsior,* one of the few women reporters in the country, I was told. The man's repartee consisted of clever jokes, double entendres, sexual gestures of the hands and face. The woman tried to look serious, but couldn't help breaking out in laughter. Briefly, she diverted the conversation to other topics: the International Women's Year Conference, and the rumor that the president's wife, just returned from Cuba, would run for office when her husband's term expired.

"She's nothing but a *tamale!*" the man shouted. (I learned that calling someone a *tamale* meant she was cheap and low-class.) The business man continued: *"El Mercurio* reported that she was in bed with Castro when she visited Havana. Of course, your papers won't print those stories, but we know it's true. Castro thinks he can fuck all our women. Well, fuck him! We don't want Castro laying so much as his pinky on Mexico."

"Bravo, bravo," Dr. Marin's mistress said. She laughed in the businessman's face. "Go on, Mr. Macho, you tell Fidel where to shove it."

"You see now why I adore her," Dr. Marin said to Rosa Elena. "She's got Tina's eyes and Tina's fire."

Rosa Elena and I had arrived at Dr. Marin's at two in the afternoon. We had been invited for lunch, but for two hours we talked and drank. I was told that this was the normal social practice. Dr. Marin told me stories about his sister Lupe and Diego Rivera.

"They had no money, but Diego would buy Aztec relics. It was a craze with him. He was an artist and he was in love with Aztec art. But there was never anything to eat in the house. Lupe was mad. Finally, she threatened to leave him, really she did. She was jealous. She threw the clay figures into a big pot of hot water, dissolved them, and served them to Diego for supper. Was he mad! Another time he came home and found her sitting on the flat, cast-iron stove with her skirt up. 'What *are* you doing?' Diego shouted. 'I'm warming your supper, dear,' Lupe said. 'My pussy is all we have to eat in the house.'

"Yes, those times were wonderful, weren't they," Rosa Elena said, laughing and blushing at the same time. "Lupe, Diego and Fedde knew Traven in Mexico City at that time, but they didn't know him as B. Traven," she explained. "In those days my husband used the name Torsvan. It comes from Thor, the Norse god of thunder and lightning. As Torsvan he was a photographer and an explorer; he told them he was Norwegian-American. Fedde didn't discover that he was Traven until many years later, did you, Fedde? Of course, almost no one had heard about Traven in the twenties. Well, about 1928 Torsvan vanished and Fedde lost track of him for twenty-five years. Then they met again before the Skipper and I were married, but by then my husband was using the name Hal Croves, and he was telling everyone that he was B. Traven's business agent."

When we finally sat down to eat at four, I had a chance to ask Dr. Marin about Torsvan.

"He was no stranger than anyone else," the Doctor said. "Diego was quite a character and so was Lupe. We were all a bit crazy then; we were young and adventurous and in love. Torsvan disappeared for long periods of time, then reappeared suddenly and unexpectedly, but that was to be expected since he was an explorer. He traveled to Chiapas once with the government expedition as the official photographer, and, later, on his own expeditions. Came back with hundreds of incredible photographs. There was no reason to suspect that he was Traven—or anyone else, for that matter—because Torsvan had what I'd call a scientific bent of mind. He was interested in machines, engineering, skyscrapers, and bridges. I would never have guessed he was a writer."

"What about Hal Croves?" I asked.

"Ah, Croves, now there was a peculiar man, neither poet nor scientist but a businessman." Dr. Marin paused a moment to ring the bell. Immediately a maid appeared with the first course, a creamy soup of tender clams and pink shrimp. While she ladled the soup, Dr. Marin uncorked a bottle of Matéus and filled our glasses.

"What did Torsvan talk about?"

"He didn't talk much," Dr. Marin said. "He was just part of the group. We did everything together: drink, eat, travel, have fun."

"What was the group?"

"Well, there was Diego, of course, and Lupe, Weston, Canessi, Tina."

"Torsvan worked with Edward Weston," Rosa Elena said. "He taught himself photography, and had his own dark room."

"You mentioned Tina before, didn't you? Who is she?" I asked.

"Tina, Tina, Tina . . . Tina Modotti," Dr. Marin warbled, as though calling her to his side. "You mean you don't know Tina? Incredible. I'm so sorry. Tina was the most beautiful woman I have ever known." Dr. Marin reached for a book on top of the radio—a finely reproduced collection of Edward Weston's photos—and turned the pages until he found Tina. She was seated in a wicker chair. Her hands, like Lupe Marin's in the portrait, were entwined, but around her knees,

not under her chin. Lupe looked like a mature woman; Tina
looked like a young girl. Her hair was raven-black and was
parted down the middle. Unlike Lupe, Tina was looking directly at us and in a coquettish way.

"Tina was also a photographer," Rosa Elena said. "She
was a fine artist, and very political, but Weston only saw her
as his pin-up girl. It's really too bad."

Dr. Marin flipped the pages again. There were portraits of
D.H. Lawrence, Nahui Olin, José Clemente Orozco, and Diego Rivera wearing a floppy hat—one eye in shadow, one eye
in the sunlight. And there were more portraits of Tina. One,
dated 1923, a close study of her face, made me want to reach
out and touch her lips. Here Tina had lost her girlish expression. Her eyes were closed, but they gave me the im-
pression that they were opening, that Weston had captured
that exact moment between open and shut.

Then we looked at a nude photo of Tina from 1926. She was
lying on a stone patio in the bright sun, her eyes closed, her
hands behind her arched back. I couldn't tell whether Tina
was asleep or sunbathing.

"You were in love with Tina, weren't you?" Rose Elena
asked, her voice betraying her own desire to be entertained by
romantic tales about Tina and Weston, Tina and Diego, Tina
and Fedde, Tina and. . . .

"Everyone was in love with Tina," Dr. Marin said. He
cupped the book of photos in his hands and lapped at her face
with his eyes. "We all worshiped Tina. She lured us on and on
and on, then signed us up as members of the Sandino Liberation Support Committee, had us going to political meetings
when all we wanted to do was make love. Only Torsvan never
came to the meetings! He knew Augusto Sandino from Tampico during the boom time in oil. You see, Sandino was on the
run for having killed a man in Nicaragua. He was an orphan,
a bastard, had no family, and he had to leave town. They were
both anarchists—Tampico was a big anarchist town in the
twenties—and they hit it off. Then Sandino went back to

Nicaragua and started fighting the U.S. Marines.* Coolidge had sent them in to protect American interests. Some interests!"

"Sandino slipped into Mexico to rally support for the Nicaraguan cause. Tina raised money—she could get a hundred pesos from a stone if she wanted—and Torsvan helped, too. The guns weren't much good, believe me, but they made Sandino's men feel a lot better."

"Tina was the organizer for the Communist Internationale in Latin America," Rosa Elena explained. "The Mexican Communists had a tough time taking orders from a woman, believe me, it was no easy job. My husband never took orders from her either, but then he never took orders from anyone, always worked alone, independent, though he was all for Sandino and against Coolidge and the U.S. Marines."

"Ah, Tina, Tina, Tina," Dr. Marin murmured. He was obviously still in love with Tina Modotti. Now he rang the bell again and the maid served the main course: baked tongue in a sauce of white onions, green olives, and bell peppers. There was rice with mushrooms, a green salad, and more wine. I began to feel that I was in one of those Luis Buñuel movies in which rich Spaniards sit and eat and drink and talk, unable to leave the dining room. So those Buñuel movies weren't surrealistic after all, as I had imagined, but realistic portraits.

Diego's oil painting of Lupe got darker and darker, with only her white dress still visible in the late afternoon sunlight. And Weston's picture of the young Tina looked more textured, more grainy. Tina seemed to have moved forward and the room backward.

"You know Stalin ordered Tina poisoned," Rosa Elena said. "She died in a taxi on the way to the hospital. My husband told me that Tina and Sandino were too dangerous for

---

*Traven's Juan Mendez, the "general from the jungle" in the novel of the same name, was inspired by Augusto Sandino. His political program is nearly identical to Sandino's and his military strategy was drawn directly from Sandino's guerilla activities in the late twenties and early thirties.

the Russians. First they let Somoza murder Sandino, then Stalin's agents killed her."

The maid was standing on tiptoe to cover the bird cages; the parrots were going to sleep. Rudolfo Usigli looked like he too was ready to be covered for the night. One couldn't tell whether he was awake or asleep, not until Dr. Marin rang the bell for desert. Suddenly Usigli opened his eyes, lit a cigarette, and began to blow smoke rings above his head. His eyes opened wider and wider; they looked like an owl's eyes.

"I missed it all," he said. I thought that he was referring to the afternoon, but he meant life in Mexico for three decades. "I was in Lebanon and Norway. There were no diplomatic affairs of any importance, but the post gave me peace and quiet to write my plays. You should read them, young man. Chelena has them in her library. So you're writing about B. Traven. Well, well, isn't that interesting. Too bad about Tina! She knew a thing or two about him. But good luck, young man—all the best luck to you in the world."

6

I didn't know whether it was day or night, morning or evening. Except for the low murmur of their voices I heard no other sound, not from the house nor from the street, and though I tried to concentrate I couldn't understand what they were talking about. My head was propped up by white pillows, and there was a dull ringing in my ears. I searched for my reflection in the mirror across the room, but I could see only a dark, cloudy surface. My back was cold. I could feel the drops of water frozen on my spinal cord, like icicles hanging from a tree. But my chest, my throat, and my belly were on fire. And my stomach was exploding.

"...every few hours...tomorrow...until," I heard him say. Then I felt the bed sag and the cool dampness of a compress on my head. There was a smell of perfume, a blur of turquoise, and her black hair brushing against my face.

I fell asleep and was immediately woken by a hand shaking my chin. "Ah, open," she said. I found a small disk on the tip of my tongue, then a cup of water at my lips. In a moment I was falling back into the white pillows, asleep again.

For the next two days I stayed in bed, swallowing pills, sleeping hour after hour. Gradually the chills and the burning sensation stopped, my temperature returned to normal, and my stomach stopped exploding. Rosa Elena drew the curtains and the bright sun filled the room. She opened the door and I felt a cool breeze against my face.

I looked at myself in the mirror; I had a stubbly beard and my complexion had turned yellow. My arms and legs were heavy, my head light, my balance unsteady. There was no clock in the room, but I learned to read the time of day or night by the sounds that rose from the street. I heard the cry of the newspaper man, the clang of pesos, the thump of a knife against a wooden chopping board. Then the traffic began. I listened to the angry horns, the squeaking of tires, the roar of engines, and the harsh cough of the exhaust.

At midday the knife and scissors sharpener arrived on the corner. I heard the wheel spinning and the grinding of steel against stone until I could almost see the sparks. In the afternoon the street sweepers descended, their thick brushes scrubbing the rough pavement, wet with cool water, then the clang and bang of cans and the smell of rotten vegetables and fruit. In the evening I heard the whistle of the tamale cart, and then at night the roar of the rock 'n' roll band from the discothèque, shoes pounding the dance floor, and the wail of the singer hitting the high notes.

Dr. Marin gave me photos of Tina, Diego, and Weston. Rosa Elena brought me a photo of Traven. Tabasco stretched out on the floor and left the room just long enough to bolt down his food, while Gigi poked her snooty nose through the door.

When I got restless I put on a robe, staggered down the stairs holding on to the railing, and collapsed in the library.

"*Hola*," a little voice said. Lost in the arms of the easy chair was a girl with long braids, a round face, and Rosa Elena's dark eyes.

"I'm Irene," she said. "I know all about you. You're getting better now. *Abuela* says Americans always get sick when they come to Mexico. She says it's Montezuma's revenge. *Abuela* says we have germs that you don't have, but I like you anyway. Can I call you Pepe? Your American name is too hard to say."

41

"Yes, you can call me Pepe," I said. "I came down to find a book."

"I'm supposed to be doing my school work, but I'm reading this instead," she said, lifting a Donald Duck comic book. "Don't tell on me. My mother will be angry." The comic had Spanish dialogue, but he was the same old Donald Duck that kids were reading in the U.S.A. and all around the world.

I started to get up, but felt dizzy. Irene offered to help me find a book, so I settled back in the chair.

"Let me see *Oil*," I said. "It's on the third shelf, near the end." Irene ran her eye down the row of books.

"The one by Upton Sinclair?" she asked, handing it to me. "Don't you want to read one of Traven's books? My mother says you're going to write his biography. Did you know him?"

"Never met him," I said. "I've only read his books."

"I tried, but they're too old for me," Irene said.

"You should try *The Creation of the Sun and the Moon*," I suggested. "It's a story about an Indian warrior named Chicovaneg; he leaves his home and his family. You see, the old sun has been destroyed by evil spirits, and the earth is in darkness. Chicovaneg wanders through the sky with his shield —he doesn't have a sword—until he has enough star-light to make a new sun. But he can never return home. He lives in the center of the sky, and while he can *see* his family and they can *see* him, they can never be together again. It's on the bottom shelf. Take a look."

Reluctantly, Irene put down her Donald Duck comic book and looked at Traven's story. I opened *Oil*. It was dusty and mildewed. "To B. Traven from Upton Sinclair" was scrawled on the inside cover.

"Too sad," Irene said. She placed *The Creation of the Sun and the Moon* back on the shelf and returned to Walt Disney.

"Try it again when you're older," I said. "Did you know Traven, Irene?"

"I can't remember, but *abuela* says he held me on his knee when I was a baby."

"Let me see the paperbacks on the bottom shelf."

Irene handed me half a dozen tattered "dime-store novels" with lurid and violent illustrations on the covers, and compelling titles like *Murder at Oak Ridge*, *The Man Who Disappeared at Midnight*, and *Bandits of Lone Gulch Ranch*. I wanted to read them because they were Traven's books, and because he had been influenced by the popular fiction of the day: cowboy yarns, detective stories, and tales of the supernatural.

Upstairs again. Petra was making my bed. Irene put the books down on the table and Tabasco wagged his tail. I taped the pictures of Tina, Diego, Weston, and Traven to the mirror. Now, when I sat in bed I could see my reflection, and their bright glowing faces. I watched them and wondered what they had been thinking and doing at the moment they were caught on film. What novel was Traven writing? *The White Rose*,—or *The Bridge in the Jungle*? What mural was Diego painting? What photos was Weston shooting, and what revolution was Tina plotting? I arranged the pictures so that the eyes carried you from the top left to the bottom left corner of the mirror. Traven looked at Diego, Diego at Tina, Tina at Weston, and Weston at Traven.

"So now you've got *your* pin-ups," Rosa Elena said, standing in the doorway. "Which one do you like best? It's Tina, isn't it? I'll take the Skipper."

"From now on I'm calling him Pepe," Irene said.

"That's good. Whenever you come to a new place you should take a new name. The Skipper believed that," Rosa Elena said. "He *had* to take aliases, it was in his blood."

"Do you know where the name Traven comes from?" I asked.

"No, I don't," Rosa Elena admitted. "But listen, B. Traven sounds like *betray*, doesn't it, sounds like *travel* and *raven* too. It could be all those things and many more. As far as my husband was concerned the more interpretations the better. Irene is a simpler name but I like it anyway; Irene is with me now until her mother comes home."

"Then she's not *your* daughter? You look so alike," I said.

"Heavens no," Rosa Elena said. "She's Chele's. I'm the

grandmother. *Abuela.* I'm the one who spoils her."

After supper I read a few chapters from Upton Sinclair's novel *Oil*, and then watched professional tennis on television. The band across the street was so loud that I couldn't sleep. I wrapped a blanket around my shoulders and got out of bed, ready to explore the room.

The closet door was rusty, and I had to move it slowly to prevent it from squeaking. In the top drawer there were nylon stockings, bras, and underpants, in the second, belts and sashes, the third was empty, the fourth had bathing suits, and the bottom drawer had cracked powder puffs and flattened lipsticks. I opened the top drawer again, pushed aside the stockings and felt a thick bundle of paper tied with a piece of string. I picked at the knot and leafed through the letters. They were signed "Hal Croves," or "the Skipper," and they were addressed to Malu one summer when she was traveling in Europe. Hal suggested what she visit in Paris, Rome, Athens. As he wrote, he seemed to be recalling his own memories of Europe: palaces, piazzas, canals, cathedrals, boulevards, and museums, and the historical events that had shaken the continent. There were other letters too, from Hal to Malu while he was traveling and she was at home. He advised her to eat tortillas and not white bread—or *colchon*, as the Mexicans called it, because it was soft and bouncy as a mattress. Hal hoped that Malu would listen less to rock 'n' roll and study more, drink *liquidos* and stop guzzling Coca-Cola.

I was having fun peering into the private life of B. Traven and his stepdaughter, feeling partly guilty about spying, but I persuaded myself that it was important for the biography. Now I knew how Traven felt about white bread, Coca-Cola, and rock 'n' roll. When I least expected it, the bedroom door opened and Rosa Elena walked in. It was too late to put the letters back in the drawer, or even hide them under the blanket.

Rosa Elena had only to glance at the letters in my hand to realize what I was reading, and where I had gotten them. But her face showed no sign of anger or disappointment, and she

didn't scold me for prying. Maybe she was glad that I had
read the letters.

"Children are always rebelling against their parents, you
know that," Rosa Elena said. "I rebelled against mine. Malu
was no different. She was on the telephone talking to friends
all day long and that drove the Skipper crazy. He threatened
to have the phone company disconnect our lines, but that
didn't stop her. And he couldn't stand Malu's music. Listen to
that." Rosa Elena paused a moment and looked across the
street. "He'd have hated what's happening here," she continued. "They're tearing down his palm trees, making the Rio
Mississippi into a highway. And that American rock 'n' roll,
it's terrible. When he first came to Mexico he heard Bing
Crosby tunes, and of course he preferred Indian flutes and
harps. Can you imagine how he felt at breakfast when he saw
Malu turning her nose up at tortillas and ordering the cook to
make her white toast? The world was coming to an end! Later, Malu wrote a fashion-and-gossip column for one of oui
magazines. The Skipper was so upset that he forced her to
stop."

"What about your other daughter?" I asked.

"Chele, well, Traven wanted Chele to become an artist,"
Rosa Elena said. She picked up the letters and placed them
back in the top drawer. Then she sat down on the bed.
"Traven loved the Mexican muralists so much that he wanted
Chele to follow in their footsteps. He insisted on art lessons.
But Chele had her own ideas. She had read Traven's books,
like *The White Rose*, and became interested in economics. Yes,
he was responsible for her ideas, but still he wanted her to be
an artist, not an economist. They had big arguments. Finally
Chele won. But Traven won, too, because she took after him.
Traven understood our girls, because he too had rebelled
against his parents."

7

We walked downstairs in the darkness. Rosa Elena disappeared into the kitchen to brew a pot of jasmine tea and I stood at the window. Across the street the discothèque had just closed; yellow Volkswagens lined the curb to carry tourists back to their hotels on the Paseo. Only a few couples strolled along the Rio Mississippi; each one was stopped by an Indian woman with a baby at her breast. Without looking into their faces, she held out her hand to beg, then slid back into the shadows.

"Come sit here," Rosa Elena said. She set the tray on the table and warmed her hands over the black teapot. Her face was softer, her eyes brighter. The shadows covered her wrinkles and made her look almost as young as she did in the portrait on the wall.

Tabasco hobbled down the stairs like an old man with arthritis that acted up on cold, damp nights in January. He looked at me, then at Rosa Elena, his eyes demanding an explanation for this late-night meeting.

"Lie down, Tabasco," I said. The dog circled round and round and finally collapsed in a heap with his head touching his tail. Rosa Elena pulled her turquoise bathrobe tightly round her waist. Her slippers dangled from the tips of her toes. She seemed awkward, embarrassed. I thought that I ᴋnew what she was thinking but was unable to say so I said it for her.

"You think that Traven was the Kaiser's son, don't you?"

Rosa Elena smiled. "My husband kept his parent's identity a secret for more than fifty years," she said. "It was traumatic, believe me. He was an anarchist and a revolutionary and his father was the Kaiser."

"It's hard to believe," I said. "It seems too unlikely." Rosa Elena reached for a cigarette and then waited for me to light it for her.

"You can believe what you want to believe," she said. "I am only telling you the truth. His father was the Kaiser and his mother was an opera singer. Von Sternwaldt was her name, I believe. When my husband and I went to Berlin in 1959 for the screening of *The Death Ship* he insisted on taking me to the Grünewald. He knew his way through the park even after half a century. 'Where are you going?' I kept asking, but he wouldn't say. We walked mile after mile. Finally we stopped in an open field and he pointed to a statue. I didn't recognize the man so I went up and looked. It was a statue of Kaiser Wilhelm II, the last German Kaiser. 'I am descended from this man'—that's *exactly* what Traven said. Later he told me that during the Munich rebellion, his mother visited him and pleaded with him to stop his revolutionary activities because he was betraying his own father."

"Maybe he made up the Kaiser story like all the other stories he made up," I suggested. "Or maybe his mother made up the story to stop his radical activities. I've heard mothers threaten to commit suicide unless their sons abandoned the left."

"My husband invented nothing," Rosa Elena said. "He was an aristocrat. I am positive of that. You could see it in his manners, in the way he held himself. They teach them those things at an early age and they never forget. The children of poor people don't act like that. My husband was raised by servants, and educated by tutors. He was obsessed with royalty. It was in his subconscious; he repressed it again and again

47

but it came out unexpectedly. When he married me and we came to live here, it was for him like returning to the luxury and ease he had known as a child."

"Let me tell you something: One afternoon we went shopping. I was tired and I wanted to come straight home, but he insisted on buying *elote*. He was a very stubborn man. If once he had decided on something there was no stopping him. He wouldn't go home without *elote*, and he was very choosy where he bought it. We went to five or six different places. Finally, he found an old woman on the corner of Cinco de Mayo and asked her for an ear with soft kernels, because his teeth weren't as strong as they used to be. 'It's all the same. Take it or leave it,' the woman said. She stuck her hand into the fire and stripped away the burned husks. 'Maybe this will suit the *señor*, she said, smearing chiles on the cob.

"I thought that she was terribly rude but Traven just laughed. 'She has the best *elote*,' he told me. 'But she is never on the same street corner. I always have to hunt for her.'

"At home Chele and Malu wanted to know what we had done downtown. 'Oh, nothing special,' I said. But the Skipper thought differently; he asked them to sit down right here on the sofa where we are sitting now. 'I'll tell you what we saw,' Traven said. And, you know, he told them a fantastic story about that old Indian woman. 'There were deep wrinkles in her face and she must have been a hundred years old, at least,' he said. 'Her hands touched the charcoal but they were never burned or blackened. She had the patience to stand all day selling *elotes* in the city.'

"By the time the Skipper was finished with his story, the girls thought that she was an Aztec princess, a relative of Montezuma himself. After that, whenever I took them downtown they insisted on looking for the '*elote* woman,' as they called her. They saw lots of old Indians, but they couldn't find the right one. 'Did you meet the *elote* woman today?' Traven would ask. 'Oh no, we couldn't find her,' Malu would say. She looked so sweet and innocent. 'Then you aren't looking in the right place,' Traven insisted. It was a little game that he played with them, of course—but there is an *elote* woman. She's still there. Maybe you will have better luck finding her than my daughters did."

"But that doesn't prove he was the Kaiser's son," I said. "It just shows he was a good storyteller."

"I tell you he was preoccupied by his father," Rosa Elena said. Tabasco began to growl; he disappeared in the darkness. "I hope that you locked the doors," Rosa Elena said. Then I heard a noise at the back of the house. There was the sound of bare feet on the stone floor. Suddenly, I saw Petra's eyes. She was holding a candle under her chin. Tabasco growled again and Herme emerged from the shadows. The two women looked as though they had done something terribly wrong and expected to be punished.

"Go back to sleep," Rosa Elena ordered. "We don't need you, don't want you." Petra looked tearful. Herme curtsied like a lady, then retreated into the darkness. I heard their footsteps on the stone floor and on the metal steps. All of a sudden there was a strange sound. Herme and Petra were giggling. "Those people are so very stupid," Rosa Elena said. "Just because they never sit up and talk late at night they think it's strange. I have to explain everything to them because they are like children."

Rosa Elena reached for another cigarette and again waited for me to light it. "Sometimes I think that I should sell this house and move to Cuernavaca," she said. "It's just too big for me. When the Skipper was alive and the girls lived home it was different. Then we needed lots of room. Lately I've thought about going away, but I know he wouldn't like it. When he was a child he didn't have a real family and he was always running away. This was the only home he ever had. That's why I don't want to sell."*

* The experiences of Judy Stone, the reporter and film critic for the *San Francisco Chronicle*, are interesting in the light of my own. Stone met Traven in May 1966. At that time Rosa Elena told her that Traven "was a Hohenzollern and that he never forgave his mother, a British performer, for telling him this when he was already involved in revolutionary activities." The following year Stone met Traven and Rosa Elena again. This time Rosa Elena told her "quite specifically. . .that Traven was the

illegitimate son of Kaiser Wilhelm II." Stone interviewed Traven and wrote two articles about him that were published in *Ramparts* in September and October 1967.

While Stone was preparing her articles, the German magazine *Stern* released a story with photos, arguing that Traven was indeed the Kaiser's son. When Stone phoned Rosa Elena for a verification, she denied having given the information to *Stern* and pleaded with Stone not to use the story because Traven "was furious and threatened to leave." In 1969, when Stone returned to Mexico to attend Traven's funeral, she asked Rosa Elena again about Traven's identity. Rosa Elena said that Traven "believed he was the son of the Kaiser" (which isn't the same thing, of course, as *being* the son of the Kaiser.)

In the course of my stay in Mexico Rosa Elena assured me that Traven *was* the Kaiser's son; at the same time she denied that she had ever told the reporters from *Stern* that Traven was the Kaiser's son. It seems that she liked telling the story, but as soon as anyone reported it she denied it, or, as in the case of Judy Stone, she put on pressure to censor the story.

While I was in Mexico Gerd Heidemann, the reporter from *Stern*, sent Rosa Elena a "sworn statement made under oath and threat of perjury." Heidemann swore that on December 14, 1966, Gabriel Figueroa, the famous cinematographer, told him that "Ret Marut, the foreigner, could edit *Der Ziegelbrenner* because he had a very influential person behind him."

According to Heidemann's sworn statement, Señora Luján herself had added that "the famous personage who stood behind Marut was none other than Kaiser William II." Señora Luján went on to say, "My husband loves Germany, but he hates it too. His trauma was that as an anarchist and revolutionary all his life he has fought his father. My husband hated his mother from the moment that she told him about his father. . . My husband told me that his mother's name was Helene, that she was a singer of Norwegian descent, that she moved to London, married an Englishman, went with him to India where she later died." Rosa Elena Luján concluded, "This is one of his traumas. . .that he was also born out of wedlock. That's why he hates his mother and his father. But the picture of the last German Kaiser hangs upstairs in his study."

Rosa Elena showed me this statement from Heidemann, but insisted that it was false, that Heidemann was a liar. Rosa Elena's interpretaion of her husband was extremely Freudian, though where and when and how she became a Freudian I don't know. There were no copies of Freud's books in Traven's library. Judy Stone told me she believed that Traven came from an aristocratic background. She felt that he had a romantic view of work and workers, a view that a real worker would never have had.

8

I moved to Tlalpan, a small village on the outskirts of the city. Though I didn't like the forty-five minute commute through pollution and traffic to the Rio Mississippi, I wanted my own place. I can't explain it, but after the late-night discussion about Traven and the Kaiser and the opera singer mother, I felt it would be best if there was some distance between Rosa Elena and me. To live under the same roof would be too tense. There was no bitterness between us; whenever I wanted, I could sleep in my room on the second floor.

Mrs. Yampolsky, or *La Señora* as all Tlalpan called her, was my landlady. I rented the top floor of her colonial-style house for $96 a month. "Mrs. Yampolsky is a Polish Jew," Rosa Elena said. "She makes delicious cottage cheese and a special almond cake. Maybe you can buy one for me."

Mrs. Yampolsky's address was number 65 San Marcos. It was located across the street from a *tienda* run by a gaunt-looking woman who sold everything from saltines and bubble gum to cold beer and razor blades. Two doors away, also on San Marcos, was another house with the number 65. The first time in Tlalpan I went to the wrong number 65. I opened the iron gate, walked up the stone path, and rang the bell. There was no answer so I waited. I waited an hour. Then I went into the *tienda* to ask for Mrs. Yampolsky.

51

"Ah, it's *La Señora* you want." The woman behind the counter offered me a toothless smile. "Why didn't you say so, *extranjero! La Señora* lives in the big house with the red roof." I looked across the street. The red tile was barely visible. The house was concealed by a high wall, but it was the only wall on a street lined with walls that wasn't embedded with broken glass, barbed wire, and medieval-looking spikes.

There was no name on the door but I rang the bell. *"Quien es?"* a voice squeaked. *"Abre, por favor,"* I said. The door opened and a young boy looked up at me, frightened I thought, because he dashed off shouting, *"Abuela! Abuela! Abuela!"* And just as he dashed off a pack of dogs descended upon me. They surrounded me, stood on their hind legs, and tried to lick my face. They weren't one bit dangerous but Mrs. Yampolsky came to my rescue anyway. Calling each dog by his or her name, she chased them away.

"I've been waiting for you," she said. "You're late." She was wearing black trousers, sturdy walking shoes, and a polka-dot shirt with short sleeves that revealed her powerful forearms.

"I was waiting next door," I explained.

"You could have been arrested for trespassing," she said.

"You should change the number," I suggested. "You can't have two number 65s on the same street."

"Nonsense! You can't change anything, not even the house numbers. Come in, come in."

The house was built of red brick. There were beautiful red brick arches, eight or nine of them that extended the length of the building, and each arch was fitted with a clear window pane that faced the garden. The floor was red brick and the walls a brilliant white. The living room fireplace had a strange opening; it looked like a frowning mouth.

We walked through the kitchen. Here too the floor was red brick. The ceiling had exposed rough-hewn beams. You could see the mark of the ax. Along the walls were large, ceramic pots decorated with Indian designs and overflowing with curdling cottage cheese. At the back of the kitchen a spiral staircase led up to the second floor.

"I'm too old to climb it," Mrs. Yampolsky said, so I climbed alone, higher and higher, going round and round. The bedroom was small, but a large window overlooked a sea of purple flowers, and the bay windows in the study looked down upon the red brick courtyard. A small, round woman was hanging up the laundry, and the boy who had run from me in fright was hiding behind a large, white sheet.

"You want it?" Mrs. Yampolsky shouted up from the kitchen. "Look at the view from the roof." I walked up one more flight of stairs and pushed the metal door hanging from one squeaky hinge. Mrs. Yampolsky's house was the tallest in Tlalpan, taller even than the church in the zócalo. To the north the downtown skyscrapers were lost in a sea of gray clouds. To the south the mountains rose sharply. There were no houses, no factories, no roads.

Tlalpan was quiet. Below me, lazy flea-infested dogs slept in the middle of the street. A block away the tortilla factory was running at full speed. I smelled the freshly ground corn meal.

"My house belonged to one of Diaz's generals," Mrs. Yampolsky shouted from the ground floor. "Then there were troubles in Tlalpan. The peasants dragged him to the zócalo and hung him from the tallest tree. There's a plaque in town to mark the spot. Come on now, what do you say, I haven't all day. A general's house and hung by the peasants too! Doesn't that appeal to you?"

I walked down the spiral staircase, faster than I had climbed it, and paid Mrs. Yampolsky the first month's rent. She gave me a receipt and a key to the front door. "Don't lose it—or else! It's the only one," she said, shaking her finger at me. We sat down at the table in the dining room. The legs and the frame were of wood, but the top was a solid piece of clear glass. I could see my own shoes and Mrs. Yampolsky's too.

"So you're from Poland, are you," I said.

"No. I am German," Mrs. Yampolsky insisted. "I was born in Germany and my parents were German. If you are so interested in my background, mister, I will tell you. Maiden name Urbach. Husband Russian. Never was in Poland. Mrs. Luján told you I was Polish, didn't she, and no doubt she told you I was a Jew too, didn't she?"

"Mrs. Luján is a Catholic and a Mexican, but does anyone call *her* a Mexican Catholic? No, of course not. That would be ridiculous—so why should she call me a Jew, and a Polish Jew to boot? To belittle me! You had better get it straight, mister, if you are looking for kosher food you won't find it here. I take no *schnorrers;* I've had too many *schnorrers* in my life, including my husband. He would give you the shirt off his back, but I'm not giving away anything for free, so you'd better have the rent the first of every month. I'm a hard-working woman and I know the value of a dollar. My husband never worked; he was an artist, a sculptor. Look, look, I want to show you." Mrs. Yampolsky handed me a small nude sculpture of a beautiful young woman. "I was much younger then, of course."

"This is *you?*" I asked incredulously. The statue must have been done fifty years ago. One hand modestly covered her left breast, the other her pubic hair. She looked like a Northern European version of the Venus de Milo. "Don't be embarrassed—look, look!" Mrs. Yampolsky said. "You must have seen a woman's body before. With that kind of attitude you won't get far with Mrs. Luján. Ah, about time. Here's Ellie with the tea and cookies." The woman who had been hanging the laundry set the tray on the table. "Pablito, come out here." With his head bowed, his eyes downcast, Pablito emerged from the kitchen. "I knew you were there," Mrs. Yampolsky said. "If you want to hide from me you'll have to be a lot quieter." Pablito and I shook hands, then he ran outdoors to play. "Now tell me, what business do you have in Mexico?"

"Didn't Rosa Elena explain?"

"Mrs. Luján tells me nothing," Mrs. Yampolsky said. "We are not exactly the best of friends. I have not seen her for a long time. Tell me, does she still wear the low-cut evening gowns that show off her bosoms? My husband would have liked her to model for him. Mrs. Luján was very beautiful; she used to have many young admirers."

"I'm writing a book about her husband, B. Traven," I said. "Have you heard of him?"

Mrs. Yampolsky's jaw fell what seemed like a good foot. Then, suddenly and unexpectedly, she broke out in wild, uncontrollable laughter. It was a clear, high-pitched laugh. She doubled over, her eyes closed, and tears streamed down her cheeks. For a moment I thought that she was going to laugh herself to death. She held her sides to keep from falling apart. Then, just as suddenly as she began, she stopped. She wiped the tears from her eyes and adjusted the strap from her brassiere that had come loose with laughter.

"I'm sorry," she said apologetically, and then in a serious tone of voice, "What has Mrs. Luján told you about her husband?"

"She claims that he was the illegitimate son of Kaiser Wilhelm II," I said.

"The Kaiser's bastard," Mrs. Yampolsky said. This time she looked as though she were deliberating a matter of life or death.

"I understood that you met her husband," I said.

"I met an old man who called himself Hal Croves," Mrs. Yampolsky said. "He was so blind he could hardly see, so deaf he could barely hear. I remember once he came downstairs from 'The Bridge' as he called it. Apparently during his youth he had spent many years at sea, or so it was rumored. But he didn't dress like a retired ship's captain, more like a Wall Street banker. He wore a black tuxedo with tails, a white silk shirt, and a black bow tie. He looked like J. P. Morgan, you've heard of him haven't you, or old man Rockefeller, the granddaddy. Then *she* came down in a black satin evening gown that exposed her bosom, and they went out to the theatre."

"You don't think that Croves was Traven?" I asked.

"Who am I to say?" Mrs. Yampolsky responded, shrugging her broad shoulders.

"Did you talk to Croves in German or English?" I asked.

"In English."

"Did he have a German accent?"

"None at all."

"If he wasn't Traven, who was he?" I asked.

"Well, maybe he was nobody, maybe he was just an old man," Mrs. Yampolsky said. "Maybe Mrs. Luján found him in Acapulco and pawned him off as B. Traven. Could be he actually was a friend of Traven's, and possibly had some of his manuscripts and a few of his possessions. Mrs. Luján knew about the so-called 'mystery' of B. Traven. Couldn't it be a hoax? Who could deny it? No one ever caught B. Traven sitting at a typewriter, writing a book. The manuscripts just appeared out of nowhere. Who wrote them? Traven? Perhaps, but what did the man sitting at the typewriter look like?"

"Why create a hoax?" I asked.

"I don't know," Mrs. Yampolsky said. "That's what *you* must find out. Mrs. Luján is a very shrewd woman. You'll have to be very careful, mister writer. I don't mean to pry into your private affairs, but tell me please, are you getting paid to write this book, or does the *gelt* come out of your own pocket?"

"I have an advance," I said.

"Very good. I wouldn't want you to throw away your own dollars on such a project," Mrs. Yampolsky said. "You know, I remember Croves as a very quiet man. *She* did most of the talking. He would whisper in her ear and then she would tell us what he had said. Why couldn't he talk to us directly?"

"He was old," I said. "He needed someone to take care of him. He knew that Mrs. Luján would continue the mystery he had cultivated his whole life."

"Couldn't anyone who knew Traven's books have said as much as Croves did?" Mrs. Yampolsky asked. "Maybe he read the books, and then talked about them and about his experiences, as though *he* was the author."

"Then you think that Rosa Elena passed off an old man, a nobody, as B. Traven? You think Croves was fraud? I've heard of such things, of course, but that's going too far, Mrs. Yampolsky."

"Don't dismiss it so lightly. That woman is capable of anything. I remember when Heidemann came from Berlin. Croves refused to meet him. He stayed in his room and let Mrs. Luján do all the talking. It was she who told Heidemann the Kaiser story. And now she's repeating it. I don't know . . . but you say you're getting paid for this work? It's puzzling. I don't know. I just don't know any more."

9

"If Traven were alive today he would write about us," the
pesero driver said. I was sitting beside him, and a fat man was
sitting beside me, his arm and half his shoulder out the window Four passengers were squeezed into the back seat of the
collective taxi, and they were all anxious to get to work on
time. It was rush hour and the streets were jammed. Our
driver was weaving in and out of traffic, passing on the left and
on the right, crossing intersections just as the light turned red.
I guessed him to be forty-five or fifty years old; a veteran
driver. He wore suspenders, baggy trousers, and a blue sweat-
shirt that read "University of Cincinnati." The *pesero* was an
old Chevy, a '63 or '64, but it was clean and quiet. It was a
stick shift, but in place of the regular plastic knob that sat atop
the stick, the driver had fitted the number eight ball from a
pool table. On the dashboard was a plastic Virgin Mary with
the baby Jesus in her arms.

When I got into the cab at San Angel the driver noticed that
I was carrying a copy of *March to the Monteria,* Traven's book
about the forced march of Indian peasants to the mahogany
forests. "Yes, indeed, if Traven were here today in Mexico
City he would write about us *pesero* drivers. You see, *hombre,*
we're in the shit, and Traven wrote about people who are up
to here in it." With his index finger he drew a line across his

neck. "Driving in this traffic is like moving through shit. Of course, in Traven's time, the people up to their necks in the shit were all in the jungle. Not so any more. There was too much shit there so they moved in with us." He wasn't using the Spanish word *mierda* but the English *shit,* as though only *shit* could convey the utter shittiness of Mexico City life.

To get from Tlalpan to the Rio Mississippi I had to take two different *peseros.* The first leg of the journey was down Avenida Insurgentes—the longest street in Mexico—past the Olympic Stadium and the National Autonomous University of Mexico, to the final stop at San Angel. Almost every week there was a demonstration at the University. The students blocked off the road, distributed leaflets, and collected money from drivers and passengers. Before the police could clear up the congestion with their clubs we would have lost an hour.

The second leg of the journey was down Avenida de la Revolución to the end of the line at Chapultepec Park. By the time I arrived at Rio Mississippi I was covered with soot, my eyes were inflamed, my ear drums were ringing. We were always squeezed together, because the more passengers he carried the more fares the *pesero* driver made. The trip was a mad race through a Mexican maze of cars, buses, trucks, trolleys, motorbikes, and crowds of pedestrians, contemptuous of motor vehicles. Yes, indeed, as B. Traven said, "Transportation is civilization."

The *pesero* drivers were always on the thin dividing line between life and death, recklessness and safety. They took big chances, and of course there were big collisions. But that was part of the *pesero* business, part of our civilization too. The driver sat behind his wheel ten to twelve hours a day, with only occasional breaks to eat, pee, shit. He not only had to be a good driver, he had to know how to repair his car as quickly as possible. Moreover, to make a decent living he had to break the laws of the road. The competition was tough. If he drove carefully he would be pushed aside by the other *pesero* drivers, each one more anxious than the next to pick up fares.

At the same time, the driver had to be constantly on the

lookout for the police. They knew that the *pesero* drivers broke the law. Most of the time they tolerated it, or turned the other way. If he was ticketed or arrested the *pesero* driver would have to pay a fine, or *la mordida* ("the bite" or bribe), which was in effect a fine that went directly into the cop's pocket—a more honest and democratic method than collecting it and handing it over to the government bureaucracy. The *pesero* drivers were not only the victims of police corruption, but of stick-up artists too, especially late at night. A thief might hold a knife to the driver's throat and demand the day's take. The driver had to be careful, because he might lose his life, as well as his money.

The driver was right. Traven would have written about the *peseros;* it was like living and working in shit. And Rosa Elena always looked radiant. She had just showered and wore her turquoise robe and fluffly green slippers. Her black hair was combed straight back and her face glowed.

"Today we'll climb The Bridge," she said. "I have some important things I want to show you." But first she had to find the key. Usually, Rosa Elena carried the key ring in the pocket of her robe or held it loosely in the palm of her hand. You could hear the keys clanging as she walked. But today the keys couldn't be found.

"The Skipper has told the keys to hide," Rosa Elena said. "You see, he doesn't want us going through his things. Even now he wants his privacy. It's such a nuisance, but I have to lock the rooms to keep *them* out. Petra I can trust, but not Herme. It's not that they *steal;* like children they don't know what they're doing. If something pretty is lying around they borrow it. They don't know if it's a diamond or an emerald, but it glitters in the sunlight so they put it in their pocket and then when it's missing they're afraid to say anything."

Rosa Elena looked behind the pile of old newspapers and under the kitchen table. She asked Petra and Herme if they had seen the keys; they looked at each other suspiciously, and turned their heads from side to side. We went upstairs, searched under the beds and along the hall.

"*Aqui, señora, aqui,*" Petra shouted. The key to Rosa Elena's office was buried in the lock; the others dangled from the ring. Rosa Elena looked at Petra as though she had taken the keys from their hiding place and stuck them in the lock when we weren't looking.

"We don't want to be disturbed, understand!" Rosa Elena said, harshly. She grabbed the keys and led me up the wooden stairway to the top floor. At last we were on the Skipper's Bridge. It had taken two weeks to climb three floors.

Rosa Elena held the ring in her hand and examined each key, trying to determine which one fit. I was becoming impatient. The ritual of the keys was annoying. Finally, she found the right one. The door opened and we stepped inside; the room was pitch black. I could see nothing, but there was a smell of mildew and hot, stale air that grated on the lungs. Rosa Elena coughed and gasped. Then she pulled the curtains and the sun streamed into the room revealing millions and millions of tiny particles of dust. Rosa Elena unlocked the door that led to the balcony. The wind rushed in and sucked the dust toward the sky.

The balcony floor was covered with bird shit and the green paint was peeling. One house plant was already dead; a sickly vine crawled along the wall looking for water. Above us a flock of birds circled not knowing where to home, now that the last of their palm trees was being removed. Below us, on the Rio Mississippi, workmen with picks and spades were digging up a palm tree as high as the Skipper's Bridge. Half a dozen trees had already been uprooted. There were deep craters in the center of the alameda and piles of dirt along the curb.

"The Skipper wouldn't recognize the street any more," Rosa Elena said. She sat down on the immense bed and ran her fingers through the black fur pelt that covered the mattress. On the wall behind the bed was another portrait of Rosa Elena. It looked like it belonged over a bar in the Wild West. Rosa Elena's lips were a scarlet red, her hair raven black. The gown revealed the curve of her breasts. She couldn't have been older than eighteen or nineteen, wearing her first evening gown. The artist had caught her youth and arrogance, and had added a touch of the vamp.

"The Skipper used to say that I was his pin-up," Rosa Elena said in a coy tone of voice. "I usually don't let people see this painting. The one downstairs makes me look more respectable, doesn't it? That's why this one is locked up here."

I let my eyes wander around the room. I was looking for the Kaiser's picture. When I was helping Rosa Elena with writing the essay "Remembering Traven," she told me that Traven always kept a picture of the Kaiser on the wall, that it was still on the third floor.

"Where's the Kaiser's picture?" I asked.

"You mean it's not here?" Rosa Elena asked. "Don't worry, I'll find it somewhere."

"Yes, I hope so; I'd like to see it." I noticed a small round alarm clock beside the bed. The case was as red as the lips in the portrait on the wall. The time read 5:40. I looked at my watch: 10:30. I picked up the alarm clock and was about to reset the time when Rosa Elena reached up to stop me. "Traven died at 5:40," she said. "I want to keep the hands like this." She stood up and ran her fingers over the calendar. It was so dusty I couldn't read the dates. Rosa Elena found a rag and wiped it clean. It was March 1969. "He died on the twenty-sixth," she said. "That morning we made a death mask of his face." She reached around and removed a cloth that revealed Traven's face. It was dark. The mouth was small, the eyes were cold, the cheeks sunken. It looked like his flesh was decomposing fast, and the bones were emerging from beneath the surface. There was a sneer on his lips.

"My husband didn't look this bad at the end," Rosa Elena said. "But as soon as death came his whole face suddenly collapsed." She covered her husband's eyes and sat down on the edge of the bed. What a morbid preoccupation with death, I thought!

"Do you know how it looked to him at the end?" I asked. "He was always writing about death in his books. Maybe he saw the Bone Man he described in *Macario,* or death as the Great Music Master who appears in *The Bridge in the Jungle*

62

and plays a tune that carries Carlosito away from the living."

"In Mexico Death isn't a man but a woman," Rosa Elena said. "She's *La Muerte*. My husband wasn't afraid of her. I remember that March we had an unexpected hail storm. He was very ill but he went outside and looked up at the sky. The Skipper fought to the end, and when death finally came he was ready. You must remember the end of *The Death Ship;* death is the 'Great Skipper' who takes Stanislav on a long, long voyage that frees him from all pain, on a ship that demands no passports or identification papers. No one is refused, not the outcasts, exiles, or homeless. So at last Traven joined his old friend Stanislav."

"He didn't get religious at the end, did he?" I asked.

"Religious no, of course not, but he was in a way spiritual," Rosa Elena said. "For Traven rebirth comes after the grave, but it has nothing to do with the Catholic Church. It's more from the old myths and legends. You see, my husband believed in a kind of reincarnation, like the Orientals, and sometimes I think that his spirit is alive today in nature, all around us."

10

Rosa Elena unlocked the doors and cabinets and invited me to explore. "I want you to see it all," she said; I didn't hesitate. It seemed that Rosa Elena had saved everything of Traven's. I tried on his eyeglasses and saw the steady decline of his vision, especially in his right eye. I sat down at his typewriters, three old Remingtons, and played with the keys. Having read *The Death Ship* a dozen times I pounded out the first sentence by memory:

> We had brought, in the holds of the S.S. *Tuscaloosa,*
> a full cargo of cotton from New Orleans to Antwerp.

"He didn't use this machine to write *The Death Ship,*" Rosa Elena said. "The Jungle Novels were written on this Remington. Most of *The Death Ship* was written before he came to Mexico. When he arrived here he was so poor he didn't have the money to buy a machine. My husband told me that he wrote *The Death Ship* and *The Cotton Pickers* by hand; he wanted those two books to be longer, but he had to stop when he ran out of paper and ink."

I poked my fingers into the dusty holes of his desk, and came out with rusty paper clips, thumb tacks, and stale chewing gum. What I liked best were the stubs of pencils that were so worn down that I could barely hold them between my thumb and index fingers.

"Why save these?" I asked. "You can't use them."

"Traven always kept a can of pencils on top of the desk," Rosa Elena said. "Once he had typed a book he went over the manuscript with a pencil and made changes. The pencils were as important as the typewriters. You remember what Traven says in *The Death Ship:* 'It is not the mountains that make destiny, but the grains of sand and the little pebbles.' So I save everything: the broken-down typewriters, the hearing aids, eyeglasses, paper clips, even the pencils. They were all an important part of his world."

In the big closet Rosa Elena had saved Traven's clothing; there were "uniforms" for all kinds of jobs and roles. She reached for a pith helmet and balanced it on top of her head, then grabbed a pair of trousers and held them against her waist. On the top shelf was a beautifully carved leather saddle, an Indian riding blanket, spurs, a bridle with the bit marked by the horse's teeth, and a Stetson hat—all the gear a cowboy would need. "Traven had several horses," Rosa Elena said. "He trained them himself, but he never *broke* them. He had so much love for animals, for all living creatures."

I reached into the far corner of the closet and pulled down one of those Chamula Indian sacks that expand as you add more and more things. This one grew smaller and smaller as I removed things: an Indian shirt, several woven belts, and a few pouches embroidered with red, yellow, and blue beads. I loosened the blue string and turned the pouch upside down in the palm of my hand. A few cocoa beans rolled out.

"The Indians wear these pouches around their necks," Rosa Elena said. "After they've been working fourteen or fifteen hours and they're dead tired, they chew on the beans, and then they can stand on their feet a while longer without falling asleep."

On the top shelf was a hammock, a sailor's cap, overalls stained with oil, and high, lace-up boots. But most of the closet was taken up with business suits. The jackets had wide lapels and the trousers had wide cuffs and baggy seats. The moths had attacked them, leaving large, ragged holes. We rummaged through the pockets, found a few old pesos, a key ring, and a daily diary for 1948, with notations like "Noche de Bellas Artes," "Peggy B.," and "sardines, string."

"The day he died the press invaded the house," Rosa Elena said. "They tramped across the carpets, the sofas, the beds, tracking mud everywhere. Malu caught one reporter up here, going through Traven's things. It was terrible. They were taking so many pictures, the flash bulbs kept exploding in my face. I couldn't see. I was sick and Malu had to take care of me. She was very good with Traven before he died. Malu wouldn't let the doctors hurt him. They kept poking him in the side; he was in so much pain from his kidney. The reporters wanted to poke him too, even after he was dead, just to touch the real body of the famous B. Traven. It was awful. And then, suddenly, they left . . . and the house was so quiet and still. The next day there were big headlines in all the papers: 'B. Traven Is Dead.' The day after that there was nothing in the press about Traven. Someone else *famous* had died and my husband was all forgotten. You see, Traven was right about fame! It doesn't mean a damned thing! He used to say that it flared up briefly like a sun spot, then disappeared, forgotten the next day. When the next day you're dead, what good does fame do you? Fame! Traven has more fame now than when he was alive, but does he care, does it do him any good? No, not at all. He didn't care about publicity, didn't want to be a celebrity, just wanted to be left alone! Look at his closet. It's so full of clothing, what a shame. . . . But why don't you try one on so it doesn't go to waste?"

I stood in front of the mirror trying my best to feel comfortable in Traven's oversized jacket. The shoulders were padded and his arms extended beyond my palms, but Rosa Elena insisted that once adjusted it would fit perfectly. So I brushed off the dust and decided to keep it.

"My husband had a split personality," Rosa Elena said. "He was Ret Marut—the German actor and anarchist. Very important that he was on the stage, that he made his life a stage. After Marut he was Torsvan—the Norwegian explorer, photographer, scientist, the man always traveling and investigating the unknown. Then came Traven the mysterious writer and Hal Croves the American literary agent and screen writer. It was a division of labor. Very sensible too. Traven was the artist who needed to be alone, Croves was the businessman who had to be among people. He used to say that I married four different men—Ret Marut, Torsvan, Traven, and Croves—and that I'd never be bored. 'But you're really in love with Marut, aren't you, confess, you think he's very handsome and romantic, don't you?' he would say. My husband rarely said *'I.'* It was a word absent from his vocabulary. It was always 'Marut did this and that'; never 'I did this and that.' He was always acting, always making up stories, even when there was no audience to watch him. He performed for himself because the true drama was in his own mind. We were just bystanders in the wings. More than anything else the play of his own imagination fascinated him. That's where he really lived, up here in his thoughts. Even when he was talking to me or to Fredde he would be more concerned with his own inner world."

"Did he ever have a nervous breakdown or crack up?" I asked.

"Come now. I'm surprised at you. You've read *The Night Visitor*. Then you know that he went crazy. He was living all alone in a bungalow on the edge of the jungle; he felt guilty about being a European. You see, Ret Marut came to Mexico to escape. He didn't want to live in Mexico. He was in hiding and he had nightmares of being arrested and sent back to jail in Germany. Gustav Landauer, Erich Mühsam, and Eugené Levine—his Munich friends—had either been killed or were in prison. Marut thought of himself as one of 'the living dead,' that's the way he put it. 'I should have died in Munich with the rest of them,' he said. He was heartbroken. His dreams were crushed. Most of the time he spent digging for relics; it was a good way to forget, so he thought, to lose himself in the remote past. But then he couldn't sleep at night. My husband made some very important archeological discoveries in Chiapas, but it bothered him, breaking into the tombs of the Aztecs and the Mayas. He was haunted by it.

"During that time in the jungle he went crazy. He didn't know whether he was Ret Marut or Torsvan, a German, a Scandinavian, an American. But then he wrote *The Night Visitor*. It's autobiographical. Then his spell of madness vanished and he became like a new man. After that he was B. Traven. With *The Night Visitor* he had found, how do you Americans say, his trademark, his signature as an author: the mystery of the jungle and the Indians, and of course himself. He was a man in love with mystery."

"And that was the only time, as far as you know, that he had a breakdown?" I asked.

"Yes, as far as I know," Rosa Elena said. "At the end of his life, the last ten years or so, he just wanted to be Hal Croves. He was old and tired; it was too difficult going back and forth from one identity to another, from Torsvan to Traven to Croves . . . It took so much energy. At the end he had his memories."

Rosa Elena opened another drawer, pulled out several dolls and held them affectionately. They were cute. "Ret Marut and Irene Mermet sold these dolls in the streets of Berlin when they were running from the police. They had no money and they were starving," Rosa Elena said. "Irene made the dolls from old rags; Marut stood on a busy corner in Berlin and sold them for a few marks. When Heidemann was here he asked me for one of Marut's dolls. He would have paid a lot of money for it, but I wouldn't give him a doll for all the money in the world. They're too precious to me; they're *my* treasure. But that Heidemann, I could strangle him. You know he took a manuscript of Traven's, *The Art of the Indians*. We've got to get it back from him and publish it ourselves because it has the most wonderful drawings and sketches by my husband."

I held a doll that had long, golden hair, fashioned of wool. She looked like a German peasant in her traditional folk costume. The doll was extraordinarily well-preserved. None of the seams were torn and the material had not mildewed. Her button eyes had not cracked or chipped.

"That was the most *difficult* time of his life," Rosa Elena said. "He slept in alleys and doorways listening for the police. Mrs. Yampolsky can tell you about that period."

"Mrs. Yampolsky? What does she know?" I asked.

"You mean she hasn't talked about Germany?" Rosa Elena asked.

"No."

"She hasn't said anything about Malu, has she?"

"No. But she talked about Hal Croves," I said. "She doesn't think that Croves was Traven."

"Oh, that's ridiculous," Rosa Elena snapped. "Mrs. Yampolsky's feelings were hurt years ago and she's never recovered. Croves asked her to translate *The Creation of the Sun and the Moon* from German into English. She did a terrible job and we told her so, but I insisted we had to give her something, poor dear, she tried her best."

"If you don't like Mrs. Yampolsky why did you suggest I live at her house?" I asked.

"Mrs. Yampolsky will be very useful to you," Rosa Elena said. "She can tell you a lot about Ret Marut and the German period. Ask her about *Der Ziegelbrenner.*"

There was a knock at the door and Herme poked her face into the room. *"Señora,* Malu is here," she announced.

"Very well," Rosa Elena said. "Now please tell Malu we'll join her in a moment."

"Señora, shall I dust and vacuum the room?" Herme asked.

"No. I do not want this room disturbed," Rosa Elena said. She chased Herme toward The Bridge, locked the door, then followed us down the stairs.

11

Malu reclined seductively on the living room sofa under the portrait of her mother. While she painted her fingernails the same shade of pink as her lips, her husband Miguel, the owner of the Campos Hermanos steel factory, read the newspaper. And Herme knelt at Malu's feet, adjusted her stockings, and slipped her toes into a rose-colored shoe. I started to say *"Yo sé que . . ."* but Malu put her hand over my mouth.

"Talk in English. The servants are very nosy and I don't want them to understand us," she said. "Herme and Petra were gossiping about you and mother in the kitchen. She lets them get away with murder." Herme couldn't understand English, but from Malu's tone of voice and her eyes, she knew that she was the subject of the conversation. Malu didn't like the rose-colored shoes; she kicked them off and sent Herme upstairs to fetch another pair.

"Now you see a real liberated woman," Miguel said. "I don't tell her what shoes to wear; she decides all on her own with that big brain of hers."

"Oh, shut up, Miguel, you've given me a headache. Now be a dear and get me an aspirin and a glass of water."

"He's really a very sweet man, and I'm crazy about him," Malu said, after Miguel left the room. "We were just talking about you, wondering why mother chose *you* to write the bio-

70

graphy of Traven. You're much younger than the others. At first I thought it would be Heidemann, but mother didn't like him. Then Johnson came from California, but he didn't satisfy her either. Of course, Judy Stone never could have done the job. Perhaps you can. I suppose you *think* you can. I'll give you all the help I can."

"Do you think that Croves was Traven?" I asked.

"Of course he was," Malu said.

"How do you know?" I asked.

"He told me," Malu said.

"Isn't it mysterious that Traven married your mother?"

"There's no mystery about that," Malu said. "They were in love."

Miguel put the aspirin on Malu's extended tongue and handed her a glass of water. Meanwhile, Herme had returned with more shoes. Malu took one look at them and with a wave of the hand dismissed Herme. "Miguel, I'll have to buy a new pair of shoes."

"What can you tell me about Traven?" I asked.

"I loved him very much and he was super good to us," Malu said. "My mother probably wouldn't like me saying this, but they had a terrific sex life."

"But wasn't he an old man when he married your mother?" I asked. "I should guess he was about sixty-seven."

"Oh, that's funny! You think you won't want sex when you're sixty-seven? Miguel won't be tired of sex if he lives to be a hundred. He wakes up every morning with a very big erection."

"How do you know Traven and your mother had sex?"

"I could hear them," Malu said. "My elder sister was already married to Julio and living in an apartment, but I was right here. I saw what went on; I heard the sounds of love-making right through the bedroom wall. You know, you can hear everything that goes on in this house if you listen carefully. The Skipper was a real romantic, but very funny too, and that combination made him extra special to me. He would make jokes about everything, including sex. Like not being

71

able to get an erection when a beautiful woman with big breasts was in your bed. Miguel would have a fit, but Skipper would laugh."

Rosa Elena had come through the door just in time to hear Malu mention erections. "Lunch is ready now, Malu, so you'll change the subject, please." Rosa Elena escorted us into the dining room; Miguel handed us glasses of tequila and offered a toast: "To the Skipper."

"Did you know him?" I asked.

"No," Miguel said. "But he sounds like a very shrewd man. He may have been mysterious, but I look at the bottom line. He made a lot of money, didn't he."

"Yes, enough to live well," I said. "But he didn't make big money, not like Norman Mailer or Harold Robbins, and you must make a lot more than he did from your factory, Miguel."

"Not as much as Malu had hoped before we were married," Miguel said. "Campos Hermanos steel was bought by a Wall Street bank recently. Malu married a multinational."

We were about to sit down at the table, when Rosa Elena shouted at Herme, "Change it immediately, it makes me sick!"

"What's wrong?" I asked. Malu pointed to the tablecloth and the linen napkins. "You can't have red and orange like that," she said. "It's impossible to eat looking at such nauseating colors, but what do *they* know about it!"

Herme and Petra cleared the plates. "Hurry up," Malu shouted. She had been talking in English but now she switched to Spanish so the maids could understand her. "We're *starving*, do you think we have all day to wait? Honestly, mother, I don't understand why you keep those two good-for-nothings any longer. They're more trouble than they're worth."

I watched the expression on Petra's face; she was terrified. But Herme was in a rage. She picked up the knives and forks and for a moment I thought she might use them, but then she lost her nerve. "Put the knife on the other side," Malu shouted. At last everything was neatly set. Petra served a soup of chicken, tortillas, avocado, and corn. Malu handed me a jalapena chile and dared me to swallow it whole.

"No, don't, it'll kill you," Rosa Elena said. "Malu's just making trouble; she loves to make trouble." Malu rolled the chile between the palms of her hands—"to make him real angry," she said—and popped it into her mouth. "The Skipper swallowed them like candies," she said, goading me on.

Rosa Elena put her hand on my shoulder. "Don't you think he's looking more and more like the Skipper?" she asked Malu.

"Oh, mother, whatever are you thinking? Are you all right? Maybe you *should* move to Cuernavaca." Herme cleared the soup plates, and Petra served the next course, pigs' knuckles under mustard sauce. Malu reached for a corn tortilla and finding them cold, sent Petra running to the kitchen. *"Caliente,"* she shouted.

"You're giving me an upset stomach," Rosa Elena said. "I don't want any more shouting." She pushed her plate away and carefully folded her napkin. "His expressions are the Skipper's," she said. "Haven't you noticed the way he *watches* us?"

"I suppose that he is becoming one of the family," Malu said. "Now I'll have to bring him a gift from Texas. Mother wants chocolate bars. Maybe you'd like a new fountain pen?"

After lunch Malu and Miguel piled their suitcases into a cab and left the Rio Mississippi for the airport. I was anxious to return to the third floor. We climbed the stairs, stopping briefly at the office. Rosa Elena made sure all the file cabinets were locked, then rummaged in the hall closet until she found a crowbar.

Rosa Elena turned the key. The air was fresher and the smell of mildew less strong. Rosa Elena stretched out on the bed, her head propped up by pillows.

"Drag it here," she said, pointing to a crate that was gathering dust in the corner. It was about six feet long, a yard wide and, say, two feet deep. It looked as though the carpenter had intended it to be used as a coffin. It certainly was the size and shape of a coffin, large enough to accommodate a man my size. I got down on my hands and knees—it was that heavy—and pushed it toward Rosa Elena. Then I used the crowbar to pry open the lid. The wood was brittle and dry and I had to work carefully so it wouldn't crack and splinter. Finally, all the nails were loose. I lifted the top plank and rested it against the wall.

Rosa Elena peered inside. I removed the top layer of newspapers—copies of *The New York Times* from 1928, and the long-defunct *New York World* from 1927—and recognized the names of Calvin Coolidge, Benito Mussolini, and Charles Lindbergh in the headlines.

"Traven would disappear into the jungle for months at a time," Rosa Elena said. "The newspapers would pile up, higher and higher. When he returned from his journey he would take one look at the headlines and say to himself, 'I didn't miss a thing, it's the same, old world.' But he liked to keep up his English, so he would read through the papers."

Under the newspapers Traven had stored his souvenirs of the jungle: the feathers of the quetzal bird, used as currency in remote areas of Mexico and Guatemala as recently as the 1930s; balls of cotton; dry, brittle tobacco leaves that crumbled in my hands; the limb of a mahogany tree; and a long, sharp thorn that I recognized. I had never seen it before, but I had read about these thorns in *The Rebellion of the Hanged*. Urbano, a lumberjack in the mahogany forest, blinds an overseer by stabbing his eyes out with a thorn, like the one I was holding.

Bows and arrows were also stored in the coffin-like box. The string was frayed, but the obsidian arrowheads were as sharp and polished as the day they were chipped and filed. Rosa Elena pulled out a shell necklace and dangled it so that the light played on the surface. "Traven collected these necklaces from the Indians along the Pacific Ocean," she said. "They're very rare. He sent them to his German publishers and they gave them to readers as special gifts. The Gutenberg Book Guild was no ordinary publishing house; their books were real works of art, like these hand-crafted necklaces."

Beneath the balls of soiled cotton was a Colt .45 and a box of shells. I picked up the revolver and felt its weight in my hand. "He had rifles too that he used for hunting, but Miguel borrowed them," Rosa Elena said.

At the very bottom of the coffin Traven had stashed a dozen or so small notebooks that recorded his experiences in Chiapas in 1926, 1928, and 1929, and his experiences in Tampico in 1924 and 1925. I flipped through the pages, noticed that they were all in English, and that the handwriting was clear. Each entry was listed by day and month, and in some cases by year too:

> Lost in the jungle in a terrible way. Late in the afternoon reach springs. Talk with woodmen. Half an hour to springs. *Tascalate* is a certain kind of paste, tortillas ground with cocoa beans roasted and ground. Refreshing when fresh. Later ferments and tastes sour.

> For the poorest supper am charged $1. Near Salvador bridge at Salvador charge for passing that bridge man or beast $0.10. Indians have to pay too.

> In Tapachula Fiesta de San at night from 12–2. Marimba plays in the colonades [sic] where sleeping. Hilario and Juan drunk. But work faithfully with high sense of duty and minding well their contract.

> Chamulas elect each year new president. 1929. I. l. [sic] president was told by government officials not to resign, stayed in office. Town was surrounded. I. l. [sic] at 10 h. president and all his family was killed. Secr'y on the phone telling proceeds when soldiers arrived Indians had disappeared none was caught, killers not known.

> *Quadrillos:* men, women and children that go to to

the monterias in big troop. He who does not pay fine
or debts is sold to the monterias. . .Chamulas when
coming to San Cristobal are taken by the authorities
by the hundreds and are sent to build the road
without money, without food.

I also found a separate piece of paper in Traven's handwriting that was dated "morning, 4 March, 1969," three
weeks before his death. The line of writing rose slightly from
left to right—a sign, they say, that the author is optimistic:

> This world with all its troubles, short comings, dis-
> appointments, pains, problems, unwelcome events,
> occasional hailstorms is after all still too beautiful to
> abandon even if you are sick and tired of life or close
> to a hopeless end. Stick it out! Keep on fighting!
> Don't give up. Spit Death in its face and turn the
> other way. The sun is still in the sky surrounded by
> stars.

"I remember that day," Rosa Elena said. "He made out his
will because he knew that he was going to die, but, you see, he
was a real fighter down to the end. Always, always, the sun in
the sky gave him hope."

Finding Traven's "last testament," as I've called it, gave me
a sense of intimacy with the author. The death mask, the clock
that was stuck at 5:40, the calendar that read March 1969, the
baggy trousers hanging in the closet—these things said "B.
Traven is dead." But the "last testament" said "B. Traven is
alive, he is here now." I could hear him spit Death in the face,
and I could see him gaze up at the sun in the sky surrounded
by stars.

12

That night I stayed on the Rio Mississippi to read the diary Traven kept in Tampico in the mid-twenties. He listed the days he had diarrhea—about three straight weeks—and the days it rained—also about three straight weeks. There were several notations about work and money.

Staying with three cotton pickers. Two mestizos. One Negro. Night horrible. No sleep. Too many mosquitoes. Too hot.

Oil camp. Dinner. Black sugar.

B. came. Is talking about job in oil camp. Go down. In camp supper. Indifferent welcome. Help drilling. 12 h. midnight meal.

Will pay 3 ps. Go up to pump station. Work till 5 h.pm. Bring back time keeper.Tells there is no job, pays one day wages. Supper. Night in camp.

Meet Mr. G. got the sack for his fault by his drilling. No word about money – support.

Got the Canadian money. British counsel [*sic*] re-
fuses.

Back to Co. with the car of the geologists. See the S's
house. No roof. With same car to farm. Cotton-
pickers gone. $. Great joy.

As a cotton picker Traven earned a "miserable peso a day,"
and that was twice as much as the Mexicans made. The cotton farmer refused to pay him the same wage as the native
laborers on the grounds that a white man, by virtue of his skin
color, deserved more money whether or not he picked more
cotton. The Tampico diary also described a broken-down hotel with a leaky roof and cots for fifty centavos a night.

There was one sentence that was enigmatic and revealing at
the same time: the Traven trademark. It almost seemed that
Traven had written the sentence to tantalize someone who
might come upon it years later. Or else he was paranoid and
felt that he had to make oblique, veiled references in his own
private journal. In any case, the sentence read:

The Bavarian of Munich is dead, black brother.

At first I couldn't believe my eyes; it was too good to be
true. The Bavarian of Munich is dead, black brother. Surely,
the Bavarian of Munich was Ret Marut. Here, Torsvan or
Traven, or whatever he was calling himself when he first arrived in Mexico, realized that his Old World identity was
dead, that he was in a strange New World of black brothers.
It was only a fragment and yet how incisive. It seemed to
crystallize a whole experience.

I wanted to know what lay behind that sentence, and what
led to the realization that "The Bavarian of Munich was
dead." Who was the "black brother?" Was he a symbolic figure or was he the Negro cotton picker that is referred to in the
diary? Did a black worker meet and befriend Traven in Tampico? Why did he call himself the "Bavarian of Munich?"

Why didn't he say "Marut is dead"? Probably for much the same reason that he kept the journal in English. He didn't want anyone to know that he was a fugitive from Germany, wanted by the Bavarian police. At the same time, by describing himself as the "Bavarian of Munich," he made himself mysterious. It was like wrapping himself in a cloak and disappearing into the shadows. He was making himself a living legend.

Tucked between the leaves of the Tampico diary were a number of important government documents, many of them identification cards. Traven had used so many different aliases, many of them variations on the same name: Traves Torsvan Croves, Traven Torsvan Croves, Traven Torsvan, Berrick Torsvan. One document dated July 1930 identified him as Traven Torsvan, age 40, date of birth 5 March, 1890, place of birth Chicago, Illinois, religion Protestant. Another document indicated that he had lived in San Antonio, Texas, in 1932 and again in 1934, with a Major J. A. Cashburn, that he had studied to be an airplane pilot, and had received his credentials from a flying school. Still another document showed that Traven was naturalized a Mexican citizen on September 13, 1951. Nine days earlier he had certified that his name was Traves Torsvan, born on May 3, 1890, that he cultivated fruit trees in Acapulco. Finally, on another sheet of paper he had practiced his signature:

B. Traven

B. Traven

B. Traven

B. Traven

B. Traven

The dates, names, and places were swimming in my head, so I turned out the light and locked the door. Tabasco followed me across the hall, sniffing the carpet. Rosa Elena seemed to be fast asleep and there was no rock 'n' roll from the discotheque across the street.

I looked at my face in the mirror, then at the photos of Tina, Diego, Weston, and Traven that were taped to the glass. I thought about Traven's birth, his parents, and wondered was he really the Kaiser's illegitimate son, the Kaiser's bastard son —or was it possible that Traven made up this story to confound you and me, his readers, all of us? And I wondered why he had married Rosa Elena Lujan, and what had been the nature of their relationship.

I had the feeling that he was watching me, playing with me, that he had left a trail of clues—some true, some false—and that he was judging me. I wondered if Rosa Elena was reporting what Traven had told her—or had she changed and shaped the material to suit her own needs and tastes? Whose stories were they? Traven's or Rosa Elena's? Or had they collaborated in their creation during the last years of Traven's life? Perhaps they had concocted a wide variety of stories. Depending on the identity and personality of the writer who came to investigate the Traven "mystery," Rosa Elena could vary her performance. Maybe what she told me about Traven conformed, in part, to her view of *me*, as well as her view of *him*. Maybe she was making it up as she went along.

Surely the old man living with Rosa Elena on the Rio Mississippi chose to remember some things clearly, distort others, even bury a few experiences. Why should he be completely honest with her after a lifetime cultivating the mystery with others?

There were Traven's stories and there were Rosa Elena's stories. And there were stories inside of stories inside of stories. There were stories told by the same storyteller, three or four or five different ways, at different times, to half a dozen different listeners, and those listeners, in turn, told different stories depending on what they remembered and what they wanted to remember. The damned storyteller had so many different identities. He was Croves! I was sure of that! Yes, B. Traven was the same as Hal Croves! I didn't share Mrs. Yampolsky's doubts.

When I first arrived on the Rio Mississippi I was surprised to find such affluent surroundings. Reading Traven's books had suggested that I would find humbler, starker surroundings—if not the poverty of the Oso Negro or the Hotel Que, then something less aristocratic. Certainly I had not anticipated servants. But gradually I came to accept the fact that Traven/Torsvan (writer/explorer, myth maker/scientist) became Hal Croves (literary agent and business representative). The man who wrote about workers, strikes, enslaved Indians, and guerrilla warriors became "The Skipper" on the Rio Mississippi, a married man with an aristocratic wife, two adopted daughters, a big house, fat royalties, and Indian servants. The vagabond in tattered trousers and shirt who had picked cotton under the hot sun with his "black brother" had put on a tuxedo with tails, silk shirt, and bow tie to play J. P. Morgan.

I fell asleep and I dreamed that I was in the library with Rosa Elena and Frederico Marin. The Doctor wanted to read a book on the top shelf. He pointed to it and asked me to reach it for him because I was taller than he. I stood on tiptoe and extended my arm, but just as I touched the book it became an old shoe in need of new soles. I turned around and saw that the Doctor was examining Rosa Elena. I was jealous. She was lying on the carpet. I thought that she wanted my help, but when I got closer I saw that the Doctor was tickling her neck. Rosa Elena was laughing. My mouth opened wide, my eyes closed, and I laughed too. But in a moment I was laughing all by myself. The Doctor disappeared and Rosa Elena was sitting in the black chair with no clothes on. Her skin was extraordinarily soft and brown and warm. I wanted to embrace her, to caress her, but the photographer asked us to smile for the camera.

At first I couldn't see the photographer's face. He was using one of those old-fashioned cameras and his head was buried under a black cloth. Suddenly, there was a flash of light and a loud bang. The photographer threw off the black hood and looked into my eyes. I had thought that he was going to be Torsvan but it wasn't him and I was disappointed. The next thing I knew Rosa Elena was shaking me. "Get up, it's late," she said. "Get up, get up, breakfast's almost ready."

13

Reading Rosa Elena's files I learned a great deal about Traven's identity as Ret Marut, the German actor, bohemian, and anarchist.* From 1908 to 1914 Marut was an actor on the German stage. He played minor roles, mostly in romantic comedy, but he also appeared in serious drama. In *Hamlet*, for example, he was one of the gravediggers. Marut was also a theater critic; he defended the new controversial work of August Strindberg and Henrik Ibsen.

Then, with the outbreak of World War I, most German theaters shut down and Marut was out of work. However, his

*I am deeply indebted to the work of Rolf Recknagel. Professor Recknagel spent ten years digging through German police records, interviewing older radicals, actors, and writers. His *B. Traven: Beitrage zur Biografie*, published in Leipzig in 1966 but never translated into English, proved conclusively that B. Traven was Ret Marut— long before anyone, including Rosa Elena, mentioned the Marut/Traven connection. Recknagel gave no support to the notion that Marut/Traven was the bastard son of Kaiser Wilhelm II. Rather, he suggested that Traven was born Charles Trefny on July 2, 1880, in St. Louis, Missouri, that he traveled to Germany about the turn of the century to study theology, and that in 1903 he was expelled from the University of Freiburg for an "immoral act." Though there are no "hard facts" to back up this hypothesis, I find it appealing because while Traven opposed organized religion he was deeply conversant with Christian theology and church ritual. He opposed Christianity with all the fervor of the ex-Christian. He detested the Church, the role of popes and priests in buttressing the established order against workers and peasants, but he regarded Christ as a brother to the downtrodden of the earth. In this sense, Traven belongs to a tradition of Christian rebels. He wanted to dismantle Rome, as well as the Lutheran and Methodist hierarchy, and return to the "original egalitarian" teachings of Christ.

problems were not so much financial as political. Marut didn't *need* a job. He told friends that he had a "private fortune" (though he didn't reveal the source of his wealth), and boasted that he never invested his money on the black market, never tried to profit from the war.

In 1912 Marut registered with the Dusseldorf police as a British subject born in San Francisco. Then, in 1914, his legal status changed drastically. As an Englishman living in Germany, while England and Germany were at war, Marut was subject to arrest, detention, or, at the least, scrutiny by the police. And in fact there was suspicion that the mysterious, enigmatic Ret Marut was a spy. He could have been held as the agent of a foreign power. So Marut changed his nationality. From 1915 on he insisted that he was an American citizen, born in San Francisco on February 25, 1882.

Apparently, Marut believed that he *was* born in San Francisco. In July 1915 he wrote to the San Francisco Department of Public Health to ask for his birth certificate. A health officer replied, "All the birth records of the City and County of San Francisco. . .prior to April 18, 1906 were destroyed in a general conflagration. . .therefore this office is unable to furnish a certified copy of the birth certificate of Ret Marut, said to have been born in the City of San Francisco on the twenty-fifth day of February, 1882." Undaunted by his failure to obtain a birth certificate, Marut applied for naturalization as a German citizen; pending a full hearing, the Dusseldorf police issued him a temporary identity card.

Meanwhile, Marut moved to Munich and began to write stories that drew upon his experiences as an observer on the Western Front in 1914. In "Der Fremde Soldat" ("The Unknown Soldier") Marut condemns a war that creates nameless, faceless human beings, and then destroys them on the battlefield. But the story is also an autobiographical reverie. It describes Marut himself—a man who has no clear identity, and no recognizable past. Like the soldier, he too is unknown.

In 1916 Marut wrote an anti-war novel *Letters to Fraulein von S.*, and published it under the pseudonym Richard Maurhut;

the man with an alias took another alias. At the beginning of *Letters to Fraulein von S.* a woman receives a letter informing her of the death of a man who "died in the service of the fatherland, never smiled, and was a kind of mysterious figure." The nameless soldier leaves Fraulein von S. a collection of letters: accounts of life on the front. The woman reads the last letter first. "I have nothing more to say," the soldier writes. "All has come to its end, my life and I. Tomorrow comes death. They can't take anything from me because there is nothing more to take, and all search would be for nothing." Then the Fraulein turns to the first letter. "I am alone, totally and absolutely alone," the soldier writes. "So alone and lonely that you can only understand and appreciate it, if you have suddenly awoken from a dream and realized in a flash that no one on earth, not one single person, not even your mother, is related to you." Once again, Ret Marut, alias Richard Maurhut, seems to be reflecting on the trauma of his own identity.

Maurhut's descriptions of the soldier's fears and dreams are matched by his brilliant evocations of the chaos, craziness, and horror of war. We see the body of a half-dead soldier, hanging from a wall of barbed wire in "no man's land," unable to get loose. The bullets of both armies sail over his head. He is in such torment and pain that he points to his heart and begs his friends to shoot him and end the misery. Out of love and friendship they oblige. (The roots of Traven's own irony and cynicism are in Richard Maurhut's *Letters to Fraulein von S.*)

The central irony of the novel involves the main character's motives. He charges into battle and in the process kills enemy soldiers. He leads his regiment to victory. But when the officers award him a medal for bravery in action he explains that he is no hero but a coward, that he charged into battle because he wanted to commit suicide. "I don't give a shit," he tells his superiors.

An ancestor to Dalton Trumbo's dying soldier in *Johnny Got His Gun*, Traven's nameless, anti-war anti-hero confronts death alone. "Behind me I hear a harmonica," he says. "A crow flaps its heavy, black wings over the emptiness, crows, caws, and is not to be seen any more. And suddenly I know it. I have nothing more to say. Everything is fulfilled. My life and I, all my thoughts are with me. Tomorrow comes death. He can't take anything from me, because there is nothing more to take. And all my searching is for nothing. I have triumphed."

The next year, 1917, Marut used part of his "private fortune" to start his own newspaper/magazine, *Der Ziegelbrenner* (*The Brickburner*). Posing as an aesthete and bohemian, Marut tried to pack in as much anti-war sentiment as the state censor would allow. In March 1918 he wrote and published this poem:

> Men fall men stand
> Men die men live
> Mothers grieve women mourn
> People make hand grenades,
> Curse in the street car.
> Children's cries are everywhere.

Under the pen name Hyotamore von Kyrena, Marut published his own *Death Songs*, haunting, lyrical poems that condemn society's attitude toward death:

> You cry for the dead? Fools that you are. Cry for the living and say to the others, Blessed are you who are dead. Why do you cry over dead ones? Why. . .Because it doesn't cost anything, because it looks good, because it is customary, because you label the one who doesn't cry as insensitive and hard-hearted, though most likely his is the most honest among you scoundrels. . .

> So cry in God's name. But I tell you there are dead ones alive who are more alive than the living ones, and among you are living ones who are dead already

since their first day of school. . .

For me it is inconsequential whether I take my last breath in an easy chair or on a dung heap. The only thing is that no one bothers me when I die, neither the anointer nor the doctor, not the magician or the high priest, nor the soft hand of the one who is waiting for me to die. Nothing is worth the agony of reading in the eyes and on the lips of the attendants the thought that soon it will be over.

As soon as you understand that death is not an end, but only a condition, only a step between events that you can follow precisely, then there will be no more slaves on earth. And of course no masters either.

In November 1918, Marut published the rhetorical prose poem "The Day Dawns":

The storm nears, the day dawns, be ready. Take the sleep out of your eyes, comrades, the day dawns. A new day. A new day? A new day??? Be ready. Think. Words, words, nothing but words invade me. Where is the deed? The new day? The blow from a club is no deed. A murder is no deed. Think. Only once, once think and the world falls to pieces. May it be. Dare to think. But words, words, nothing but words invade me. Split the old world into a hundred, thousand splinters. Make them equal to the sands of the desert so that not a single piece of the old wall remains to darken the sunlight of the new world. Don't clutch onto words. Don't stick to the old wisdom.

Work. Full, complete, inconsiderate work. The superior ones, the timid ones, the cautious ones, the overly cerebral ones will detain you enough. Think.

Only thinking makes you free. Only thinking makes
you godlike. Reflect. Take the sleep out of your eyes,
comrades. Everyone stand up for his own affairs. His
own affair is that of humanity. The storm nears. The
day dawns. Reflect.

Readers wrote to Marut complaining about his style and
language. When one subscriber told him to modulate his
"blunt, coarse language," Marut replied, "One can't shovel
shit with an elegant lady's hatpin." When another reader
complained that an issue was late in the mail, Marut wrote
that he "could not come out punctually, and even if I could I
wouldn't." He explained that there was no assurance that
subscribers would get the full number of issues that they had
paid for, that he would "murder *The Brickburner* with a laughing heart" as soon as he noticed "signs of arteriolsclerosis in
the pages of the magazine."

Throughout 1918, as German troops suffered loses at the
front and as the workers' movement grew at home, Marut became more outspoken politically. In December 1918 he
printed and distributed the pamphlet "The World Revolution
Begins." Marut's irony and cynicism were now overshadowed
by his new-found hope and optimism. He thought that utopia
was on its way.

Marut still defined himself as a solitary individual, but he
began to throw out lines of communication to other individuals, groups, and organizations. He was less suspicious of others, more willing to join in collective political activity. "I
belong neither to the Social Democratic Party, nor to the
Spartacus Group, nor to the Bolsheviks," Marut wrote in
1919. "I belong to no party. . .because I see membership in a
party as the reduction of my personal freedom." However, he
noted that—although he wasn't a proletarian—he "welcomed
the dictatorship of the proletariat" because it would "deliver
the people from the dictatorship of monopoly capital, and the
dictatorship of militarism." Marut went so far as to praise the
newly founded Soviet Union, a sentiment he later regretted.

"Once I wished that the light of the world would come from Germany. But now it comes from Russia," he wrote. Marut warned the Communists to be prepared for an attack by the Social Democrats. "They are already asking for war against the Bolsheviks," he cautioned.

With the end of World War I, Marut considered closing down *The Brickburner*. However, when the Socialists came into power he saw that the magazine had a new role to play. The Kaiser abdicated the throne and fled the country; the Socialists were in power. But Marut insisted that no fundamental changes had been made. The state looked more modern, but still tyrannized the individual; the Social Democrats promised freedom, but delivered new laws. "The Social Democrats brought no revolution of the proletariat but a revolution of the capitalists," Marut wrote. "They went the way that every party in Germany has gone that once had revolutionary aims; they are dissolute and spiritually in rags."

Marut launched an attack on the Social Democrats, and all parties that defended the state. "The single individual, not the state, is the most important," he told his readers. Marut's hero was Christ—not the Christ of the popes or the priests, but the Christ of Lenin and Rosa Luxemburg. "Christ didn't know the state," Marut proclaimed. "He only knew humanity. Christ was a communist."

In the winter of 1919 Marut emerged from his cultural isolation. He held a public meeting for *Brickburner* readers, though he didn't permit them to meet him. Characteristically, he stood in the shadows so they couldn't see him, but could only hear him read his poems and essays. There were a few sympathetic listeners, but most of the people in the audience were conservatives who had come to disrupt the meeting. They accused Marut of betraying Germany to the British, French, and Russians. From behind the curtain Marut insisted, "It took more courage to edit a newspaper like *The Brickburner* than to lie in the trenches. If there had been two hundred papers like *The Brickburner* during the war, Germany wouldn't be in ruins today." The conservatives finally succeeded in ending the meeting abruptly, but Marut escaped before the audience could see his face in the light.

Following this meeting, Marut emerged as a public figure. The anarchists and some of the Communists created a "Council Republic" in Munich and Marut joined the new government because, as he explained, "The Council Republic is a prerequisite for the reconstruction of culture, because it makes possible the liquidation of the state. A month later, the German army, backed by the German state "liquidated" the Council Republic and twelve hundred Munich citizens. Marut's dream of the "world revolution" was crushed. Not utopia, but hell, seemed to lie ahead.

14

Saturday morning before breakfast, I went shopping with Mrs. Yampolsky. We had made a deal; she needed me to cart her groceries home from the open-air market, and I needed her memories of World War I Germany and her information about Ret Marut. Mrs. Yampolsky was a storehouse of information, but it was extremely difficult to pry it loose. She had been a socialist in Germany, the United States, and Mexico. The police kept files on her in Berlin, Chicago, and Mexico City. (Curiously, Mrs. Yampolsky's journey paralleled Marut/Traven's journey from Germany to the United States to Mexico. After nearly fifty years of being in the same places at more or less the same time, they finally met in Mexico City in the late 1950s—and didn't like each other.)

"The police are still interested in me," Mrs. Yampolsky said. We were standing in the middle of the street surrounded by fruit and vegetable sellers, though they might just as well have been CIA agents, from the way Mrs. Yampolsky eyed them. Each peddler sold only one type of fruit or vegetable: either mangoes or oranges, chilies or tomatoes. There were at least two hundred separate stands, including those selling flowers, chickens, fish, and beef. The price and the quality differed from stand to stand; Mrs. Yampolsky insisted on getting the best quality at the cheapest price, and that meant going to each stand and haggling with the peddler.

"Oh, yes, they are still interested in me," she repeated. "A few years ago my passport expired. I went to the office and filled out the forms. Then the consul interviewed me. 'How long have you been a member of Americans for Communism in Mexico?' he asked. I told him 'Never'—because, you see, there is no such organization! They just make it up and anyone they don't like they accuse of belonging to it."

"Sounds like a B. Traven situation," I said. "It comes right out of the pages of *The Death Ship,* Mrs. Yampolsky."

"So what if it sounds like Traven? It's the truth and Traven wrote good, truthful books. Yes, they are still interested in me, so I wonder why you too are so interested, mister writer."

"I'm not interested in you," I said. "I'm interested in Traven, Marut, Croves, whatever you want to call him, he's the same man."

"I think that you are more interested in Mrs. Luján," Mrs. Yampolsky said. "If you *shmooz* around with those rich people all day and night you will never write the biography of B. Traven. That takes hard work."

When we got back to Mrs. Yampolsky's house, my labors began to be rewarded. There was still more work ahead—peeling and cutting potatoes, onions, and apples—but the more I worked, the more Mrs. Yampolsky confided in me.

"You couldn't trust Ret Marut," she insisted. "He didn't belong to any party or group, always worked alone. Very suspicious!"

"But he was against the war," I said.

"He was anti-Semitic," Mrs. Yampolsky said. "He blamed the Jewish journalists for starting the war, then he blamed the Jewish bankers for trying to stop the revolution in Russia. Oh, yes, Marut was against the war and for the revolution, but all the time he was against the Jews and for the Germans."

"He was against both the Jews and the Germans," I said. "He was against all national groups."

"But the Germans discriminated against the Jews," Mrs. Yampolsky said.

"True," I said. "And Marut attacked anti-Semitism. He detested it, but he also felt that Zionism was as bad as Germanism, Americanism, Russianism. He was against all patriotism and nationalism."

"See what Marut says about Moses," Mrs. Yampolsky said. I turned the pages of *The Brickburner* and found the March 1920 issue, printed underground when Marut was on the lam, wanted for treason by the German police. Marut told his readers that Moses wasn't a Jew at all, but the illegitimate child of Pharaoh's daughter, the Pharaoh's bastard grandson. Curious interpretation, isn't it, in the light of Rosa Elena's claims about her husband's parentage. "The revolutionary leader of the Jews was not a Jew, but a royal Egyptian," Marut declared. "So all great leaders are foreigners."

"Sounds to me like he's talking about himself, as well as Moses," I said. "He's thinking about his own illegitimate birth, his father the Kaiser, and his being an aristocrat and an outsider in the German revolution."

"Sounds to me like you are dreaming," Mrs. Yampolsky said. "Sounds to me like Marut was anti-Semitic. When the Jews have a great hero, a liberator, like Moses, Marut says he's an Egyptian prince. Very suspicious. Could be Marut was an agent. Why was he allowed to publish *The Brickburner* during the war when all the other newspapers were forbidden? Why was Rosa Luxemburg in prison when Ret Marut was free to come and go? Answer me that?"

I knew that Rosa Elena would have said it was because Marut was the Kaiser's son, and even though he was a bastard and an anarchist, he still received favors from his father. I didn't offer Mrs. Yampolsky that argument. Instead, I reminded her that *The Brickburner* was censored. Marut had to submit each issue to a state bureaucrat in Munich. In all the issues articles were banned. Every issue was forbidden for export, though Marut managed to smuggle copies of *The Brickburner* across the German border into France, Austria, Holland. Also, he was not allowed to put up posters in the streets of Munich advertising *The Brickburner*.

In 1917 and 1918 Marut was prohibited from publishing articles about the conditions endured by French prisoners of war. Marut had seen POWs used at the front to haul munitions under heavy fire. Under the terms of international law such treatment was illegal; naturally, the German censor could not allow Marut's exposé to be read by the German people.

Not only articles, but single words, phrases, and images were censored. Marut was prohibited from describing the members of the Reichstag as "gentlemen" because it was felt that he used the word derisively. He was forbidden to print verbatim a speech by Kaiser Wilhelm II—no commentary added—because the censor claimed that "when published in *The Brickburner* the speech acquired a different meaning than when published in the Munich *Nachrichten*."

Marut's bitter fantasies were also censored. In 1917 he had written:

> One day a film will be shown: the World War or 9,000,000 dead, 25,000,000 crippled, six oceans full of the tears of women and children, charming comedy in five acts, in the main roles Henny Porten [a popular young German actress], Liza Weise, Hindenburg, Lloyd George, and Woodrow Wilson. In the epilogue the film will show us the executions, but I know already that none of the guilty will be present.

The Munich censor was offended by that scenario and tore it from the page scheduled for publication.

After the Kaiser was overthrown and the Social Democrats came into power, the old censors lost their jobs and new censors were quickly appointed to fill their posts. *The Brickburner* still had to be submitted for approval. "When the Social Democratic regime decreed the relaxation of the censorship I knew that meant the tightening of the censorship," Marut wrote. "With every new regime that announced a relaxation of censorship, a sharper censorship was imposed."

"Marut's attitude toward the censor was perverse," Mrs. Yampolsky said. "He admired the censor and sneered at his readers."

"Yes, that's true," I said, finding common ground with Mrs. Yampolsky at last. "Marut did enjoy his confrontations with the censor. He made himself into a kind of Dostoevskian hero—the arch rebel—at war intellectually with the arch bureaucrat. Marut was the underground man. You see, Mrs. Yampolsky, what I think is that if the Kaiser had a bastard son, and if that son became a revolutionary, he might very well have turned out to be Ret Marut."

"That's a mighty big *if*," Mrs. Yampolsky said. "And you can't excuse his anti-Semitism."

"I don't excuse it; I'm trying to understand it. He was living in a society that was profoundly anti-Semitic. Because Marut was mysterious about his past, readers of *The Brickburner* accused him of having Jewish ancestry. Of course, he denied it passionately, claimed there wasn't a drop of Jewish blood in his past. But look, Marut's anti-Semitism comes from the fact that people suspected him of being Jewish, and because there *was* genuine mystery about his parents. If he had something to hide maybe it was because there was Jewish blood in the family."

"And what happened to your hero Marut?" Mrs. Yampolsky asked. "Disappeared! Ran away! Left his comrades in prison."

"He went underground rather than be executed," I said. "That's no crime."

"Well, what did Marut publish when he was in this so-called underground?" Mrs. Yampolsky asked. "Garbage. He went off the deep end. He even claimed that he invented the theory of relativity before Einstein. What nonsense! Just taking away from the Jews again. *The Brickburner* became a science-fiction magazine. And fairy tales too. The 'Khundar' story he wrote is so bad I feel ashamed, even for him."

Again, I had no basic disagreement with Mrs. Yampolsky. As a fugitive Marut wrote and published several strange

94

articles in *The Brickburner*. In one issue he argued that there
were no straight lines anywhere, that everything was a spiral,
a curve. Marut offered a geometry of the universe, and at the
same time a personal philosophy. "I am alone. I am the sun.
I am the center of the universe. I am god," Marut wrote. Mrs.
Yampolsky thought he was crazy. And maybe he was.
Without a past, a family, a homeland, running from the police, living underground—all these factors precipitated a
crack-up.

In the final issue of *The Brickburner* Marut published "Khundar," a story about a wandering minstrel who is both beggar
and king, prince and pauper. Again, Marut seems to be writing disguised autobiography, a fable about himself. And writing "Khundar" enabled Marut to exorcise his own demons.
After he published the story he closed down *The Brickburner*,
and never wrote again under the name Ret Marut.

"Marut was Marut. Traven was Traven. Croves was
Croves," Mrs. Yampolsky said. "They were three separate
people, don't make them into one." Ironically, when Rosa
Elena insisted that Marut/Traven was the Kaiser's son I was
dubious. But the more Mrs. Yampolsky claimed it was impossible that Marut was a bastard prince, the more probable
it seemed to me. Unconsciously and unwittingly, Mrs. Yampolsky was persuading me of things I didn't want to believe.
Now, it seemed that Traven the anarchist and revolutionary
was haunted by the identity of his aristocratic parents, illegitimate birth, and stigma as an orphan and an outsider. I
saw a strong record of these feelings in Marut's writings on
Moses and in his short story "Khundar"; and later, in
Traven's *The Night Visitor* where the humble Indian charcoal
burner is also the royal Indian prince, and in *The Creation of the
Sun and the Moon,* where the humble Indian becomes a deity—
the sun king.

As Marut and as Traven he tapped the source of the basic
human myths and legends, and infused them in his own writings. Marut/Traven wrote about wanderers and exiles who
return home. He wrote about the dead who are resurrected,

about paupers who are really princes, and princes who are common peasants. Marut/Traven wrote about doubles, twins, brothers. In *The Death Ship* Traven's two heroes, Gales and Stanislav, are both orphans, sailors, both homeless, both without identity and family. They are soul-mates, brothers, and yet they are also fundamentally different. Gales is an American: optimistic and hopeful. Stanislav is, as his name suggests, a Slav; he is fatalistic, cynical, pessimistic. Behind Stanislav is Ret Marut, the Old World actor and anarchist who died in Munich when the revolution was crushed. Behind Gales is B. Traven, the New World explorer and proletarian who was born in Mexico among the Indians of the mysterious jungle.

Loss and discovery, death and resurrection, riches and poverty—these are the basic themes in Traven's books, from *The Death Ship* to *Macario*. Surely, they emerge from his own experiences, from his sense of himself as a prince turned proletarian, a vagabond who found a home, a dead man who was reborn, a nobody who wanted to live with the gods. But I couldn't convince Mrs. Yampolsky. "Marut was a scoundrel," she said. "He had nothing to do with the Kaiser or B. Traven." That was her final word and she was determined to make it *my* final word, to wean me from the ideas I had acquired from Rosa Elena.

15

Most of Mrs. Yampolsky's guests had known Hal Croves; the others had heard a lot about him and about the mystery of B. Traven. All of them had read Traven's books and each had his or her own theory.

Humberto, for example, wondered why Croves had not protested the massacre of citizens at Tlatelolco in 1968. "If Croves was Traven, then wouldn't he have raised his voice with the others? There were many writers and artists who went to jail," Humberto explained. "Even José Revueltas, and he was already an old man."

Humberto had wavy hair, a gentle smile, and warm eyes. I liked him immediately. He was a heavy-set, middle-aged man, a bachelor who lived with a group of artists and writers in La Casa de la Malintzin—the House of the Malintzin, the Aztec woman who became Cortés's mistress in 1519. That was, of course, a long time ago, but Malintzin (or "Malinche," as Cortés called her) was still a hot topic of conversation in Mexico. "She collaborated with the Spanish and betrayed the Aztecs," Humberto said when he gave me a tour of the immense walled house now almost five hundred years old. "Today we say that anyone who betrays another is a 'Malintzin.' You see, she's a kind of national disgrace."

Humberto sat at the head of the table. To his right was

Marianne, Mrs. Yampolsky's daughter, and to his left, Arjen, Marianne's Dutch husband. Marianne was a short, heavy woman; most of the time she looked grim, then suddenly she would break out into wild laughter, like the laughter of her mother.

Like Humberto, who studied clay, and like Arjen, who worked in irrigation, Marianne was employed by the Mexican government. She was responsible for two new and controversial school textbooks: one in biology, the other in history. In Monterrey, parents led by a zealous Catholic priest and funded by industrialists carted the textbooks into the streets and burned them, rather than let their children read about birth control or look at the illustrations that portrayed Mao, Che, Fidel, Allende.

Marianne had taught Rosa Elena's daughters at a school for the children of the Mexican elite. Malu she detested, Chele she loved. Marianne didn't hide those feelings, but she guarded her views about Hal Croves and Rosa Elena. "If I were you I would talk to Maria de la Luz Martínez," Marianne suggested.

"Who's she?" I asked. My question sent Marianne into peals of laughter. But she wouldn't say another word about Maria de la Luz even though her mother pleaded with her to tell me all she knew. "If Rosa Elena didn't mention her I suppose she had good reason," Marianne said. "I think that I'd better keep my mouth shut. My only suggestion is that you write the book as a mystery story with you as the detective. You could have all the suspects on a train in Chiapas and you could unravel the mystery as we're stuck in the jungle."

Marianne's husband Arjen had a big grin on his face. "Marianne has a secret, Marianne has a secret," he teased in a sing-song tone of voice, until she kicked him in the shin.

"I think you should write a book about Mrs. Luján," Arjen continued, to Mrs. Yampolsky's annoyance and to Marianne's delight. "Isn't that what she really wants? Doesn't she think she's more important than he?"

Across the table from Marianne, Dr. Perralta was filling a

tortilla with *carnitas* and chilies. Dr. Perralta, or Pepe, as he was called, was Marianne's first husband, and Hal Croves's physician in the fifties and sixties.

"Was Croves Traven?" I asked Pepe.

"I don't know," he said. Pepe spoke slowly and deliberately as though he had just examined a patient and was offering his medical opinion. "The circumstances are very suspicious," he continued. "Whom do we believe? Rosa Elena? Marianne? Señora Yampolsky? You? Everyone has a different reason for believing or disbelieving the story. I have my ideas too. Maybe you will not like them, but I'll tell you anyway. In his books Traven defended the Indians, didn't he? But Croves was quite a different man. He and Señora Luján had Indian servants in the big house on the Rio Mississippi and they did not treat them well. Croves ordered them about. I tell you it was an ugly thing to see and hear. A shock to me."

"As his doctor, Croves must have confided in you," I said. "He must have told you his medical history, how old he was, where he was born, the facts."

"He told me, but I don't know whether his story is true or false," Pepe said. "There was something peculiar. What he said about his age didn't conform with what his body told me when I listened to his heart and his lungs. But who knows? Maybe his mind played tricks on him. If he really was Traven then perhaps his health can be explained by all those years in the jungle. They can take a terrible toll on a man's body, and age him in a moment."

"Don't you have Croves's medical records?" I asked.

"I don't know if I have them any more," Pepe said. There was a touch of mystery in his voice, the infectious Traven mystery. Everyone who had come in contact with him seemed to have caught it, from Rosa Elena to Maiu, Federico Marin to Pepe Perralta. "I wasn't his doctor at the end," Pepe said. "Rosa Elena fired me and hired a specialist. The last time I examined Croves was ten years ago, 1965 or so. Even if I still have the records it doesn't prove that Croves was Traven. If what you say is true, then Traven lied to everyone: police, immigration, his friends, and his wife too. Do you think that such a man would tell the truth to his doctor? Perhaps he would if he thought that his life depended on it. But sometimes a man doesn't know if it's a question of life and death. He thinks that he has a few more years to go, that he doesn't have to tell the truth, not yet anyway, and then the next day, when it's too late, he dies and takes his secrets with him to the grave."

Mrs. Yampolsky's friend Isabel had a theory too, the most infuriating theory I had heard yet. "Traven's novels were written by Esperanza López Mateos," Isabel said.

"That's absurd," I shouted. "Esperanza was a translator, not a writer. Anyway she couldn't have written *The Cotton Pickers, The Death Ship, The Treasure of the Sierra Madre* because she was too young to hold a pencil in her hand when those books were published in the twenties. Besides, no woman could have written those books. There are hardly any women in Traven's books and the few who do appear are either bitches or prostitutes. Traven was always complaining about women, how you can't trust them, how they'll cheat on you. He was a woman-hater most of his life."

"Then how do you explain the fact that no Traven books appeared after Esperanza's death?" Isabel asked.

"He was deeply disturbed by her death," I said. "And by 1951 he was already over sixty, perhaps even seventy years old. Of course, *Aslan Norval* was published in 1960, nine years after Esperanza's death, and during the fifties and sixties he worked on screenplays. Novels didn't interest him any more; the movies did. After the popular appeal of *The Treasure of the Sierra Madre* he wanted to take Hollywood by storm. Movies were the way, he decided, to reach the masses."

"Isn't it curious that *Aslan Norval* is unlike every other Traven book," Isabel said. "Some critics claim it's a fake. There are no Indians and no workers; the main character is a beautiful young woman married to a lecherous old man."

"Yes, of course, it's curious," I said. "But it's no forgery. It's the sort of book you'd expect Traven to write after living with Rosa Elena on the Rio Mississippi. I read a letter he wrote in '55; he said, 'If something doesn't sound mysterious or sexy nobody reads it and everybody prefers the comics.' *Aslan Norval* was an attempt to attain popularity by appealing to sexuality. At the end of his life Traven craved popularity. He had made it big with *Treasure* and he wanted to make it big again before he died."

"What about Tlatelolco?" Humberto asked. He had returned to his theory. "If Croves was Traven, why didn't he protest the massacre? José Revueltas was an old man, too, but he defended the students and went to prison for it. Have you read Revueltas's books? No? Well, you should; he really describes torture and brutality, makes *The Rebellion of the Hanged* look like a picnic in the jungle."

"Traven lived through the 1919 massacre in Munich," I said. "There were as many people slaughtered then as there were here in 1968. Traven lived through a lifetime of massacre: Munich in 1919, the Nazis in the thirties, Stalin's Siberia, the Indians murdered in Chiapas, then Tlatelolco in '68. Protest! Traven protested—but he felt that there was no escape. Oh, sure, he was always dreaming about paradise and utopia. He had that anarchist spirit of innocence, and like him his characters dream of heaven, but where do they end up? On death ships, floating infernos, or the hell of the jungle labor camps. Oh, Traven protested all right. But he knew that there would always be torture, slavery, dictatorship.

"Remember what he says in *The Cotton Pickers,* Humberto? 'The whole world is a jungle. Eat or be eaten! So it goes round and round. Until there came a world disaster or a revolution and the whole circle would begin again.'

"And in *The Death Ship* he notes sadly, 'The people who were tortured yesterday, torture today.' I can understand his silence on the Rio Mississippi. What could he have said that would have stopped the army from slaughtering the people?"

Humberto didn't have an answer. No one did. I didn't either. It was late. The house was quiet and peaceful, except for that crazy bird at the window.

Mrs. Yampolsky's guests slowly departed. Humberto shook my hand affectionately and offered his help. Pepe grinned from ear to ear. "If you're going to write about Traven you'll have to have a sense of humor," he said.

16

Monday morning on the way to the Banco de Mexico to cash a B. Traven royalty check from European sales, I asked Rosa Elena about Maria de la Luz Martínez.

"I'm not hiding anything from you," she said. "It's only that if you go to see Maria de la Luz you'll never get away. I know what I'm talking about. I've had problems with her and her brother. He still comes here once a year to ask for money. And I give it. What other choice do I have?"

The bank was crowded. I filled out the withdrawal slip and stood in line. "As you can see, I'm a rich woman," Rosa Elena said. "I don't hide my wealth from you and I'm not hiding anything else from you. I deserve the money. I took excellent care of the Skipper, believe me. He had only the best. Malu and I were his nurses to the very end. I can still remember that day perfectly. He started to talk in a whisper. I had to put my ear to his lips to hear. A tear dropped from his eye and landed in my palm without breaking. It was a perfectly round drop. Then he took my hand, kissed it, and said, 'All my life I've been alone, but now *mi vida*'—that's what he called me—'I'm surrounded by your love.' "

Now we were at the head of the line. Rosa Elena handed the cashier the check and collected her money. As far as the international banking network was concerned there was no mystery. Hal Croves and B. Traven were the same man; Rosa Elena Luján was the widow and she was entitled to the money. No one else had come forward and claimed to be the legitimate heir.

"Let's go spend the money," Rosa Elena said. On Reforma we hailed a *pesero* and headed for the post office.

"Where does Maria de la Luz live?" I asked, unwilling to drop this line of investigation.

"Oh, in the same place," Rosa Elena said. "She never moves. Stubborn as you. Oh well, if you insist. My husband met her in '27 or '28; she owned a plot of land in Acapulco before the big hotels arrived. It was very beautiful then. Traven rented a bungalow and some land. There was no running water and no electricity but he liked the primitive surroundings. He worked as a cashew farmer."

At Juárez and Reforma we left the *pesero,* and walked across Alameda Park. A band of young boys surrounded us and demanded the opportunity to shine my shoes. I ignored them, but Rosa Elena felt sorry for them, so I sat down on a bench and waited until the boys decided which one would shine my shoes. One boy claimed he had spotted my shoes first. Another insisted that he had asked first. Finally, Rosa Elena picked out the smallest, most ragged boy and asked him to shine my shoes. He stuck filthy pieces of cardboard inside my shoes to protect the socks from the polish. Then he opened his box, removed an oily rag, a bottle of some unknown substance, and went to work. While we were sitting on the park bench a woman came by selling lottery tickets. Rosa Elena bought twenty-five pesos' worth, and insisted that each ticket have the number 9, "the Skipper's lucky number," she said.

"Why don't you want me to talk to Maria de la Luz?" I asked.

"Talk! Talk to anyone you want," Rosa Elena said. "But I'm telling you if you go to Acapulco you'll be risking your life. And even if you go back to the States you won't be free of Maria or her brother. He'll come looking for you, get money from you—and more, lots more, believe me."

I handed the shoeshine boy two pesos, which he wrapped in the folds of his rag and stuffed into the box. My shoes didn't look polished, but the boy beamed as though he had done an extraordinary job.

The central post office was a beautiful old building, modeled after a *palazzo* along the canals of Venice. We climbed the wrought-iron steps and followed the numbers until we reached M-2701. "Traven taught me never to have mail delivered at home, but always to a post office box," Rosa Elena said. "That way it's harder for them to trace you." I reached into the box and pulled out the letters, some of them addressed to Hal Croves (six years dead) and others to Rosa Elena. We walked downstairs, crossed the street to Sandborns' House of Tiles, and sat down in a booth.

I opened the mail. A professor in Arizona wanted to know if Traven's books were written in English or German. "We'll tell him they were written in both languages," Rosa Elena said. A student in Berlin writing a Ph.D. asked if Traven had read *Moby Dick*. "Of course he did," Rosa Elena said. "He read all the books about the sea. You're the expert on American literature. You answer that one." I watched the Traven "mystery industry" in action, and took my place on the assembly line, turning out tales and legends about the man and his work.

Rosa Elena was feeling unusually relaxed and happy. She sipped her lemon coke and unwound, spun story after story.

"Every Father's Day I used to give the Skipper a present," she said. "In part that was because I was never sure about the day of his birth; he gave so many different dates. But it was much more than that. At first it was subconscious. Then one year I gave him a dictionary and on the inside cover I wrote: 'To my father.' I had not consciously decided what to write. It just came out like that, and I was surprised by my words. Then I thought about it and I realized that my love for the Skipper was like the love of a girl for her father. In Spanish we say *incesto;* I don't know the English word."

"It's the same. Incest," I said. "Did that disturb you? You

seem to think about incest often." (Rosa Elena had told me several stories about aristocratic Mexican women and their sexual relations with their sons.)

"I had a real love for Traven," Rosa Elena said. "He was a kind, fatherly man and I respected him more than I did my own father. Our relationship was passionate, sensuous. I didn't mind staying at home taking care of him. I didn't want to be a liberated woman, because he was a real man. The incestuous feeling didn't trouble me, but all the different names and identities did. He was Marut, he was Torsvan, he was Traven, he was Croves, and he was driving me crazy. I wanted to know the truth. Who was he *really?* He had lied to everyone, to Irene Mermet, Esperanza, Maria de la Luz, but I was his *wife*. I was different from the others, and I wanted the truth. I couldn't stand all the different stories. How could he not tell *me* the truth?

"I even thought of going to a psychiatrist but I knew that I couldn't tell the psychiatrist my fears. I had to keep Traven's secret from everyone, even if it meant I would go crazy. But eventually I learned to live with him, and with all his different identities. I don't think he could have told the truth, even if he wanted to. I forgave him. It was so tangled in his mind that even he didn't know the truth any more."

For the first time I felt sorry for Rosa Elena. I saw her as a victim of Traven, and the Traven mystery. She had put up with him and his craziness. Now she deserved to reap the benefits.

From Sanborns' we took a cab to Malu's apartment. Miguel was at work; Malu was unpacking after her Texas vacation. She greeted us in a bikini and high-heeled shoes, embraced her mother, then turned her face to the side and said, "Come give me a kiss." I gave her a peck on the cheek and sat down on the couch.

"I've brought you presents from the States," Malu said. She unzipped a suitcase stuffed with Milky Ways, Almond Joys, Hershey bars. And there was more Texas loot: one suitcase was crammed with new shoes, another with jars of caviar, frogs' legs, goose-liver pâté.

"We had a marvelous time," Malu said. "Miguel went water-skiing every day, and as you can see I went shopping. The States have really changed since I was there last. Everything is much cleaner and more modern. The shopping malls are wonderful. But mostly I was struck by the fact that the Jews are taking over. You see them everywhere in positions of power. They control most of the banks and corporations now."

"That's absurd," I said.

"What about Kissinger? He's a Jew," Malu said.

"The Jews do have a lot of influence," Rosa Elena said. "They are very shrewd in business. You know that most of the New York publishers are Jews." She unwrapped a Mars bar, took a small bite, and passed it to me.

Malu stood on the zebraskin rug and preened in front of the mirror. "If the American Jews don't give up their wealth and power it'll be like Germany," she said.

"That's anti-Semitic," I said.

"Malu, you're not against the Jews, are you," Rosa Elena said.

"Ooh, I think we've hurt his feelings," Malu said. "He needs a girl friend. Obviously he hasn't had enough sex in Mexico, don't you agree, mother?"

"Well, yes, but he has lots of work to do reading the papers of Traven," Rosa Elena said. "I've introduced him to Louisa, but he doesn't seem to like the type."

Late in the afternoon we left Malu's and took a *pesero* down Reforma to the Museum of Modern Art. Rosa Elena had been invited to attend an exhibit of Robert Motherwell's abstract expressionist paintings. As *La Viuda de Traven* ("Traven's widow") Rosa Elena has an official government status, and was invited to cultural and political events. Shortly before I had arrived in Mexico City she and Malu had been guests of President Luis Escheverría at Los Pinos. For a month afterward Malu boasted that the President was a fan of Traven's and wanted to make a film about his life.

Now, Rosa Elena and I drifted through the Museum of Modern Art, looking at Motherwell's canvases, bewildered by the enigmatic titles. Rosa Elena introduced me to the director of the gallery, to Octavio Paz, to various friends and acquaintances. The U.S. Ambassador was moving through the crowd.

"Ever since the CIA went into Chile, we don't like him very much," Rosa Elena said. "Of course, my husband never attended affairs of this kind because there were always government bureaucrats who wanted to pump his hand and slap him on the back. Years and years ago he was friendly with López Mateos, Esperanza's brother. During the workers' strike he told López Mateos—Mateos was the Minster of Labor then—to keep the troops in their barracks and pay higher wages to the workers. Traven had an influence on government policy. But in '58 when Mateos was elected President, Traven refused to see him again. That was his principle. He couldn't continue his friendship with Mateos as long as he was President."

The U.S. Ambassador mounted the stage and gripped the microphone in his hands. He was a handsome man, tall and thin, with silver-gray hair, like the silver-gray tones in Motherwell's paintings.

We stood under the klieg lights and listened to the Ambassador talk about the friendship between Mexico and the United States, between the peoples of both countries, and how Robert Motherwell's paintings symbolized that love and friendship. B. Traven had never wanted presidents or ambassadors to use his art for their political purposes, and yet it had been, still was, as Motherwell's art was now being abused.

I looked at Motherwell's canvases, but all I could see was Chilean blood, not love between the peoples of the Americas. I knew it wasn't Motherwell's fault, as it wasn't Traven's fault that the President of Mexico had used his books to defend Mexican society. Traven and Motherwell were both betrayed by the politicians. Under different circumstances I was sure that I would be able to appreciate Motherwell's art, but not with the Ambassador holding forth on Democracy and Freedom.

17

On the third floor, under a stack of dusty books about Mayan art, I found what was probably Traven's first draft of *The Death Ship*. It was handwritten in the English language; the grammar and syntax were rough and clumsy. Several sections in the manuscript made me feel that it had been written in England. One long passage, missing from published versions of the book, describes the main character in the British Museum Reading Room, researching the history of the *Yorikke*. In addition, the narrator complains about England, her "fogs, her nasty colds, her hunting the alien, and the stupid ever-smile of her arch prince."

I collected all the manuscripts, typescripts, and printed editions of *The Death Ship,* and, step by step, compared them. It was fascinating to watch the growth of the novel, to see the changes in Traven's ideas, language, and craft.

One key development was the evolution of the narrator. In the handwritten manuscript that I found on the third floor (it was a welcome surprise for Rosa Elena too), the narrator was nameless, anonymous. Then Traven gave him the name "Gale." Later he added an *s* making him "Gales," and finally he assigned him the first name "Gerard." So Gerard Gales came into existence.

The choice of the name was logical. B. Traven translated

"Marut" which in Hindu mythology meant "god of the wind" into English, and came up with "Gales." But there was another reason. In Rosa Elena's office I found several issues of a magazine that had been published in Mexico City from 1917 to the early 1920s. The title of the magazine was *The International Monthly for Revolutionary Communism;* the editor was an eccentric North American radical and member of the IWW named Lynn Gale. Traven's hero Gerard Gales is also a North American and a member of the IWW. He is based on the real-life Lynn Gale. Jumping from manuscript to typescript to printed book, I saw how Traven transformed his nameless, faceless narrator into a radical with working class identity. Moreover, in the first draft, the narrator has a deep streak of arrogance and elitism. But with each revision Traven made him less aristocratic, more a common victim of injustice, and at the same time, an angry proletarian rebel.

I also noticed that Traven became more and more dissatisfied with Gales and his story, and was finally compelled to introduce Stanislav Korzinowski. If you look at *The Death Ship* you'll see that Traven doesn't introduce Stanislav, the fatalistic Slav sailor, until the book is at midpoint. Since Stanislav is a major character, essential for Traven's story, it is strange to meet him so late in the journey. His tardy arrival almost throws the book off balance, as Traven noted. Fifteen years after he had written *The Death Ship,* he observed that if he were to write the book again he would drop the early section about Gerard Gales and begin with Stanislav. "Stanislav is the real hero of the book," he wrote.

In the handwritten manuscript there is no Stanislav, but there is a German Communist named "Berthold," a character probably based on a revolutionary Marut had known in Munich during the days of the insurrection. Traven describes Berthold as

> a genuine comrade. . .He was a Bolshevik and he
> told me once he had done a good bit to make him
> and a hundred thousand of his fellow countrymen

such. He tried several times to convert me, yet soon he gave it up saying "You are not fit for you are lacking the proper foundations." Yet he was very near to catch me, not by his eloquence but by his never-ceasing kindness and willingness to help me whenever I faced trouble.

Looking at the drafts of *The Death Ship* I came to appreciate why Traven had to create Stanislav Korzinowski—though "create" is not the best word to describe the process. More accurately, Traven drew Stanislav out of his own divided personality and complex experience. In the very process of writing *The Death Ship* Traven discovered the power and significance of his own story. His original blueprint of the novel was now inadequate, and he had to change course. What began as a tale of one rather happy-go-lucky sailor who loses his identification papers because he spends the night in bed with a Dutch girl, was transformed into a bitter indictment of the mad world of modern bureaucracy.

Stanislav has no papers, not by a fluke, but because of World War I. The war robs him of his identity, his home, his past, his human rights. Stanislav belongs to the vast "army" of displaced persons. He tells the unsuspecting, innocent Gales:

> Every night there is going on, at all European borders, a lively exchange of unwelcome travellers. Men and women and children. The Germans kick out their Jews, and their undesirable foreigners, and Bolshevists and communists and pacifists, across the Dutch, the Belgian, the French, the Polish, the Swiss, the Danish border, just like nothing. And of course, the Czechs, the Poles, and all the others do exactly the same in exchange.

I saw that in the manuscript version of *The Death Ship* Traven was anxious to hide his past as Ret Marut, the bitter, angry European anarchist and fugitive. So he created the character of Gerard Gales, the comic American sailor, as a cover. With each revision of the text Traven added descriptions of the United States to persuade his readers that Gales was indeed a genuine native-born sailor, and that he, Traven, was truly an American author. For example, in the original manuscript Gales has few American connections and no American relatives. But in revising the novel Traven gave him an "Aunt Lucinda, who had never been away from her native town, Jetmore, Kansas."

Traven developed Gales into a richer, more complex character, but he was still never complex or deep enough to allow Traven to convey the pain, horror, and betrayal he had experienced in Europe from 1914 to 1922. So he gave birth to Stanislav; and once Stanislav was on the deck of the *Yorikke,* Traven could put into his mouth ideas and opinions that would have sounded peculiar coming from a cheerful New Orleans sailor with an aunt in Jetmore, Kansas.

Gales does mention the brutal side of American life—prisons like San Quentin and Leavenworth, southern lynchings, deportation of subversives, and the marines invading Latin America—but only in passing and always with a sense of humor. Gales makes jokes about death. Stanislav has a more pessimistic viewpoint; death isn't all that funny in his eyes. Like his creator Marut/Traven, Stanislav knows the horror of World War I, the corruption of European socialism, the betrayal of the working man by the financiers, generals, and politicians, from Lloyd George to Woodrow Wilson and Hindenburg. In fact, Stanislav's opinions are lifted, with minor changes, from the essays that Ret Marut published in the pages of *The Brickburner.* For example, Stanislav tells Gales (it could just as well be Marut speaking):

> Workers, and all those what is called "proletarians of the world unite," they are more patriotic than the kaiser's generals ever could be, and more narrowminded than a Methodist preacher's wife. . .They

are educated that way. They can't help it. Was the same when the war broke out. Karl Marx on their book shelf, and the guns over their shoulders, marching against the workers of France and Russia. There will still have to pass five hundred years before they won't fall any longer for worn-out slogans.

By putting these words in Stanislav's mouth, B. Traven risked recognition by Germans who knew Ret Marut and had read *The Brickburner*. Most readers didn't see or hear the similarity. But a few, including Erich Mühsam, the Munich anarchist and poet, did. As early as 1926 Mühsam suspected that the author of *The Death Ship* was none other than Ret Marut, his sly old friend and mysterious comrade. Several editors at the Gutenberg Book Guild also assumed that Marut was Traven, but lacking definite evidence, and in sympathy with his motives for anonymity, agreed to keep his identity a secret.

Comparing the manuscripts and typescripts of *The Death Ship* I also observed how Traven made the *Yorikke* into a symbolic ship, a ship of mystery. In the first draft, Traven tells us that the *Yorikke's* home port is Bergen, Norway. But he soon realized that a mysterious ship, like a mysterious man, couldn't have a home port. So the *Yorikke* became a ship undefined and unfettered by place. It mirrors Gales's own soul. "There was a secret hidden somewhere," Gales says when he first sees the *Yorikke*. "She did not want to betray her birthplace. So you're like me, I thought, without a proper birth certificate. Bedfellows, hey!"

Traven also transformed the *Yorikke* into a timeless ship:

> When the *Yorikke* was still a virgin maiden the language spoken by her crew was Babylonian; later it was changed to Persian, then to Phoenician. . .After the Roman Empire was destroyed. . .the language on the *Yorikke* was a mixture of Italian, Spanish, Portuguese, Arabian, and Hebrew. This lasted until after the Spanish Armada was knocked out. Then

French influence became more dominant. . .At
Abukir the *Yorikke* was on the side of the French, and
old man Nelson took her as a prize. He sold her to a
cotton-dealer and shipping agent in Liverpool, who
in turn sold her to English pirates who worked the
Spanish main.

With each step of revision, Traven made it clear that all countries and all ports have their death ships, that death ships exist
today, no matter what presidents and parliaments may say
about progress, civilization, and justice in their official
decrees.

What intrigued me most about the handwritten manuscript
of *The Death Ship* were three short sentences that Traven
censored, probably because they revealed too much about
himself:

Great men always have some secret as to their personality, always have something to hide as to their
past. Not necessary that this secret has to be a
murder or a holdup. Nevertheless, it is his secret that
gives a great man a shade of mystery which is essential for his power over the average.

In Traven's hands mystery could be elitist and aristocratic,
or democratic and egalitarian. This passage from the manuscript set me wondering all over again about Traven and the
Kaiser. Did Traven have a secret? Was there something in his
past he had to hide? Or did he fake it? Did he consciously
create a mystery where none existed so that he might become
a "great man" with "power over the average," as he put it.

Initially, Rosa Elena insisted that Traven was the Kaiser's
son, an aristocrat who descended the class ladder, became a
proletarian, and wrote about the lives of workers. But Rosa
Elena also insisted that Traven was a genuine proletarian, and
not an aristocrat slumming among the workers to gather material for a working-class novel. She wanted her Traven both

114

ways: prince *and* pauper. "He was a proletarian who had to go to sea to earn his living," she said, seemingly not conscious that she was contradicting herself. What to believe? Was he a rich boy pretending to be a pauper? Or was he a poor boy creating a mystery about a princely past?

The aesthetic structure of *The Death Ship* added fuel to the great debate. By comparing the texts I could more fully appreciate the novel as a retelling of the traditional rags to riches story. Life on the *Yorikke* is cast in proletarian rags. And Gales loves it. He becomes a true proletarian. After his first stint of hard, uninterrupted toil he exclaims:

> Now I was initiated and a true member of the *Yorikke*
> . . .I had become so dead that no feeling in mind,
> soul, or body was left. . .The time came, though
> slowly, when I began to get my own ideas again. No
> longer did I swagger about the bucket in a dazed and
> unconscious state. I began to see and to understand.
> Rebirth had taken place.

Rebirth for Ret Marut was rebirth as a proletarian on a death ship, after life as an aristocrat.

But the *Yorikke* isn't the only death ship in the novel. In the port of Dakar, Gales and Stanislav are kidnapped from the *Yorikke* to the *Empress of Madagascar,* a transatlantic luxury liner. At first it appears that Traven's heroes have climbed from proletarian rags to aristocratic riches. Aboard the *Empress* they live "like Balkan kings in Paris." But that is an illusion. "The end of the world" is near; the *Empress* is also a death ship. The captain scuttles her on the rocks to collect the insurance. The crew perishes so that the stockholders may profit. Floating on a raft in the sea (like Ishmael at the end of *Moby Dick*), Gales longs for the life-giving rags of the *Yorikke.* On a proletarian death ship there is the possibility of rebirth and resurrection. But on the aristocratic *Empress* there is only shipwreck and the grave. For Traven, life and the proletariat are as inextricably connected as death and the aristocracy.

It would seem that Marut/Traven knew aristocratic life aboard ships like the *Empress,* and also proletarian life aboard ships like the *Yorikke.* In *The Death Ship* Gales is catapulted from the *Yorikke* to the *Empress.* I suspect that Marut/Traven's life was the reverse, that he fell from life aboard the Empresses of the ocean to life aboard the Yorikkes of the seas. So, too, Marut's voyage was from Europe to America, not from America to Europe—the direction the ocean gales drive Gerard Gales. B. Traven the artist had an uncanny habit of turning things inside out and upside down. As Stanislav says, "Everything is head under foot." By falling Marut found himself. The lonely orphan discovered a universe of lonely orphans, men without homes, families, or countries, among the workers of the world.

18

"I don't give a shit what you think, motherfucker," Chele shouted. She was talking on the phone with a comrade. Rosa Elena and I were in the kitchen listening. "My girls have the most awful language, but of course they learned it all from the Skipper, and he cursed like a sailor," Rosa Elena said.

Chele and Malu were sisters, but they looked and acted like polar opposites. Chele was dark, Malu light; Chele was gloomy, melancholy, Malu was bright and cheerful.

Chele slammed the phone and threw her sunglasses across the table. Her dark eyes were inflamed. She was crying, her lips trembled, her hands shook. "Those bastards had a meeting without me," she said.

"That's what happens when you work with a group," Rosa Elena said. "And that's why the Skipper always worked alone, independently. But you insist on belonging to the *Punto Critico* (*Critical Point*) collective." She picked up a copy of the magazine—there was a picture of Che on the cover—and threw it on the pile of old newspapers. "I don't see why you waste good money on the magazine any more." Rosa Elena turned to me, putting her hand on my shoulder. "My daughters have their own private banker. With Chele I am financing the revolution; with Malu I am financing big weekends in Texas and Acapulco. The money goes right through my fingers like a sieve. By the time I die there won't be a peso left for them to inherit."

Chele sat down, wiped her face, and applied mascara and eye shadow. Petra filled our coffee ups, Herme swept the floor, Rosa Elena chased a fly out the window. I listened to the sounds of the street: the hum of the sharpener's wheel, the ring of the workmen's picks and shovels as they broke the earth, the squeal of rubber tires, and the policeman's shrill whistle.

"The *Punto* collective doesn't think we should bother with the peasants any more," Chele explained. "They want to organize factory workers. That is always the fault of the left in Mexico. They don't give a shit about the people in the countryside. So what if they're starving." Chele was indeed B. Traven's spiritual daughter. She had his sense of anger and irony, his dedication to the peasants and the poor of the countryside, and his skepticism about the privileged industrial workers of the urban centers.

Soon the *Punto Crítico* collective arrived: Huberto, Pablo, Teodoro. All three men wore dungarees, boots, faded blue shirts, yet in spite of the "uniform" they managed to look distinct. Huberto wore a wide-brimmed hat and a white scarf, Pablo had a bushy beard and a receding hairline, Teodoro wore small, round glasses. I assumed that he was trying to look like Leon Trotsky, but Chele whispered that he "fashioned himself after Flores Magnon, the Mexican anarchist who had spent time in prison in Los Angeles."

We sat in the living room, under the portrait of Rosa Elena. "Before we get into an argument, we've got to talk about our financial problems," Teodoro said.

"Let's talk about the peasants," Chele insisted. "If you only want to write articles about factory workers and union strikes then I don't want another issue of the magazine. It's that important! I know you haven't read Traven because you never read novels—you think they're bourgeois—but you damned well should study his books. Then you might learn something about imperialism, you sons of bitches. Don't you realize the corporations *own* our land! And you don't want to organize the peasants. You're fucked!'"

"Soon there won't be a stinking peasant left," Pablo said. "Mexico City is ten million people already. The land will be worked by machine."

"Not while there's labor for five pesos a day," Chele said. "Mexico will always be one big plantation for the Americans."

"Dead wrong again," Huberto shouted as he twirled his mustache. "It's going to be one big factory from the Rio Grande all the way to Guatemala and every Mexican old enough to walk and talk will be a proletarian. Don't tell me different, Chele, because you've a very idealized picture of the peasants, living here in the Zona Rosa, going to the countryside on weekends to do research. It's very unreal, and Traven's novels were written forty years ago. It's all changed. We're living in a different world."

"When it comes to my money we're living in the same world," Chele said. "It's O.K. to spend it on the magazine."

Teodoro stood up, insulted. "Maybe we should leave until you calm down," he said. The three men picked up their briefcases and filed out the door. Chele was in a rage. She put on her dark glasses, went into the kitchen, and to my surprise asked her mother for a check.

"I hope it isn't for *Punto,* not after that argument. You're too good for them," Rosa Elena said.

Chele didn't say a word. She folded the check, stuffed it into her pocket, and invited me to see her apartment. On the way Chele intentionally took me past the headquarters of the CGT, the General Confederation of Laborers. On the sidewalk a group of men were smoking and laughing. They were caricatures of union bureaucrats, especially one fat man who was having his shoes shined by a young, barefoot boy. His hair was greased back, and when he smiled you could see his gold teeth.

"Union organizers," Chele said. "They've turned their backs on the peasants too, but of course that's to be expected because the building is owned by the CIA and the men are bought off by the CIA." (Philip Agee's book about the agency had just appeared, and there were other revelations about the CIA in Mexico. Chele wasn't talking off the top of her head.) "We've proven that. The union rents one floor of the building. Look at them. Some revolutionaries! We call them *charros* [cowboys]. Don't they make you angry? Union bureaucrats! That's what we'll become unless we go to the countryside to organize the peasants. And who knows what *you*'ll turn out if you don't go to the countryside either. You must! If you are writing about Traven you must get out of Mexico City. Go to Chiapas! You can't understand Traven if you live in the Zona and don't see the Chamulas in San Cristóbal. Mexico City is so Americanized, the music, the discothèques, the food, and the unions too. Traven said that unions were necessary to maintain the system. They police the workers for the capitalists. And strikes don't achieve anything either unless they're general strikes by all the workers against the entire system. Get out of Mexico City. Go to Chiapas. Then you'll know what it means to be underdeveloped, to be a colony. Then you'll understand Traven."

(Chele was right about Traven and unions. In *The White Rose* he says that "Unions exist for a good reason: both capital and labor need them. . . .Without unions the struggle between capital and labor would be fiercer. . . .When adequately paid and decently treated, this army is eager to fight any system that threatens their liberty to work for capital. In this way, unions are the best mates that capital ever had." B. Traven was a proletarian novelist, but with a twist: he was bitterly critical of trade unions and believed that they betrayed the proletariat.)

We took the elevator to Chele's apartment. Irene was lying on her stomach reading a "Little Lulu" comic book. "Irene, get over here," Chele shouted. I thought she was going to swat her daughter. Irene came to the table, opened her school book, and began to write her exercises. Chele poked her nose in the kitchen and scolded the maid: "No comic books, no television until her homework is done."

We sat down in the living room. Chele put a record on the turntable, and soon I heard the sound of flutes and harps.

"It's very depressing being a Luján and a Montes de Oca in the left movement," Chele said. "I feel schizophrenic. What should I do? Pretend I'm a poor girl? I like to live well. Is that such a terrible crime? Whenever the collective comes here for a meeting they make me feel guilty. Huberto pretends to be penniless, but his family has money too, only he is ashamed. Mother knows the check is for the magazine. I'm not fooling her."

"Tell me, how will we make a revolution without money, and where will we get it?" Chele asked. "Not from the peasants. They're starving. If you take it from the government you're bought off. A friend of mine, Paqueta, from a very wealthy family joined the guerrillas. They kidnapped a banker and got three million pesos' ransom. A million pesos they gave away in the poorest neighborhoods so people could buy beans, tortillas, milk, rice. A million pesos they used to buy arms. And a million pesos the police found under Paqueta's bed when they arrested her. Of course it was never returned to the bank. You know you can't succeed as an urban guerrilla, not in Mexico City. And some of the so-called left groups are created by the government to confuse us. Paqueta, I don't agree with what Paqueta did, but some friends of mine—all women—and I are trying to have her released from prison."

In the afternoon Chele's ex-husband Julio arrived to take Irene for a walk in Chapultepec Park. He was a short, heavy man; he looked uncomfortable, embarrassed. I nodded hello but he didn't return the gesture. He stood in the hall until Irene was ready.

"We separated after '68," Chele explained after they had left. "Julio thought that our demonstrations were the work of the CIA. I was hiding one of the student leaders in our apartment and Julio was insanely jealous. So we divorced. Now he's happily married with three kids. Oh, he's very good to Irene, I can't complain. It wasn't his fault; I'm just not the monogamous type. How could I be? A Montes de Oca and a

Luján in the revolution. Schizophrenic!"

Chele turned the record over and tossed me the album. On the cover a group of Indian musicians in red and blue *sarapes* played their flutes and harps. "Get out of Mexico City. Go to Chiapas. Go to Traven's world," Chele said. "You must see something other than this rotten life in the Zona."

19

The optometrist adjusted the eyeglasses so they fit snugly round my ears and nose. The lenses were mine, the frames were Traven's. I had rummaged through the old glasses on the third floor until I found a pair that made me look like a German university student. "They went out of fashion when I was a boy," the optometrist said. "But if that's what you want."

I did. Wasn't I wearing Traven's trousers and shirt, and didn't I have my hair cut so it resembled his. So why not wear his eye glasses. A professor of mine at college thought he was Bertolt Brecht and cultivated a Brechtian appearance, so why couldn't I think I was B. Traven and look like Traven too. I wasn't going to do anything by halves. Might as well take the leap, rather than crawl into the role inch by inch.

"I think they look silly," Rosa Elena said. "They looked silly on my husband and they look silly on you. You're as much of a clown as he was. Always acting, always performing. You know, I think that you like mystery as much as he did."

We took a *pesero* from the optometrists office near the Zócalo to the American Embassy on Reforma. Rosa Elena and I were applying for all U.S. Government files on B. Traven, Ret Marut, Hal Croves, and T. Torsvan. Under the Freedom of Information Act, Rosa Elena was entitled to see FBI, CIA, State Department dossiers on her late husband.

At the entrance to the Embassy we were stopped by a young marine with a crewcut and a collar so tight that his Adam's apple leapt into his throat. We showed him our identification papers, filled out the necessary forms and were escorted upstairs. Half a dozen people were already waiting, so we sat down on the hard wooden chairs. The room was dead quiet. On the right was a photo of President Gerald R. Ford, and on the left an American Flag. Two marines stood guard at the door.

While we were waiting Rosa Elena told me the story of her family. I wasn't sure if I was listening to a factual account or to a movie scenario. When I closed my eyes I saw a picture that resembled *Gone with the Wind*.

"Traven was planning to write the history of the Lujáns," Rosa Elena began. "All Mexican history is in our family. After we finish the biography we'll write the book Traven was going to do. My ancestors owned large tracts of land in the state of Coahuila, and they would have had much more if the Texans hadn't robbed thousands of acres from us." Rosa Elena raised her voice so that the marines could hear her story too.

"My father, like his father, was an army officer. Not like today's soldiers. He was disciplined. A bachelor until he was thirty-four and then he met my mother. She was only fifteen, but right away they got married, even though she didn't love him, and nine months later her first baby was born. Still, she didn't love him, and not during the revolution either, when my father fled across the border to Texas. My mother stayed at the *hacienda*. The revolutionary armies made our home their headquarters. The soldiers camped in the living room, cooked on the patio, turned everything upside down. They had no manners at all, so my mother complained to the commanding officer, a Pole named Kosterlitzski, a real gentleman."

"What was a Pole doing in Mexico during the revolution?" I asked.

"You had a Pole fighting in your revolution, so why shouldn't we," Rosa Elena said. "Kosterlitzski was a gentleman. He ordered the troops out of the *hacienda* and into the fields, where they belonged from the start. Kosterlitzski respected my mother. She was a young woman, very beautiful, and very passionate. Her husband was across the border in Texas, and, well, you know what happens under those circumstances—a handsome army officer, a lonely woman. My mother fell in love with this Colonel Kosterlitzski.

"My father didn't know anything was going on, but he arranged to go by ship to the Yucatán, and my mother went there to be with him, not because she loved him, but because he was her husband and the father of her children. She was a very brave woman to cross Mexico in the midst of the revolution, bullets flying everywhere." (I could almost hear the whistle of bullets.) "They settled in the town of Progreso and that's where I was born. They say that there is no progress in Progreso and it's true even to this day. Some things never change. You'll see that when you go to Chiapas. It's the same as it was when my husband first went there.

"In Progreso my father was living under an alias, but some of the rebel soldiers recognized him and locked him in jail. They were going to hang him. Imagine! My mother was desperate. She went to the commanding officer to plea for her husband's life. . ."

"Señora Luján," a marine shouted. "Señora Luján, please go into the office, it's your turn now."

We shook hands with the American Vice-Consul and filled out the forms. Rosa Elena swore that her husband had used the names B. Traven, Hal Croves, Ret Marut, and T. Torsvan, that he died on March 26, 1969, that he resided at Rio Mississippi 61, and that she was willing for me to see all government papers pertaining to her husband.

"He must have been a strange man with so many different names," the Vice-Consul said casually. She had never heard of B. Traven.

"My husband was a writer," Rosa Elena said casually.

"Oh," was all the Vice-Consul replied. She looked skeptical, but signed her name and affixed the official seal of the U.S. Government.

The marine escorted us downstairs. Outside, a long line of Mexicans were waiting to obtain visas that would enable them to work legally in the fields of Texas, California, the Pacific Northwest. Some of them were barefoot, most of them wore tattered pants and shirts.

"Last summer I came to the embassy with my sister," Rosa Elena said. "The sister who is dying. You remember—the one who wouldn't let you look at her. Anyway, when she and I arrived at nine in the morning there was already a long line of people applying for visas. They had been standing in the cold all night. 'They're as stupid as sheep,' my sister said. 'What do you mean?' I asked. 'The Del Prado Hotel is around the corner,' my sister said. 'They ought to take a room for the night, get a good sleep, and come here first thing in the morning all refreshed.' You see, my family doesn't understand. They are so removed from the real world, they think everyone has money to stay at the Del Prado. It's very hard for all of us, but especially for Chele, because she goes and talks to the poor people. She tries to live as they do, but it's not easy. Chele lives in two worlds—like my husband, in that respect. Malu has it much easier. And I, well, I have some of Chele and some of Malu in me. I'm in both worlds too."

"What happened to your father?" I asked. "You were telling me a story."

"Oh, yes, my father. Well, it may be difficult to be a Luján in a world of peasants and soldiers, but it isn't easy to kill us. We are survivors! My mother went to see the commanding officer for the Yucatán. And you know what—he turned out to be none other than that handsome Polish officer, Colonel Kosterlitzski, I was telling you about! Of course, Kosterlitzski spared my father's life. It was the biggest disappointment of his—my father's—life. You see, he had been in his prison cell expecting to die a hero's death, when all of a sudden he was saved. He thought he was going to die a martyr's death, that the church would make him a saint, and now he was nobody. He didn't want to live any more. He knew that something suspicious had happened between my mother and Colonel

Kosterlitzski. Why else would a revolutionary soldier spare a
Luján?"

"My father came home and crawled into bed. He was so
ashamed. He drew the curtains, refused to eat or drink, so my
mother had to nurse him back to health. He was like a little
baby boy. Finally, she fell in love with him. Don't ask me why,
but she did. It was romantic love at last. My father got better
and came out of his room, and eventually made his peace with
the revolution. And the revolution made its peace with him.
He became a government bureaucrat in charge of the customs
offices along the border of Mexico and the United States. Oh,
yes, we are survivors!"

Rosa Elena and I had arrived at the Rio Mississippi. The sky
was dark. It looked like rain. She took out her key ring and
unlocked the door. Tabasco came out to greet us. Malu,
Miguel, Irene, and Chele were in the backyard, standing round
the statue of the Skipper, talking and drinking tequila, oblivious of the coming storm. Suddenly the wind turned cold
and the dark sky opened. Icy hail stones pelted us and we were
driven indoors for safety.

20

The galleys of *The Kidnapped Saint* arrived by air mail from New York, and Rosa Elena and I went to work, making additions and corrections. The book contained the essay "Remembering Traven" that we had worked on in January, eight short stories by Traven, a sentimental section from an otherwise grim novel *The White Rose,* and Ret Marut's essay "In the Freest State in the World," written from underground in 1919 and translated into English for the first time.

"In the Freest State in the World" offers the best explanation I know why B. Traven was preoccupied with death and resurrection. In 1919 Marut was sentenced to death, had accepted his death, and was then "miraculously" saved, reborn. The story goes like this: he was arrested by soldiers armed with machine guns at the Maria Theresa Coffee House on Augustenstrasse in Munich. The soldiers were from Berlin; they had marched to Bavaria to crush the Council Republic.

Marut was searched for weapons (in much the same way that Gerard Gales describes himself being searched for weapons in *The Death Ship*), thrown into a car, and taken to the Ministry of War for interrogation. One soldier held a pair of Browning automatics under each of Marut's nostrils, another accused him of treason: inciting soldiers to mutiny against their officers, insulting the leaders of the Social Democratic

Party, and advocating the use of force and violence against the Bavarian government.

The soldiers asked Marut to sign a confession; he refused. So a long string of witnesses filed before him, and swore that he had committed dozens of criminal acts. The soldiers assumed that he was guilty, and were prepared to recommend the death penalty, but first there was the formality of a "trial." Marut was taken to the Royal Palace. In a large hall a lieutenant was acting as judge, jury, and prosecution. Each case was disposed of in three minutes, each defendant to be shot or sentenced to a long prison term. Just before Marut was to be tried for treason a prisoner assaulted a guard. Chaos broke out and Marut escaped.

"In the Freest State" describes this series of events. It was written while Marut was in the countryside, talking to peasants and workers about the revolution in Munich, and about his dream of a communal society. Marut had counted himself among the dead, and now he was alive again. He was resurrected. In case readers missed the connection he was making, Marut spelled it out. He was following in the footsteps of He who was dead and resurrected. Marut noted that he used "a form of persuasion which is the only one that produces worthwhile results, a form that is very old and that was also used by Christ—namely, talking person to person, talking to the smallest gatherings or groups of people."

Marut's arrest, death, and resurrection appear in a changed form in *The Death Ship*. Gerard Gales is captured by soldiers, searched for weapons, jailed, and sentenced to be executed. Gales too counts himself among the dead. And like Marut he too escapes. However, Gales escapes the grave by making a joke. His own sense of gallows humor saves him. He gets his jailors to laugh at him and then release him. Before Gales is to be shot he is given a last supper. Licking his plate clean he tells his executioners, "For a dinner like that I wouldn't mind being shot every day in the year. I am sorry that I have only one life to be shot." The guards roar with laughter and decide that such a funny prisoner ought to live.

The Kidnapped Saint galleys contained another story—"Reviving the Dead"—that also testifies to Traven's preoccupation with death and resurrection. Here a young Mexican is unconscious, and on the brink of death, but Traven manages to keep him alive by applying hot stones to the soles of his feet. Then a Spaniard arrives, pushes Traven aside, and changes the treatment. The result: the Mexican dies. Traven concludes:

> In that village it is declared that I can awaken the dead, though until now I have never awakened even one dead person. But the proof that I can awaken the dead is evident beyond all doubt in the opinion of these people. For even the simplest and most unassuming Indian will grasp this fact: If in every respect I do the exact opposite of that which kills a person, then the result must always be: a revival of the dead.

Two stories in the volume, "Submission" and "The Diplomat," provoked lengthy discussion between Rosa Elena and me. "Submission" describes a Mexican macho who breaks his haughty, independent wife. At the end of the story they consummate their marriage by making love. Traven writes:

> Even though in a household or a marriage it is not completely settled who is in command, still, in bed in which a man and woman lie side by side, the question of who gives the orders and who has to obey is never discussed because it does not exist so long as the laws of nature are not set aside by some outside interference. Because in this situation satisfactory results will follow only if the man is in command and the woman subjects herself to his orders willingly and with anticipation.

I was annoyed and disappointed by Traven's insistence that the woman obey willingly. Rosa Elena said, "Traven was always in command in bed. It's the only way to have sexual pleasure. I know some of the men today don't believe that, but they are fooling themselves. I hope that you aren't going that way. And if a man and a woman want to have a child, then the man must be on top." I argued with Rosa Elena, but she would not change her mind.

She was critical of "The Diplomat," a short story about the theft of a wristwatch by Porfirio Díaz. "Traven wrote that story soon after he arrived in Mexico," Rosa Elena said. "He didn't know much about our history. Díaz was corrupt, yes, and he stole the land of the Indians and sold it to foreigners, but in his personal life he was a very honest man. He would never have taken another man's watch, as Traven claims." So we changed the ending of the story to fit Rosa Elena's view of Díaz as a corrupt dictator who was moral in his daily life.

Five of the stories in *The Kidnapped Saint* were translated from German to English by Herbert Klein and his wife Mina. Going through the papers in Rosa Elena's office I had come across a correspondence between Klein and Traven in the 1930s. Klein reviewed *The Death Ship* for *The New Republic,* and Traven offered him his views on publishing, publicity, the reading public, and American culture. "A decent critic may not earn as much as a noisy columnist and Broadway gossip," Traven told Herbert Klein, "but he will last longer and earn his living when all those town criers are buried and forgotten."

When Klein wrote to ask why Alfred Knopf didn't advertise his books, Traven replied:

> I write to propagate ideas, not to make a profit. My books came to readers precisely by the same means They came to you, that is, individual recommendation. . .Mr. Knopf does not advertise my books outside of the trade press. This is according to my specific instructions. My work carries all the publicity I

131

need and all I want. If my books are not considered
good no publicity can make them any better.

Even when his books were banned and burned by the Nazis,
Traven did not want his publishers to advertise the fact. He
thought that it would influence readers unfairly to buy his
books. "Prohibited books usually make big sales, mostly
though undeserved," he wrote to his British editors in 1933,
the year the Nazis raided the Gutenberg Book Guild and
seized his works. "I hope to gain only through fair propagan-
da and decent means."

Traven also suggested to Herbert Klein that his talent was
not in translating, but in reviewing and journalism. Klein had
lived in Berlin until Hitler's triumph; Traven hoped that he
would write "a kind of *Ten Days that Shook the World,* that
would describe the rise of Fascism."

Rosa Elena found Klein's translations of Traven's stories
awkward and archaic and asked me to make them smoother,
more idiomatic. So I spent a week going over *The Kidnapped
Saint,* changing words, rewriting passages, then reading them
out loud to Rosa Elena. "He told me exactly what changes he
wanted in these stories before he died," she said.

By the end I felt that I knew the book by heart. Words and
phrases were spinning in my head. "With your shirt sleeves
rolled up and the pencil in your hand, you really do remind
me of Traven," Rosa Elena said. "We've changed the stories
exactly as he would have done. Now you can say that you
know him. You chose the words he would have chosen. You
see the world as he saw it. Well, now we can go to the post
office and send the galleys to New York. Then you ought to
take a vacation. Maybe we can go to Cozumel together."

21

"They're going to destroy it," Mrs. Siqueiros said.

"They're like the Nazis," Rosa Elena said.

I was standing on a chair, hammering a nail into the wall. We were standing on the second floor and David Alfaro Siqueiros's widow had brought Rosa Elena one of her husband's prints. The original sketch had been used for a mural that Siqueiros had painted in Santiago, Chile. Mrs. Siqueiros had learned that the dictatorship was going to destroy the mural on the grounds that it was "subversive." Immediately she made prints; whenever she visited friends she brought one along and asked them to hang it in their homes, "so that my husband's art might not die at the hands of the dictator Pinochet." Rosa Elena was honored.

"Traven and Siqueiros were such good friends," she said, more for my benefit then for Angelica Siqueiros's.

"But they were always arguing," Mrs. Siqueiros said. "Traven never liked the Communist Party."

"What else do good friends do but argue," Rosa Elena said. "My husband never did agree with Siqueiros's political ideas, but as an artist and a human being he respected and loved him."

"There were good times too," Mrs. Siqueiros said. "Remember the party when he came out of prison?"

"I remember when Siqueiros went into prison," Rosa Elena said. "My husband was furious. He didn't want to help Siqueiros and the Communist Party get into power. 'That would just mean a new dictator,' Traven said. But he did everything he could to get Siqueiros out of prison."*

"They did have their disagreements," Mrs. Siqueiros sighed.

"Yes, don't we all," Rosa Elena said. "It's sad. You know, Federico Marin is very sick. The old crowd is slowly dying. First Diego, then my husband and Siqueiros. Federico will be next."

Chele climbed the stairs, a pile of books under her arm. For the first time in weeks she wasn't wearing dark glasses; her eyes were bright.

"It's too nice to be indoors. Let's go someplace," she said.

"I'm exhausted," Rosa Elena said. "Why don't you two spend the day together? Play tourist. I'll even give you the itinerary Traven made for Bernard Smith when he came to Mexico in '36. It's almost forty years old, I know, but it's still good, because the museums and historical sites don't change."

She fumbled with her key ring, unlocked the office door, and searched through the files. I had heard about the itinerary that Traven prepared for Smith in 1936 but hadn't come across it on the third floor and assumed that it was lost. I had never met Bernard Smith, but I knew that he had worked at Alfred Knopf in the thirties. Smith was the editor responsible not only for publishing Traven's novels in the United States—*The Death Ship* in 1934, *Treasure* in 1935, and *Bridge* in 1936—but also for rewriting the books to make them readable. Traven had submitted his manuscripts in English; the syntax, grammar, and language smacked of German. Smith felt that they were unpublishable in that form, but because there was

---

*In the early Sixties, Traven wrote a scenario about Siqueiros that portrayed him as an heroic artist persecuted by an unjust state, but never destroyed. Even in his prison cell he continues to paint murals. Siqueiros returned the compliment by including Traven in a mural he painted in Chapultepec Castle.

a wide interest in proletarian fiction, and because Traven's books were, in Smith's words, "truly proletarian," he worked out an arrangement with Traven whereby he "treated," as he called it, about a quarter of the text. Traven liked Smith's work. He felt that Smith respected his style, manner, and especially his ideas. Moreover, in the early thirties Traven was anxious to reach American working-class readers. In 1935 he noted:

> The American worker is, in my opinion, as intelligent as the Scandinavian, the Dutch, and the German worker. So why should he not buy the same amount of books, the kind intelligent workers prefer. . .We have to make it clear that a good book is of a higher and of a more permanent value to him than to watch two boxers getting their noses smashed up. Of course, if the publishers cannot give the workers books he would like to read but offer him just the same old murders in the garbage can which are offered to all the baboons we cannot expect him to realize that there are such books.

So Traven submitted his manuscripts, Smith "treated" them, Alfred Knopf published them, and a small circle of American readers bought the books. (Only after *Treasure* became a movie in 1948 did Traven become a best-selling writer in the U.S.)

In addition to this publishing history, I also knew that Bernard Smith and his wife had come to Mexico in 1936 in hopes of meeting B. Traven. Traven never appeared, but he sent a friend, whom he identified only as "Mary," to serve as their guide. He prepared an itinerary for Smith, demanded that Smith leave it with "Mary" when the journey was over, and not take it back with him to New York. Smith abided by Traven's rules. When he returned to his office at Knopf he noted that the most exciting part of the trip was the "feeling that Mr. Traven was actually nearby at all times. He was secretly looking on." I knew Smith's feeling well. B. Traven was still nearby at all times, secretly looking on.

"I've got it," Rosa Elena said, storming through the door. She handed me the folder marked "Smith." There was a cover letter, and more than thirty single-spaced, typewritten pages outlining what Smith and his wife should eat and drink, what *not* to eat and drink, what movie houses to go to, what museums and churches. Traven certainly did know Mexico City. His itinerary would have made an excellent tour guide for Americans.

Chele and I took the itinerary and drove to the Zócalo. Then, following Traven's instructions, we walked to the Merced, an immense market that served the entire city, over ten million people, and made Les Halles in Paris look like a corner grocery store. Workers were unloading mountains of tomatoes, bananas, mangoes, pineapples, while armies of flies attacked the stinking heaps of garbage in the streets. Inside there were thousands of stalls—fruit and vegetables arranged like pyramids—and old Indian women sitting on high stools, fanning themselves and watching us. There was no high pressure saleswomanship. They knew we had come to look and not to buy.

From the Merced we walked to the Ministry of Education. Mothers and children crowded the benches in the open courtyard, waiting to see one or another petty bureaucrat about this or that problem at school, and seemingly oblivious of the national art treasures that Diego Rivera had painted on the walls fifty years earlier. The colors were still strong—dark blues, bright reds, rich browns—the same strong colors in the shirts and the blouses of the mothers and children sitting on the benches. The expressions were remarkably similar too. A young boy sitting on his mother's knee looked like the boy eating a tamale in Rivera's mural.

I flipped the pages and read from Traven's itinerary:

You should look at the frescoes from every angle pos-

sible, even across the patio and you will note how
Rivera has taken into consideration every bit of sur-
rounding to achieve what he meant to do. Note that
the colors and also the motifs differ according to the
light which falls upon the picture. Where it is dark as
along the stairway and at certain nooks on the
ground floor the colors and motifs are more gloomy,
while at other places where the bright daylight is
falling in, there is a great amount of optimism and
victory in colors and motifs. Where the light is
brightest there are gay fiestas celebrating victories
and abundance of good things. I have found that visitors and critics never seem to see these details and
just look at the stories in the pictures.

From the Ministry of Education we drove to Juárez, and
climbed the steps to the Del Prado Hotel. Tourists were sitting
in the lobby, smoking, drinking, reading their guide books,
and gazing at Rivera's "Sunday Afternoon in the Alameda."
At the center of the mural I recognized a portrait of José
Posada in black hat, black tie, black trousers, and black shoes.
Rivera made him look more like an undertaker than an en-
graver and artist. Death was at Posada's arm. She was an
elegant woman. Her face was a skeleton and on her head she
wore an exotic hat. Holding Madame Death's other hand was
Diego as a small boy, wearing breeches, a Panama hat on his
head, and carrying a frog in his pocket. Behind Diego was
Frida Kahlo, his wife after his separation from Lupe Marin.
Frida held the yin/yang symbol in her hand.
Following Traven's advice I noticed Diego's use of color and
shape, the light pastels, the gentle waving lines of the trees.
And now I could also appreciate that Traven had the eye of
the artist. The Jungle Novels were his murals of Mexican history. There was a story, a plot, but there was also fantastic
color, line, pattern, rhythm. Yes, Traven had achieved with
the written word what Diego had achieved with paint and

brush. In the Jungle Novels there was even that clash of optimism and pessimism, darkness and light, that Traven observed in Diego's murals.

By now it was two in the afternoon and Chele and I were both starving. At Prendes a waiter with an old, wrinkled face seated us in the back.

"Chele, Chele, *aqui aqui*," we heard a voice whisper. It was Rudolfo Usigli and he was squinting at us. "Federico's very sick," he said, lowering his cigarette holder. "I don't know how much longer he'll last. Tell me, young man, have you written the biography of Traven yet? No, I guess not. Remember what I told you? Surrealism—that's the answer. Surrealism. Well, enjoy your lunch, I'm off to the hospital to see Federico."

The waiter brought us dark beers and *quesadillas*. He beamed joyfully. "I've worked forty years," he said. "Tonight I'm retiring. I feel like a new man already." The beer stung my teeth, the *quesadillas* and *salsa* burned my tongue.

"You seem happier today," I said.

"Things are going better with the collective," Chele said. "We have a woman's caucus now so the men don't treat us like shit any more. I'm getting along better with mother too. She likes working with you on the biography."

"Listen, Chele, I've been wanting to ask you something about Traven. Why didn't he protest the massacre at Tlatelolco?"

"He was very old," Chele said. "But in '68 he came alive again. He could hardly walk, but he made his way to Reforma, watched the demonstrations, and listened to the speeches. He supported the students, but there wasn't much he could do. He was very sick. Five months after Tlatelolco he died. Maybe the massacre brought his death on faster. Mother was terribly depressed. I was sick. Only Malu pulled us through. She loves us, loved the Skipper too, as though he were her own father."

138

22

On March 26, 1975, the sixth anniversary of B. Traven's death, I did a radio program about Traven on Mexico City's English-language station. The listening audience included business executives at the North American branches of IBM, Ford, General Motors, ITT, older retired folks living on pensions and savings, and younger exiles and dropouts from gringo America.

I opened the program by talking about Rosa Elena, the Luján family, and Rosa Elena's life with Traven. Then I played a recording of Hanns Eisler singing in German Traven's "Song of the Cotton Pickers" that was sung by Wobbly organizers in the twenties:

> Cotton is worn by king and prince,
> Millionaire and president,
> But the lowly cotton picker
> Sweats to earn each bloody cent.
> Get going to the cotton field,
> The sun is moving up and up.
> Sling on your sack,
> Tighten your belt—
> Listen, the scales are turning.

Then I read from Traven's books. Since *Treasure* was his best-known work I started with it. I chose a section near the end. *Treasure*, of course, has plenty of action: gun fights, firing squads, train robberies. I wanted a different kind of action. So I read the description of Dobbs's isolation in the desert, and his inner psychological drama. Dobbs has taken Curtin's and Howard's gold; he thinks he has killed Curtin and he begins to feel guilty (Bogart does a fine job interpreting Dobbs's fear, hallucination, and craziness in the movie):

> Suddenly Dobbs noted that everything about him was silent. He had never taken any notice of the fact that nature in the tropics, as noon approaches, becomes drowsy and falls asleep. Birds cease to sing and no longer fly about, insects become quiet and hide away under leaves and other shady places. . . Even the wind goes to sleep; the leaves no longer whisper.
> Dobbs felt this growing silence like something strange happening in the whole world. It seemed to him as though trees and leaves became petrified. Their color turned from green to a dull dustlike gray. The air felt strangely heavy, and the atmosphere appeared to have turned into a gaseous lava.
> Thick sweat broke out all over his body. He had the sensation that if he did not move that very second, he also might become petrified, like everything else around him.

Next, I read from *Bridge*. Carlosito has been fished out of the river, put to rest in a coffin, and carried to the cemetery. The school teacher, who is supposed to give the funeral oration, gets drunk and falls into the grave. It is the second *fall* in the book—the first being Carlosito's tragic fall into the water. The drunken school teacher's fall is comic.

I held the book in my hands, and moved closer to the microphone:

The fall of the respectable teacher. . .makes the funniest show I can imagine. But not a single person, man, woman, girl, or boy, laughs at the teacher. I, for one, usually have great difficulty keeping from laughing. . .I cannot help it that I see most things in a funny way, and if I fail to see fun in supposedly sacred performances or speeches, then I can see only the irony in them. And yet here I do not laugh. . .nobody laughed; neither did I, because I was one of them, and it was my boy who was to be buried just as he was the child of everybody present. No teacher was struggling to come out of the grave into which he had fallen. I saw only a great brotherly love for his fellow men which had dropped into the grave and was struggling hard to get out again. I can laugh at a thousand things and situations—even at the brutalities of fascism, which as I see them are but a ridiculous cowardice without limits. But I can never laugh at love shown by men for those of their fellow men in pain and sorrow.

I closed the book and looked around the studio. It was hushed. The technicians at the controls had been moved. I paused a moment, then led into *The Death Ship*. The *Empress of Madagascar* has gone down beneath the waves. Gales and Stanislav are floating on a raft in the midst of the ocean. This is the scene that the editors at the Gutenberg Book Guild found unsatisfactory and suggested that Traven rewrite. Traven refused. He wrote his editor:

I take it that you have never spent a few days on the sea, near the equator, bound to the wreckage of a ship. If you were, you would find the ending the only one possible. He who could write another ending was never shipwrecked and lonesome, his last companion washed away, and who sees and feels everything around him only as a dull dream. . .The

writers of earlier cultural eras made it easy for themselves. They let everybody die. Even in *Hamlet*,
Polonius, Ophelia, King and Queen, Laertes and
Hamlet all die. That is one end. I cannot do this. We
are not Werthers, not Romeos and Juliets. We have
to live. We have to bear it.

Traven was right not to change the ending of *The Death Ship*.
It's a beautiful, sad, lyrical piece of writing:

Dark thick clouds were tossed above us like so many
torn rags. The storm seemed to grow into a greater
rage so as not to be laughed at by the thundering
and roaring waves.

Through these rags of clouds we could see, for a
few seconds, the shining stars that, in spite of all the
uproar, called down upon us the eternal promise:
"We are the Peace and the Rest." Yet between these
words of promise we could see another meaning:
"Within the flames of never ceasing creation and
restlessness, there we are enveloped; do not long for
us if you want peace and rest: we cannot give you
anything which you do not find within yourself!"

The vast distances toward the horizon and the im-
mensity of the sea shrank when the mist closed in on
us. The sea became smaller with every minute, until
we had the illusion that we were floating on an in-
land lake. As time went on, even this lake narrowed
more and more. Now we felt as if drifting down a
river. We had the sensation that we could touch the
banks with our hands. The walls of mist seemed only
to veil dimly the river-banks.

The reading was over. Then the telephone lines were
opened, and listeners called in with questions and comments.
One woman repeated the story that Traven was none other
than Jack London, that London had faked his own suicide,

then went to Mexico, and took a new name and identity as B. Traven. I explained that there were similarities between B. Traven and Jack London—both were illegitimate children, both went to sea and wrote about the sea. Traven had once told the Gutenberg Book Guild editors that both he and London "are really proletarians. Both grew up in proletarian circumstances. . .in the turmoil of proletarian quarters in big industrial cities, both worked in all kinds of professions and occupations, not to study the proletariat but because they had to make a living. Both are Americans. Both lived a similar life in the same countries under similar conditions influenced by self-education and by similar sentiments. The lives of Jack London and B.T. are far more similar in every relation than ever would be concluded from reading both their books."

Another listener called in and said that she had known Traven under the name Torsvan when he lived at the Hotel Panuco. "A very quiet kinda guy," she said. "Though he did have ladies up to visit, and they'd party. Oh, he was quite a ladies' man."

It wasn't until I left the studio and walked toward the Rio Mississippi that I became fully conscious of the selections I had made from Traven's work. I had not read passages about the state, exploitation, or proletarians. Instead I had chosen descriptions of death, loneliness, hallucination, lyrical passages, and passages that modulated between laughter and tears, the bitter and the sentimental.

Then I realized that my image of Traven had changed. He was not the man I had seen (or had wanted to see) when I first arrived in Mexico City. The romantic revolutionary living with the downtrodden peasants of the jungle had vanished, and in his place was a complex man with fears, doubts, conflicting emotions and identities. Sometimes I didn't like him. He was cranky, opinionated, difficult.

The books changed too. Each time I read them they suggested different moods, feelings, ideas. I heard new voices, saw new shapes and forms. As I grew and changed, the books grew and changed.

Rosa Elena was sitting upstairs, still listening to the radio; Tabasco was lying at her feet. Rosa Elena wore her turquoise robe and her fluffy slippers. She looked older. Her hair wasn't as thick or as black as it had seemed, and there were dark lines under her eyes.

"You've reminded me of things I didn't want to remember," she said. (I didn't know whether she was performing or speaking from the heart). "You see, I've been living so much of my time in the past. It's very hard to escape. Now I'm feeling very sad and melancholy."

In the evening I went to *La Peña* in Coyoacán to hear Angel Parra, a Chilean singer and guitarist who had been arrested by the junta. Following world-wide protest Parra was released from prison and came to Mexico. Thousands of Chileans were living in exile in Mexico and *La Peña* was their cultural home.

"Most of the refugees stay out of politics," Chele had told me. "They don't have Mexican citizenship and they're afraid of being deported. And, of course, the Chileans who escaped and managed to get here are mostly upper class. The working people weren't so lucky; they didn't have the money or the connections. It's sad. The Chileans here have jobs at the University or in the government. Many of them don't like Mexico. They're snobs, won't eat the food, complain about the dirt, the tiny apartments, and the lazy servants. They've known persecution, and yet they turn around and persecute the Indians here."

The stage darkened for a moment, then the spotlight illuminated Angel Parra. He was a thin, wiry man. He smiled, but it was only a surface smile, and it lasted only a moment. Parra had thick black hair that reminded me of a horse's mane. His shirt and blue jeans hung loosely about his frame; he looked like a concentration camp survivor. When he held the guitar and plucked the strings his hands shook. When he opened his mouth to sing his voice trembled.

Parra looked directly into the spotlight. He never closed his eyes, never blinked, never looked directly into anyone's face. I stared at him impolitely. I saw a small square of light reflected in his eyes, and I felt drawn into his song. He was a powerful singer. His hands moved slowly across the body of the guitar, and the words echoed across the crowded room. I didn't realize that the song was ended until the audience applauded. Still, Parra didn't smile or blink his eyes. He waited for the applause to die down before beginning his next song.

When the performance was over I returned to Tlalpan. "They say that the Mexican government opened *La Peña*," Chele had said. "Now they can watch all of us. They make it public and they control it. Everyone thinks that the Mexican government is against dictatorship. People tell themselves, 'Aren't we lucky, we have a *peña*. It could never be like Chile here.' They forget so quickly."

It was a warm night. Tlalpan was asleep, but Mrs. Yampolsky was still wide awake and playing a hot hand of solitaire on the glass table. She offered me tea and cake, wouldn't let me go to sleep. She insisted on playing canasta, so we stayed up until two A.M. After she had beaten me viciously I climbed the spiral staircase, set the alarm clock, and fell asleep immediately. But I woke after a short nap. The watchdogs were howling. Apparently a burglar had tried to enter the house and they had frightened him away. Mrs. Yampolsky turned on the spotlight and looked in the garden. No one was there.

At first I didn't remember my dream, but then the barking of the watchdogs reminded me. I was dangling from a rope. Below me dogs snarled in anticipation of my fall. I was terrified. I could feel their sharp teeth in my flesh. I descended lower and lower, the barking became more violent, until finally it woke me.

I closed the window, covered my head, and soon I was asleep again. It must have been a deep sleep because when I woke again I felt completely rested—and not only rested, but restored. There were still several hours before sunrise, but I was so charged with energy that I couldn't go back to sleep.

Except for my right arm. It was under the pillow. I had fallen asleep with the weight of my head on my arm and now my arm was asleep. The rest of my body was shot through with electric current. I lifted the pillow with my left hand, and I looked at the other hand, the sleeping hand. It wasn't my hand, not my arm either. It was someone else's arm, a stranger's. And then it struck me. I knew immediately. I had seen it before in the pictures and paintings that hung on the walls at the Rio Mississippi.

I don't know if it was the late hour, the barking of the watchdogs, or some strange trick of my eye, but staring up at me was Traven's right arm. His arm! It wasn't a dream. I was wide awake. And I didn't seem to be hallucinating. Everything else in the room was normal, ordinary. Nothing else had changed. Except for the arm and the hand. I looked out the window. The dogs were the same. They were sniffing along the fence.

I felt as though someone had played a nasty trick on me—maybe Mrs. Yampolsky, maybe Rosa Elena, who knows whom. They wanted to tease me, make fun of me and my preoccupation with B. Traven. So I started to laugh. Might as well enjoy the joke. After all, it could have been a lot worse. I could have woken up with his face, or his mind inside my body. Now that wouldn't have been so funny.

I tossed and turned and I remembered that I had been warned by friends and family not to get carried away by the subject, by Rosa Elena, and to keep my nose to the biographical grindstone. "Don't get sidetracked," my father had said. "And, for heaven's sake, don't start thinking you're Traven. It was bad enough when you thought you were Joseph Conrad! Don't get involved in Rosa Elena's affairs. Write the book and come home!"

It had started out harmless enough. I was going to write Traven's biography. I admired the man and his books. But then I took the process a step further. I began to imitate him. I put on his trousers, his shirt, his glasses. I became greedy. I wanted the treasure. I wanted to *be* Traven. And now someone or something had given me a taste of what it was like to be Traven. Just a small sample—his right arm, his hand, his writing hand.

I didn't like it. I was reminded of that saying, "Don't wish for anything unless you really want it." Well, I didn't want it. It wasn't funny any more. It wasn't a game. I closed my eyes and hid the arm under the covers. No, I hadn't seen anything out of the ordinary. I was asleep. I was really sleeping and dreaming. I'm sleeping, I'm dreaming, I told myself. I'm asleep, I'm asleep, I'm asleep.

PART TWO

I will come like the storm that covers the wasteland. You who wake in the morning with murder already in your thoughts, I will judge you, so beware. I will come with thunder and lightning.

—Ret Marut, 1919

I would rather prefer to remain where I am staying now, because I am doing fairly well down here, thank you, and I feel somehow like a mouse in the larder with the cat thrown out.

—T. Torsvan, 1941

Forget the man! What does it matter if he is the son of a Hohenzollern prince or anyone else.

—Hal Croves, 1966

23

Outside Mrs. Yampolsky's house I caught the bus; at Tacubaya I changed for the metro. Through the train window I saw the remains of the old aqueducts and canals, and then and there I decided that the ancient Aztecs had solved the water and transportation problem far better than the modern Mexicans and their North American accomplices.

At Navarra I got out of the train and walked to the bus station. Half a dozen carwashers were in the street waiting for work. On every block in Mexico City the carwasher was always in the street—bucket, brush, and rag in hand—awaiting orders to lather and scrub someone else's steel and chrome. He was a Mexican institution, as much as the bullfighter.

Usually the carwasher was a refugee from the countryside; an Indian from a remote village, driven by hunger into the city. Now, in exchange for washing cars in the street, he could eat rice and beans and a corn tortilla. The car provided the Indian with a job; it saved him from starvation.

Watching an Indian scrub the muddy tires of a Pontiac, I thought of Malu. Malu never used the words "auto" or "car" —they were too ordinary—but always the Spanish word *coche*, which literally translates as "coach." Malu thought of her vehicle as an enchanted coach and she its princess. But she was a very rude princess, always at the horn, honking, honking, honking for someone to get out of the way, for Petra to fetch a pair of shoes, or wash *el coche*.

One's car had to be clean, as one's house had to be clean, one's clothes had to be spotless, and one's hands and face immaculate. To be clean meant to be modern, efficient, "American," but especially it meant *not* to be Indian. Mexico City was anxious to be sanitary. It thought that the more it washed its face with Ivory or Dial, the more often it had its dresses and shirts dry-cleaned, then the less Indian it would be, the more civilized it would become. Mexico City was trying hard to bleach itself white. Fortunately, there were hundreds of thousands of "dirty" and "uncivilized" Indians who could be hired to keep the capital clean. The women would vacuum and dust the big houses; the men would wash and polish the big cars; the boys would shine businessmen's shoes and their sisters would wash and dry dishes. But the dirt would not go away and the Indian would not vanish.

I was leaving Mexico City, but I told myself that it wasn't Rosa Elena or the specter of B. Traven who were driving me away. It was the car, the tyranny of the street, the reign of terror imposed on the pedestrian, and the threat of collision and death. The Indian from the countryside seemed able to endure Car City. Maybe he would even triumph over it; maybe he would convert the gringo machine into an Aztec chariot and resurrect the pyramids. Maybe. But I couldn't survive. I had to escape to the very countryside from which the Indian had fled as though from a living hell.

To survive in Mexico City people built walls. Perhaps in other cities around the world they are metaphorical walls more than anything else. But in Mexico they were thick walls of stone and cement. People locked and bolted their medieval doors against the savage invaders, trained watchdogs, hired night watchmen, and paid Indian boys to keep their eyes open and guard against car thieves. Mrs. Yampolsky had her wall. Rosa Elena had hers, too. But I didn't feel safety behind their high walls any more; rather, I felt danger. I had to travel, and maybe that too was Traven's doing. Hadn't he explained to the Gutenberg Book Guild editors:

> I must travel. I must see things, landscapes, and people before I bring them to life in my work. I must travel to jungles, and primeval forests, to visit Indians, distant ranchos, and to unknown, secret, mysterious lakes and rivers.

"It would be best for you to get away for a while," Dr. Pepe Perralta suggested after I told him about my five A.M. hallucination. He examined my arm, listened to my story and my heartbeat, and was not in the least surprised or shocked. "It happens," Pepe assured me. "I have patients who hallucinate on a regular basis. To think that you are Traven is quite natural, given the circumstances. Remember you've been living at his house, with his widow, reading his books and papers, and Rosa Elena has said that you remind her of Traven. I'm only surprised that it didn't happen sooner. A patient of mine was writing a book about Zapata, ended up thinking he was Zapata, and his wife and daughter committed him to an institution in Puebla—but you have a long way to go before you reach that point."

Pepe's wife Marie Louise offered her advice too. "Why don't you fuck Rosa Elena," she said casually. "That would probably solve your problem—and hers—all at the same time." Pepe blushed. "No, I don't think that is the best medical solution," he said. "You should travel. Get away."

When I told Rosa Elena that I was leaving for a short trip I thought that she was going to break down and cry. We were sitting at the table in the breakfast room. She was wearing her turquoise bathrobe and fluffy slippers. I looked into her eyes and suddenly I had the feeling that I was abandoning her. "I wish I could travel with you," she said. "But there are so many things to do here, and the girls need me. I'll miss you terribly, but go without me. Besides, you wouldn't want to travel with someone the age of your mother anyway."

I remembered the look on Rosa Elena's face, and the sound of her voice as I asked the man at the window for a one-way ticket to Cuernavaca. He handed me a scrap of paper with the number nine (now forever identified in my mind as Traven's lucky lottery number) scrawled in the upper left-hand corner. It didn't look like a bus ticket, but I was assured it would get me to my destination.

I stuffed the ticket into the brim of my hat and sat down on a bench. I suppose that one bus station is like another. This was the third-class station, the cheapest and therefore the one used mostly by Indians. Passengers arrived and departed. Families and friends saw travelers off, or welcomed them home. An old man strummed a guitar. A shoeshine boy looked for scuffed or muddy shoes. A young woman clutched her books. Buses pulled in and pulled out of the station, unloaded and loaded. They were like ordinary American schoolbuses, but they were painted blue instead of the traditional yellow.

No sign or name indicated the route or destination, but most of the travelers seemed to know which was his or her bus. I had to ask half a dozen times before I found the Cuernavaca-bound bus. Seat number nine was by the window. In front of me an old woman held a baby pig in her lap. It was a beautiful pig. The skin was a bright pink, and the corkscrew tail was cute. Across the aisle a man had several oil paintings of the saints—Matthew, Luke, Peter, and one of that modern saint, Che Guevara.

A young kid walked up and down the aisle hawking white shoe laces for 50 centavos. Then, suddenly, the driver turned the ignition key, pressed the accelerator pedal, and the kid scampered off the bus. The engine choked and sputtered. I opened *El Dia* and looked at the sports page; the Mexican baseball season was in full swing. I heard the driver release the brake and close the door. The pig squealed and the old woman had to hold him so he wouldn't escape. Then the bus pulled into the street.

Someone sat down in the seat next to me. I felt the weight of a body, and lowered the newspaper to take a look. He was a gringo, a white man probably in his late seventies. He was thin, wiry, balding, and his few remaining wisps of hair were white. His face was bright red from the sun, his eyes a cold blue, his nose thin and arrogant.

Do you see him? He wore round glasses that would have fallen apart at the hinges, except for a rusty safety pin that attached the arm to the frame. His pants were spattered with oil and mud. Instead of a belt he wore a thick cord that was knotted in front. His shirt was white yet it wasn't clean. No amount of cleaning could have removed the spots and stains. The old man wore sneakers, but instead of laces he had used string to hold them together.

Between his legs was a yellow and blue basket. He reached inside and took out needle and thread. His eyes were good; he was on target first try.

"They say that a rich man has a tougher time getting into heaven then a camel has passing through the eye of a needle," the old man said. He had a strange accent. Was it Texas? The Middle West? I couldn't place it. "It's not true," he continued. "Rich people just widen the eye so they can walk through, don't even have to stoop over."

The fact that he was an old white man and dressed so shabbily made him unusual. Occasionally one will see a dignified old white man, usually a Spaniard, on a third class bus, but even that is rare. A poor white man, a North American dressed in rags is practically unheard of. The old man looked like a drifter, a hobo who hadn't been told that the day of the drifter was long past, about fifty years ago. He was an anomaly, a relic of a bygone age.

You see, he looked like B. Traven, or what I imagine B. Traven looked like. No, not the Traven who lived at the Rio Mississippi with Rosa Elena, but the Traven I imagined after I had read *The Death Ship* and *The Cotton Pickers*. It was as if the Traven of *The Cotton Pickers* had never stopped picking cotton, never stopped being a vagabond and a Wobbly troublemaker.

"Where are you from?" I asked. The old man couldn't be bothered. He was stitching his tattered shirt. I wanted to ask him about his life, to get his story, but I felt inhibited. Whatever I asked would offend him. He was cranky. If Traven was sitting beside me, wouldn't he be acting precisely as this old man was acting: aloof, indifferent, and yet enigmatic at the same time, with his casual remarks about rich people, camels, heaven, and the eyes of needles.

I knew that I wouldn't get along with Traven, as I wasn't getting along with the old man. He made me uncomfortable. Traven would be as cool to me as he had been to all the journalists and photographers. He might even be nasty. Might throw me out of his house. Traven didn't want *me* to write his biography. Hadn't he told his German publishers:

> My biography would not disappoint you, but it is my own private affair, and I want to keep it to myself. The biography of a creative person is completely unimportant. If the person cannot be recognized and understood in his works, then he isn't worth a damn, and neither are his works.

I wondered what I was doing writing the biography of a man who didn't want a biography, who fought all his life for anonymity and privacy. Wasn't Rosa Elena betraying a trust? She knew he needed anonymity—and yet now she wanted us to write his biography. I felt like an invader, a trespasser! I had gone through his papers, books, clothing, and I knew that he wouldn't have liked that. He would have resented me deeply for poking through his pockets, trying on his trousers, snooping around like a detective on a case.

We were at the top of the mountain. The driver pulled into a clearing on the side of the road. The old man got out, walked along a dirt path, then disappeared behind a corn field.

24

Cuernavaca was hot. I took off my jacket, unbuttoned my shirt, and waited for the Belfridges. I waited a half-hour. When Cedric and Mary didn't arrive I took a cab to their place in Lomas de Atzingo, high in the hills, above the dust and noise of the city.

Like Rosa Elena, like Mrs. Yampolsky, the Belfridges and their neighbors had walls, though the walls of Cuernavaca weren't nearly as high as the walls of Mexico City. Clearly life was more peaceful here. Behind the Belfridges' wall was a large house, patio, swimming pool, finely manicured lawn, and flower garden. I felt like I was back in suburbia.

The Belfridges weren't home, but the cook told me that they had gone to town to pick up an American—presumably me. I stashed my luggage in the closet, and changed into a swimming suit. At the pool there was a strong smell of coconut oil and tequila. Guests lounged in the sun, preoccupied with their newspapers and magazines, air-mailed from New York.

Edita Morris was sitting in the shade, under an umbrella, typing at a plastic portable. I knew Edita from New York. Now she looked older; her forehead was wrinkled, her hair grayer, but her eyes still had a look of youth and joy. Edita was traveling through Latin America with a photographer, exploring slums and shantytowns, recording in word and image the invisible, unspoken wretchedness of the continent.

"But, of course, you know. You've read Traven," Edita said. "Hunger, misery, torture: it never ends, no matter how many books we write about it."

While I was swimming the Belfridges returned from town. Mary was surprised to see me. She stood at the edge of the pool, hands on her broad hips, her white shirt flapping in the breeze. As it turned out Mary and Cedric had gone to the first-class bus terminal to look for me, and I had been waiting at the third-class station.

Cedric Belfridge was a tall man with a large head, large hands and chest. But he was unimposing and quiet. He smoked his pipe, spoke softly, and didn't intrude, not even in his own home.

Cedric was an expatriate. In the late forties and early fifties he had been a New York newspaperman and editor who defended unpopular causes. The House Un-American Activities Committee subpoenaed him to testify about the people and the causes he defended. Belfridge refused to cooperate. He was arrested, jailed, and then deported as an undesirable alien. Cedric Belfridge was literally an un-American, an "outside agitator." He was a British subject, and had no American passport or papers. Shades of Ret Marut/B. Traven, and the Gerard Gales of *The Death Ship* who is refused entry to the United States and is deported from Holland to Belgium, from Belgium back to Holland, to France and then to Spain. I think that B. Traven would have liked Cedric Belfridge if for no other reason than because he was deported from the States. Bedfellows!

After his deportation Belfridge drifted south. Mexico took him in, as it had taken in B. Traven and Leon Trotsky, the veterans of the Spanish Civil War, and the survivors of the Chilean holocaust. Twenty years later Cedric was living a comfortable life in Cuernavaca, writing books, entertaining friends, and still denied the right to make his home within the borders of the United States.

I had met Belfridge in New York in 1973. He had written a

book about the victims of McCarthyism (or Nixonism, if you prefer), people who were investigated, arrested, deported, executed during the years 1945–1960. When the book was published the U.S. State Department granted Belfridge a six-week visa to visit the States, but stipulated that he could only speak about people and events from 1945 to 1960. If he forgot to censor himself and carelessly spoke about events or people in, say, 1961, his visa would be rescinded and he would be immediately deported. Cedric Belfridge was living testimony that, after half a century, *The Death Ship* hadn't lost its bite.

The Belfridges ran a vacation resort in Cuernavaca. Their guests—most of whom were progressive-minded and prosperous—regarded Cedric as a poor, tragic victim of McCarthyism; they took pity on him, and patronized him. Cedric didn't seem to take offense, but Mary did. She dished out her own special brand of nastiness as fast as her guests patronized "poor, old Cedric."

I'm sure that Mary wouldn't agree—Cedric probably wouldn't, either—but it was my feeling, and I think it would have been Traven's too, that arrest and deportation had invigorated Belfridge. Having to start life over again in a foreign country must have been difficult. And Cedric had certainly been done a terrible injustice. I don't mean to romanticize deportation and exile. Too many people in too many countries are destroyed or crushed by investigation, deportation, arrest, exile. But then some rare people aren't. Adversity seemed to invigorate Cedric as it had invigorated Ret Marut/B. Traven. Traven thrived on adversity; his art sprang from it.

Ret Marut, you recall, was a mediocre, though angry young actor, poet, and journalist in the Germany of World War I. Arrest, a sentence of death, escape, the underground, hard labor at sea, and finally exile in Mexico transformed him into B. Traven, novelist of extraordinary power. In my view, deportation and exile had similarly freed Belfridge from broken-down dogmas and New York radical provincialism, instilled in him a deep consciousness of Latin America, and revealed its invisible hunger, torture, and death. It was the best education he could have received, as toil and deprivation was the best education Ret Marut received.

Traven believed that the downtrodden, the poor, the persecuted was a more interesting individual than the privileged, the rich, the powerful. "I have discovered and learned through suffering," he wrote in 1925, "that the worker, the proletarian, is a thousand times more interesting and many-sided person than Rockefeller, Morgan, Coolidge, Gloria Swanson, Tom Mix, or Mary Pickford."

In *The Death Ship* Traven argued that people who were arrested, deported, exiled, had a strength and a courage denied to decent, law-abiding citizens. "Ordinary men have their birth certificates and passports and paybooks in fine shape," he wrote. "They never make any trouble for a bureaucrat. But there would be no such thing as the Most Glorious God's country if half of the pioneers and builders of the great nation could have produced passports and could have passed Ellis Island like the Prince of Wales. Ordinary people can never fall over the walls, because they never dare climb high enough to see what is beyond the walls."

Unlike B. Traven, Cedric Belfridge didn't argue that he was superior to the "ordinary men." He was more modest, less bombastic and less arrogant than B. Traven. But Traven's status as a deportee and an exile was double-edged. It fed his elitism, but at the same time it gave him membership in the human family of exiles. It provided him with a common identity. Here was a major source of his writing. Traven's characters, including the autobiographical Gerard Gales, are exiles to the bone. They are uprooted, dispossessed, lost. Traven's exile enabled him to understand the plight of the migrant worker who was robbed of his country, nationality, legal and human rights. It enabled him to understand the plight of the Indian who was robbed of his home, land, tribe, and cultural identity.

But B. Traven's characters are not eternal exiles. Like him they find new homes, families, comrades. Gerard Gales, the stranded sailor and nobody, joins a crew of nobodies aboard the death ship. He becomes a member of the society of lost souls, and undocumented proletarians.

In *The Bridge in the Jungle,* Gales the wandering gringo is adopted by a Mexican village and the Indian peasants. But first he must experience the deep pain of exile, the feeling of guilt about being a white man in a nation of dark-skinned people. On the malevolent night that Carlosito falls from the bridge and drowns in the river Traven wonders:

> Where is the world? Where is the earth on which I used to live? It has disappeared. Where has mankind gone? I am alone. There is not even a heaven above me. Only blackness. I am on another planet, from which I never can return to my own people. I shall never again see green meadows, never again the waves of wheat fields . . . I cannot come back to the earth, my true mother, and never shall I see the sun rise. I am with creatures I do not know, who do not speak my language, and whose souls and minds I can never fathom. One, only one out of this crowd has to stand up at this moment, only one has to point his fingers at me and yell: "Look at that man! Look at him! He is the white, who has not been invited to come here, but he came nevertheless. He is the guilty one. By his blue eyes and by his skin of the pale dead he has brought the wrath of our gods upon us poor people. He is a gringo. He has brought us misfortune and sorrows."

Before I left the United States I had a romantic idea about life in Mexico. I thought that I was going to get away, to escape. I envisioned Mexico as a land of small villages and pure peasants. In no way was I prepared for what I found. I had an idealistic notion of exile, derived in part from reading books by North Americans and Europeans in Mexico: John Reed's *Insurgent Mexico,* D.H. Lawrence's *The Plumed Serpent,* and Traven's *The Cotton Pickers.* I assumed that I would be in immediate touch with the land, the people, the spirit of the place. I felt that Mexico would embrace me, that I would embrace Mexico. I would find the modern Pancho Villa, ride with him across the burning plains, disappear into a cool jungle paradise and become one with the Indians. It wasn't that easy. After three short months of exile the dream vanished.

I knew, at least in part, how Traven must have felt. I was lonely. I too was on a strange planet, cut off from my family, friends, my people and culture. Now, for the first time, I could appreciate Rudyard Kipling's lament from India for the "lost heritage of London . . . the roar of the streets, the lights, the music." Suddenly I sensed the lost heritage of New York, the roar of the streets, the crowds, and especially the music. Things, places, and people I had wanted to escape from now seemed highly desirable. Yet, at the same time, I could appreciate B. Traven's and Cedric Belfridge's ability to survive and grow in a strange country, among people of a different race and culture.

Belfridge could have settled in comfortable London or Paris. Traven probably could have settled in San Antonio or Los Angeles; in the early thirties he spent several months a year in Texas and California. But Traven went against the grain. He remained on the periphery, rather than migrating to the capital. The artists and writers of our day tend to flock to New York, Paris, London. They visit or tour the tropics, the outlying islands, the remote villages, but they return to the metropolitan centers. Now I too felt that need for the metropolitan center, for intellectual discussion, cultural affinity, political battles.

B. Traven had the stubborn strength to survive away from the literary capitals of the modern world for half a century. Almost all his dealings with his editors was done by mail, and until the sixties he never spoke with them on the phone, or met any of them in person. It's an unusual way to work; I don't think I could do it.

Behind the walls of Rosa Elena's house on the Rio Mississippi, behind the Belfridges' wall, I felt comfortable—but beyond their walls I was among "foreigners," "strangers." I knew what it was like to feel guilty because I too had white skin. Hadn't my country, the people of my race and nationality ruined Mexico? Didn't the Indians see me as an ambassador of conquest? I was sure that the Indians hated me, and I was afraid. I found myself becoming afraid of them, sometimes hating complete strangers—the man on the *pesero* who glared at me, or the shopkeeper who charged me fifty centavos more for bananas than she charged the Indians.

I think that I knew how Traven felt when he feared that an Indian would point an accusing finger at him. No one pointed a finger at me, and yet I expected to see the finger leveled at me, to hear the Indian denounce me as "the evil gringo."

Traven lived here for half a century. In the fifties he became a Mexican citizen and married a Mexican woman. Only once, in 1959, the year the film version of *The Death Ship* premiered in Berlin, did he return to Germany, the land where he had spent the critical, formative years of his life. I knew that I couldn't survive in Mexico for fifty years without going back to New York or San Francisco every few years—unless going home meant, as it meant for Traven, going to prison and the gallows. If Traven had returned to Germany in the late twenties the Nazis would have arrested him, and sent him to a concentration camp along with Erich Muhsam, his old friend and survivor from the Munich insurrection of 1919. Traven was lucky. Mexico was his salvation. Erich Muhsam was gassed by the Nazis.

After three months I was already homesick. Traven too had been homesick for the "green meadows" and "waves of wheat fields," but he conquered his homesickness, fear, and hostility. He came to love the Indian. I mean *love*. There was respect, admiration, friendship, but also love. Perhaps there were strains of romantic love, nostalgic love, idealistic love. Still it was LOVE. And that's rare. In our age it is extraordinary for the European, the North American, to love the Indian. There are people in love with the idea of the Indian, or the idea of the primitive, but to actually love the people, to accept them, their prejudices and weaknesses, as well as their virtues, that is unusual. There are people who dress like the Indian, who imitate the Indian, but that isn't love. More and more it looks to me like self-indulgence. He who can afford to play Indian doesn't understand the Indian reality.

Before I left the Rio Mississippi I looked at Rosa Elena's pictures of Traven in the jungles of Chiapas. Traven never went native as I had hoped to do. He emphathized with the Indian, but he didn't wear *huaraches*, a *serape*, or an Indian shirt. He wore leather boots, a white shirt, pleated trousers, and a pith helmet to protect him from the sun. He looked like a proper, upstanding white man in the jungle. Like a sahib. Once I left Mexico City I wouldn't be caught dead looking like Traven. No pith helmet for me. With Rosa Elena's help I bought a Chamula shirt and belt. I didn't want to be mistaken for a gringo. I wanted to pass for Indian, and I was thankful that I had black hair, and a dark complexion that grew even darker under the sun. For blue-eyed, blond-haired Traven there was no possibility of passing for Indian, and perhaps that inability to pass was his salvation. Unable or unwilling to manipulate appearances, he was forced to make fundamental, underlying changes. He had to learn to love the Indian. Only then did exile become home.

Ret Marut never had a family. B. Traven found his in Mexico. He adopted the family of Mexicans as his own. Curiously, in books like *The Death Ship* and *Treasure,* when he wrote about Europeans and North Americans, his characters have no parents, no children, no family. They are orphans. However, as soon as he sunk roots in Mexico and wrote about Indians, Traven's characters automatically found themselves with family relationships. It seems that only by writing about people of a different race, culture, and nationality, was Traven able to envision and accept characters with parents. And what's more, he was able to write about love, love between husband and wife, man and woman, parents and children.

In the Jungle Novels one has the unmistakable feeling that Traven regards Andres and Celso, the exploited Indian oxcart drivers and lumberjacks, as his blood brothers. He shares their lives, their misfortunes, grief, and joy. Better than I can, Traven explained how he felt in a letter he wrote to the Gutenberg Book Guild in 1927:

> I regard the Mexican Indian and the Mexican proletarian, who is 95% Indian, as my deepest friend, closer than my own brother. I know the courage, devotion and sacrifice (unheard of in Europe) of the proletarian Indian in his fight for deliverance into the light of the sun. It is a fight for liberation that has no equal in human history. Until today I was unable to make the European working man understand a single part of this fight for freedom. It can't be done in a simple narrative form. Confronted with the immense cultural, economic and philosophical accomplishments of the Indian, all the tools of the poet and writer fail. I am hard pressed, both socially and emotionally, to empathize with this fantastic cultural event, and give it form in words and glowing pictures.

I could understand the plight of the Mexican Indian proletarian, and support his "fight for deliverance into the light of the sun," but I did not feel that he was my deepest friend, closer than my own brothers. I knew that for me *not* to feel like an exile in Mexico I would eventually have to follow Traven's path. I would have to accept the Indian worker as my brother and comrade. And what had I done so far? I had found a home behind the affluent walls of the Rio Mississippi. I knew that I could enjoy traveling in Mexico, but sooner rather than later, I would have to return to my home in the States.

25

I spent much of my time in the Belfridges' library. I read John Turner's *Barbarous Mexico,* a book as influential as Harriet Beecher Stowe's *Uncle Tom's Cabin. Barbarous Mexico* was an exposé of slavery in the Yucatán, and helped spark the 1910 revolution against Porfirio Díaz. Traven read it when he arrived in Mexico fifteen years later, and it shaped his books about the persecution of the Indians. I had always thought that Traven's descriptions couldn't be surpassed, but Turner's accounts of the brutality inflicted on the Indians were even more gruesome. They made my flesh crawl.

Rereading *The Rebellion of the Hanged* I had the feeling that as Traven wrote it he relived the Munich Rebellion of 1919. With the benefit of historical hindsight he understood the reasons for the failure of the 1919 rebellion. And through the character of Martin Trinidad, a school teacher turned revolutionary, Traven expressed his political ideas.

Martin Trinidad often sounds like the Ret Marut who edited *The Brickburner.* "If you want to make a revolution, then carry it through to the end, because otherwise it will turn against you and tear you to shreds," Trinidad advises. Later, he sounds like Ret Marut, the German fugitive who had no papers and no passport, when he insists:

If you want us to win and stay winners we'll have to burn all the papers. Many revolutions have started and then failed simply because papers weren't burned as they should have been. The first thing we must do is attack the registry and burn the papers, all the papers with seals and signatures—deeds, birth and death and marriage certificates. . .Then nobody will know who he is, what he's called, who was his father, and what his father had. We'll be the heirs because nobody will be able to prove the contrary. What do we want with birth certificates. . .I've read a mountain of books. I've read all that's been written about revolutions, uprisings, and mutinies. I've read all that the people in other countries have done when they become fed up with their exploiters. But with regard to burning papers I have read nothing. That's not written in any book. I discovered that in my own head.

No matter what he was writing about, B. Traven was haunted by papers, birth certificates, passports, by his identity and the identity of his father.

Cedric Belfridge was a B. Traven fan too. "My favorite Traven novel is *Government,*" he said. At first that surprised me because most North Americans prefer *Treasure,* but given Belfridge's troubles with governments it was a logical choice. "It's a terrible title for a novel, isn't it," he said. "When I recommend it to friends they cringe because they think it's going to be a boring sociological study. Heavens, no! It's simply fascinating, isn't it, the best book I've ever read on how governments work, any government—American, Russian, Mexican, German, Chinese. When you get down to it they operate more or less along the same lines. At least that's been my experience, and I've lived all over the world. Sometimes one government may seem a bit better than another, but in the end they all rely on force, and the threat of force, don't you agree."

167

Most of *Government* is about tyranny, but there is also a short section of the book about the democratic form of government practiced by the "Pebvil Indians." Cedric labeled that section as sentimentality. Traven explains that the Pebvil Indians elect a new chief every year. The chief receives no pay and no privileges for holding office; he is responsible for any mistakes he makes. Traven describes the inauguration ceremony for the new chief; it's a fascinating rite. The chief-elect sits on a chair without a bottom. Under the seat the tribe builds a hot fire. Traven explains:

> The fire under the chief's posterior was to remind him that he was not sitting on this seat to rest himself but to work for the people; he was to look alive even though he sat on the chair of office. Furthermore, he was not to forget who had put the fire under him. . .and that it was done to remind him from the outset that he could not cling to office but had to give it up as soon as his time was up, so as to prevent any risk of a life-long rule, which would be injurious to the welfare of his people. If he tried to cling to his office they would put a fire under him that would be large enough to consume both him and the chair.

And Traven goes on to suggest:

> Workers would be advised to adopt this well-proven Indian method of election, particularly with the officials of their trade unions and political organizations and not only in Russia, where it is most necessary. In all countries, too, where Marx and Lenin are set up as saints, the militant working class could achieve success much more surely if they lit a good fire yearly under their leaders' behinds. No leader is indispensable. And the more often leaders are put on red-hot seats, the more lively the political movement

would be. Above all things, the people must never be sentimental.

I agreed. Stalin, Mao, Churchill, Roosevelt, Nixon—they should all have been made to sit on the Pebvil Indian hot seat.

Traven cautioned against sentimentality, and yet throughout his life he indulged in it. When he first arrived in Mexico he thought that it was the promised land, and maybe it was after the hell of World War I Europe. In *The Death Ship* Traven asked rhetorically:

> Where is the true country of men? There where no-body molests me, where nobody wants to know who I am, where I come from, where I wish to go, what my opinion is about war, about the Episcopalians, and about the Communists, where I am free to do and to believe what I damn please as long as I do not harm the life, the health, and the honestly earned property of anybody else. There and there alone is the country of men that is worth living for, and sweet to die for.

In the mid-twenties Traven was under the illusion that Mexico was "the true country of men." He believed that the Mexican Revolution of 1910–1920 had abolished slavery, servitude, dictatorship. In *Land in Springtime,* the book based on his travels in Chiapas in 1926, he went so far as to say that Mexico was entering an era of freedom and democracy un-precedented in world history. He insisted that in Mexico, the workers and their trade unions, the Indians and their tribes, and *not* the police, army, bureaucracy, were shaping the nation's destiny. There was no corrupt leadership, no in-grained profit motive, no individualism among the people, Traven wrote. He was in heaven.

This optimism is reflected in Traven's first three books about Mexico: *The Cotton Pickers, The Treasure of the Sierra*

Madre, and *Land in Springtime.* Unlike *The Death Ship*—his farewell to Europe—these three books conclude with the proverbial happy ending. In *The Cotton Pickers* Gerard Gales laughs at everything. Even the rumor that he's a fugitive and a troublemaker is cause, not for alarm, but for laughter. In Mexico death-ship paranoia vanished and Traven literally sang for joy:

> The sun smiled and blazed. Everything was green— the land of perpetual summer. Oh, beautiful, wonderful land of everlasting springtime, rich with legend, dance and song! You have no equal anywhere on this earth.
>
> I couldn't help singing. I sang whatever came into my head, hymns, and sweet folk airs, love songs and ditties, operatic arias, drinking songs and bawdy songs. What did I care what the songs were about? What did the melody matter? I sang from a heart full of joy.

Can you imagine Ret Marut singing for joy in the street of Munich? No! But in Mexico, at least for a few years, he sang as though nothing else mattered. He was drunk with dreams of paradise.

At the end of *Treasure* there's no singing, but Howard, the old gringo prospector, sways back and forth in his jungle hammock. The Indian women feed him when he's hungry, and love him when he's feeling lonely. He has none of the gold that he had dug in the Sierra Madre, but in his eyes, and in the eyes of his creator B. Traven, he has a treasure far more valuable: the friendship, respect, and love of the Indians.

In *Land in Springtime* Indians emerge on center stage of Traven's work for the first time; they are Adam and Eve. In Traven's eyes they are natural, uninhibited, free of European sexual neuroses, and the political disease known as capitalism. Traven did live with an Indian tribe that knew no private property, no individualism, and no egotism—at least not as he had known them in Europe. These communal tribes gave him a glimpse of utopia. As a European anarchist Marut believed in a society with no police, no army, no jails, and no private property. In the pages of *The Brickburner* he urged people to discard their material possessions. "The day you wrap your feet in rags, instead of buying shoes and stockings, then the capitalist's pale countenance will be shot through with fear," Marut wrote in 1921. Five years later, among the Mexican Indians, Traven saw what he had wanted to see his whole life: a people who were free of the tyranny of commodities and the state. Traven's Indians were part real, part fantasy. He recognized a communal spirit that actually existed, but he magnified it, idealized it, assumed that it would spread across the land, that Mexico would indeed become a "land in eternal springtime."

Then, suddenly, the Mexican springtime became the Mexican season in hell. In 1927, on his second trip to Chiapas, Traven discovered that debt slavery still existed, that the extermination of the Indians was a thriving business, and that the Mexican government hadn't the slightest intention of withering away. Rather, it was growing more dictatorial day by day. "In Latin America dictatorships come and go," Traven explained to a European literary agent. "Right now there are five or six countries under a dictatorship, and the rest are under a semi-dictatorship. Mexico has only one political party, and only members of that party are elected to Parliament or any public office, with one or two so-called independents tolerated so as not to make the whole machinery not too obvious."

So, Traven fell from paradise to hell. The deeper he penetrated the jungle, the more torture and tyranny he saw. The Indian workers were sacrificed to the god of mahogany. For every tree that was felled an Indian fell. Those who survived became *trozas,* stumps of men, like the stumps of mahogany trees in the mutilated jungle. With this new outlook Traven decided against translating *Land in Springtime* from German into English or Spanish. Until his death he insisted that it not be published in the United States or Mexico.

In his next books Traven described, not paradise, but hell. In *The White Rose* he wrote about the violent destruction of the Indian commune "Rosa Blanca" by C. C. Collins, a North American oil tycoon. Collins is an unusual character in Traven's theater because he isn't a worker, a fugitive, or an exile, though he *is* an orphan with a mysterious past. C. C. Collins is the one success in Traven's world. Everyone else becomes poorer, more impoverished. Collins rises from rags to riches like a Horatio Alger hero, but Traven shows that his riches bring rags to the Indians, his life is their death.

In the first four Jungle Novels—*The Carreta, Government, Trozas,* and *March to the Monteria*—Traven wrote about massacre, enslavement, and torture. But he was careful how he did it. After his battles with the Munich censor during World War I, after his arrest in 1919 on charges of inciting treason and mutiny in the pages of *The Brickburner,* Traven knew that his writing could cost him his life. Accordingly, he took precautions. He hid his identity. When he traveled in Chiapas he was T. Torsvan, the Norwegian photographer and explorer. No one knew him as B. Traven the novelist. Under his alias, he visited the big *haciendas,* saw the Indian slaves building the roads, chopping the mahogany forests, picking the coffee beans.

Another precaution was embedded in the books. For his own safety Traven made the setting of the story ambiguous. Sometimes the books appear to be in the past, sometimes in the present, sometimes in a twilight zone that hovers between past, present, and future. Depending on who he was talking to and when he was talking, Traven offered different explanations of the Jungle Novels. Of course! He wouldn't have been Traven if he didn't contradict himself. Thus, Traven said that the Jungle Novels "described the conditions of peonage and debt slavery under which the Indians suffered in Díaz's time." But he also insisted, in almost the same breath, that "the essential part of the story is happening all the time. When a paper needs pepping up its circulation a sensational story is published about the cruel conditions in which the Indians are forced to live at the camps. The government sends a commission of three or four men to investigate. When that commission arrives everything looks rosy and the commission reports that the paper exaggerated its story. Before the commission is actually back in the capital, the conditions at the camp are worse than ever. And since this is so, Traven wanted his story to be timeless and that's why he refrained from mentioning the name of the dictator.''

Traven denounced governments for most of his life, and yet in 1951 he became a Mexican citizen and accepted the authority of the Mexican government. This was a dramatic turnabout. As late as 1941 he boasted that he had never applied for Mexican citizenship and didn't want it. Did Traven compromise his beliefs? I think he did. 1951 was a turning point— just as 1919 (the year of the Munich rebellion) and 1927 (the year he discovered the hell of Mexican slavery) were key points in his life. In 1951 Traven's writing career was over. He was still sitting at the typewriter, adapting his novels for the screen, but that wasn't original or creative work. Traven's last masterpiece was the tale of an Indian named Macario who evades Death, the Bone Man, three times before he is finally captured.

Macario is a humble woodcutter, but like Gerard Gales, Doc Cranwell, and Howard, he is also a miraculous doctor. He brings the sick and the dying back to health and life. But when Macario is called upon to save the Viceroy's son his medicine fails. The Bone Man takes the boy's life and Macario's too.

Macario is Traven. He is the magician, death's sly opponent, a man of mystery, and at the same time a humble traveler. In *Macario* Traven bids farewell to the world. Here, for the first time, his hero is conquered by death, by the Bone Man. Gerard Gales escapes death by firing squad, death by deadly toil on the *Yorikke,* and death by drowning on the capsized *Empress.* Andres, Celso, Juan Mendez, and Martin Trinidad escape death in the hellish jungle and death on the battlefield. But for Macario there is no escape. His time is up. And his creator B. Traven knew that he didn't have much time left either.

In 1950, the year *Macario* was published, Traven was at least sixty years old, and perhaps as old as seventy. He was becoming increasingly conscious of old age and death. In 1951, Esperanza López Mateos, his translator and closest friend, committed suicide. I found a note she had written to Traven in June 1951, shortly before she took her life:

> Man I need you. I'd wish you to be around the corner. . .There are worlds of important things not to tell you but to hear from you. Believe I do need!

After her suicide Traven wrote:

> Mexico, no the Americans have lost one of the most wonderful and extraordinarily highly gifted women with dear Esperanza.

With his career as a writer over, his friend Esperanza dead, and his own death weighing upon him, B. Traven became a Mexican citizen. Had he forgotten that Mexico was also a repressive state, that Mexican citizens were persecuted? I doubt it. I suspect that he accepted the country that had accepted him for fifty years. He was old; his spirit of defiance against authority and authorities was fast crumbling.

In 1952 he met Rosa Elena. Five years later they were married. In *Rebellion* Traven wrote, "We live with a woman we love, we give her children. That's being married. Do we need papers to prove it?" For almost seventy years Traven saw no reason to sign marriage papers, as he saw no reason to have documents proving citizenship. But by the time he died he left all the crucial human documents—will, marriage certificate, citizenship papers, contracts—all but one; the elusive, mysterious certificate of his birth. Officially, legally, the man who died had never been born.

26

"Hey man, sit down, *come on*, gotta rap to you, it's gonna be a far-out trip." I had boarded the bus to Oaxaca City and was looking for a seat, but I didn't want to sit next to *him*. However, there was no other choice. I threw my backpack in the overhead rack and swung into the seat.

"Fantastic! Name's Lafcadio," he said, reaching out to shake my hand. I noticed that he wore four or five big, gaudy rings, but his hands were filthy, his fingernails encrusted with grime. It was difficult to judge how old he was. He looked like he had been traveling by time machine rather than by bus. There were deep lines etched at the corners of his mouth and his eyes.

He was tall and thin, almost emaciated. He wore embroidered blue jeans and a bright yellow shirt. His hair was long and blond, and he wore a shell necklace with delicate carvings of animals. Lafcadio noted me staring at it. "Magic man very heavy picked it up in Palenque two years ago. You want your old lady to get pregnant you touch her with this man and that baby is on its way no shit I ain't jiving you go ahead touch it go on man it won't hurt you. Feel good don't it that's some heavy shit ain't it man. Say, this your first time?"

"I've never seen a necklace like this before," I said.

"Shit no man your first time to Oaxaca. Oaxaca is something else. Oaxaca is beautiful. It's magic, last of the great magic places on earth. It's the magnetic force, sucks you down into the heart of the cosmos. And the Indians of Oaxaca are something else. They will blow your mind man. In Mexico City the Indians are gringofried, like burgers, but down here in Oaxaca they're beautiful. Wait till you rest your eyes on the market and that's just the start. I'll show you the ruins and the tombs. You go down there in the cool darkness, feel the Aztec power and you know it's gonna rise again all the way up to the stars. Now what'd you say?"

"I've been in Mexico City," I said.

"Mexico City! Hell that's worse than Tokyo and New York shacked-up together, but ain't half as bad as Calcutta. You ain't seen a city till you been to India Jack. That's a mean fuckin' place and I mean mean."

"You travel a lot?" I asked.

"I am travel," he said. "I love travel, eat travel, sleep travel, shit travel, fuck travel, smoke travel, and I'll die travel."

"Where do you get the money?" I asked.

"You're pissin' in the wind Jack. Don't need no bread to travel need to cut loose. Oh yeah sure back in let me see was it '64 or '65 can't recollect exactly, but anyway I inherited some bread. My dad died. It blew me away because we were tight. I loved him. My mom was gone so he left me all he had. Yeah quit my job haven't worked since July 12, '65, that's right it was '65. Now I sell shit: rings, jewelry, incense. Wanna buy a ring? No—well I got some good smoke can let you have it for twenty-five dollars, a steal man. We'll get high together, I'll show you the place, my old lady's down there now waitin' on me. She's one hell of a bitch! Bitching! We can fix you up with a nice *señorita*, a *gorda*. You like Mexican pussy don't you? Well what in the hell do you do man?"

"I'm writing a book about a mysterious novelist named B." but before I could finish, Lafcadio said "Traven. Well ain't that something else. B. Traven. Now that cat had something goin' for him. Talk about mystery! Old Ben Traven had a mainline to mystery. I read his stories. Shit, Traven knew that Indians vibrate with the heart of mystery. Am I right Jack? It's all round us but we don't see it. Am I right! We got too much city poison in us. They don't and Traven knew it and that's why he came down here from Chicago and lived among the Indians. Ain't no mystery in Chicago. Talk about supernatural! What's that freaky haunted house story of his, *The Night Visitor* right, where that old Indian comes up out of the grave. Spooky. I believe it too honest man the dead come alive in Oaxaca you better believe it or you'll be knocked back on your ass before you know what hit you. And that story about the kid lifted out of the river; the Indians know how to bring the dead back to life. We've lost the art, too much machine too much thinking. Old Ben Traven's one hell of a magic man. A shaman. You don't believe me just wait and see."

Beyond the window the scenery was bleak. There was mile after mile of desert, sand, rock, and cactus; no houses, no gas stations, no hotels, no people. Fortunately we were riding first class, and the bus was air-conditioned. Lafcadio talked the whole way to Oaxaca. When he wasn't talking to me he walked up and down the aisle talking to the other passengers, trying to sell them rings, incense, handing out chewing gum to the kids, and flirting with the *gringas*.

Listening to Lafcadio I remembered Rosa Elena's words. "The hippies are doing today what my husband did many, many years ago," she told me. "I like the hippies, don't you, and I know that the primitive way is better. I would like to live much more simply than I do, but how can you escape after you've been in the habit. My husband was unusual; he could throw away material things and live with nature like the hippies do today."

Was Traven a hippie? No, absolutely not. I was ready to admit he was the Kaiser's bastard son, anyone's bastard son, but not a hippie.

Not only Lafcadio but many hippies I met in the States and on the road were anxious to claim Traven as their ancestor. They read his books and interpreted them in the light of their own experiences. And in that regard the hippie is no different from any other reader. Everyone mines a book for his or her own ore.

Of course, there *are* similarities between B. Traven and the hippies. For a start, B. Traven was a deeply spiritual man. He was vehemently against churches, priests, the dogmas of organized religion, but he revered Christ and Buddha in much the same way as the hippie reveres them. Traven had a profound sense of the mystery of life. For him all life was sacred, especially the lives of human beings, but also the lives of trees, plants, animals, and all creation. Traven was opposed to everything that would rob life of its mystery, its sacred wholeness—and that meant opposition to bureaucrats, commissars, overseers, dictators, generals. Like the hippie, Traven believed that the Indian appreciated the sacredness of life. The Indian understood spirituality. The Indian was in touch with the mystery of life, life that has no beginning and no ending, but is eternal, that sweeps us up into its timeless cycles. We are but a small part of the infinite mystery of the cosmos.

Treasure is the Traven book that comes closest to the hippie ideal. Howard, the old prospector and surrogate for B. Traven, rejects civilization, cars, money, and (if you can believe it) the radio, and settles in a "commune." He adopts the Indian way, defends the sacredness of life, peace, and love. Like Howard the hippie is anxious to reject civilization, to live in a tribe, or a small village without the hassles of the city. But he is often unconscious of his own prejudices. He thinks that he has left his hang-ups behind him in Port Huron, Wichita Falls, or Tucson, but he carries them with him in his backpack and his brain. (My own backpack and brain were loaded down with hippie dreams; I don't exempt myself.)

Lafcadio, his hippie friends, all of us, would do well to listen carefully to Gerard Gales in *The Bridge in the Jungle*. Gales claims that "One becomes a philosopher by living among people who are not of his own race and who speak a different language." I agree; so would the hippie. Lafcadio left his own people, his own race, and went to live in Mexico. But B. Traven does not advocate dropping out. As he explained, *The Bridge in the Jungle* is not "an escape story. The author has never entertained the idea that civilized man return to the simple and primitive life led by the people he talks about."

In *Bridge* Gales tells us:

> Experience has taught me that travelling educates only those who can be educated just as well by roaming around their own country. By walking thirty miles anywhere in one's own home state the man who is open-minded will see more and learn more than a thousand others will see by running around the world. A trip to a Central American jungle to watch how Indians behave near a bridge won't make you see either the jungle or the bridge or the Indians if you believe that the civilization you were born into is the only one that counts. Go and look around with the idea that everything you learned in school and college is wrong.

This seems to be the hippie creed: drop out of school, reject your education, and look around the world with an open mind. But too often the hippie, like the affluent tourist he disdains, has a closed set of beliefs. He believes that the Indian is poor because he *wants* to be poor, that poverty is morally superior to riches. For Traven the Indian is poor primarily because he is robbed, because he is exploited. For Traven the Indian is a proletarian, a worker. To understand the Indian, Traven says, we have to understand labor. But the hippie in Mexico is uninterested in labor. He or she is escaping from the factory, the warehouse, office, or kitchen. He or she doesn't want work but the absence of work.

When the Indian wants to leave the village and go to the city to find work, the hippie thinks that the Indian is selling out, becoming corrupted. It is then that the hippie argues that *he* is a truer Indian than the Indian. The hippie sets himself up as the moral and spiritual model from which he judges the rest of the world. He feels that he knows what is wrong with civilization, that he must preach his sermon to the Indian. And so the Indian often regards the hippie as just another white man in the tropics. He is another outsider, invader, crusader buying his goods, and telling him what to do, what is good and what is bad.

The hippie tends to be a non-violent pacifist. He likes the Indian when he is gentle, silent, meek. But when the Indian becomes a guerrilla, when he takes up arms against his oppressor, then the hippie is "turned off" and withdraws his approval. He feels that the Indian is using the weapons of the enemy, and that he is therefore becoming like the enemy. Sometimes the hippie admires Che Guevara, and dreams about living with the rebels in the jungle. But the hippie idea of Che is highly romanticized. The hippie thinks of a peaceful campfire in the jungle, and of bullets that don't really hurt. And even when the bullets kill it isn't so bad, because in death Che becomes Saint Che, the hippie martyr.

For B. Traven the guerrilla expedition is no joyful adventure. It is warfare; it is brutal and violent, a struggle for survival. But he does not condemn the Indian guerrillas. In *The Rebellion of the Hanged* he tells us:

> The rebels were not to blame for their ideas of death and destruction. They had never been allowed freedom of expression; every possibility of communication and discussion had been denied them. . .The workers, the peasants, all the humble people, had been deprived of every right, and had only one duty: to obey. Blind obedience was inculcated in them by lashings until it became their second nature. . .Thus it was not savagery that drove the Indians to assassination and pillage. Their acts could not be taken as proofs of cruelty, because their adversaries and oppressors were a hundred times more savage and cruel than they when safeguarding their

interests. . .Rebels are not to blame for the dis-
agreeable consequences that rebellions bring in for
those who have everything. Those responsible for the
acts of the rebels are men who believe it possible to
mistreat human beings forever with impunity and
not drive them to rebellion.

B. Traven and the hippie walk the path of mystery, spirituality, and magic together, but when they reach the crossroads
of labor, exploitation, and armed rebellion they part company. The hippie searched for utopia, blinded to the reality of
this world. B. Traven dreamed of utopia, but never lost sight
of hell.

27

In Oaxaca I saw more signs of political activity than I had seen in Mexico City. Slogans on the walls denounced President Echeverria as an assassin, and expressed outrage at the death of Lucio Cabañas, the school teacher from Guerrero who had turned guerrilla. Twenty thousand government troops had combed the mountains for two years before they caught him in a remote village, threw him against a wall, and executed him. That was late in 1974; by the time I arrived in Mexico in January 1975 Cabañas was already a legendary figure. Folk songs and poems had been written about him. He had joined the long list of slain martyrs.

I had come to Oaxaca to visit Bodil Christensen, a Danish woman who had known Traven from 1927 to his death in 1969. Both Rosa Elena and Mrs. Yampolsky insisted that Bodil was a warm, friendly person, and, what's more, that she would tell me the truth.

In Rosa Elena's office I discovered the Torsvan/Bodil Christensen correspondence from 1948, another crucial year in Traven/Torsvan's life. In 1948 Luis Spota, a Mexican journalist, shadowed Torsvan, intercepted his mail, and followed him to his house in Acapulco. In part this was Traven's own fault. Two years earlier, in 1946, John Huston wrote Traven asking for help in the filming of *Treasure*. Traven explained that he would be in the jungles of Chiapas, but that he would send his representative Hal Croves. (As late as 1946, Traven was still creating new identities and new aliases.) Croves met Huston and was put on the payroll at $150 a week.

During the making of *Treasure* Croves's identity was revealed, and *Life* announced that Croves was Traven. Croves insisted that the story was untrue, that it was a Warner Brothers publicity stunt to drum up interest in the film, then premiering in the States. "Traven could not be Croves," he said. "Traven would never have been hired for $150 a week. Traven was a famous writer and would have demanded at least $1500 a week." Croves vanished, but Luis Spota was hot on his trail. In 1948 he invaded Traven's house in Acapulco and told him, "I know you're B. Traven." Traven denied it, played games with Spota, even served him a feast of wild goose. Spota published his story in the press and Traven/Torsvan/Croves's cover was blown. Hundreds of people arrived at the cashew farm in Acapulco to see the world-famous celebrity whose film *The Treasure of the Sierra Madre* was fast becoming a box-office hit. "The whole thing was a most unwelcome publicity, this we admit," Traven noted sadly in August 1948, "but it was unavoidable; some day it had to come."

Bodil Christensen read Luis Spota's article about the mysterious B. Traven, and though she had not seen him for years, wrote to him expressing her love and friendship, and offering help. "As you are a strange man, I don't expect you to answer this letter," Bodil wrote, "but if you should want to, I would be very happy." Seven days later, on August 11, 1948, Traven replied:

> Your letter arrived at a moment of deep depression. We know of some sixty letters, some with money in, some with postal money orders, which are still missing. I always thought that only the Yellow Press of the U.S. produced that stinking sort of heels, but now I see that Mexico has them too.

When I said that I was in a state of depression, I mean that the whole place was besieged. . .The place is not mine, it belongs to Mrs. M[artinez]., as everything else that is around here. We don't live under the same roof even. You can only imagine perhaps how big the lies are that skunk is telling about us. . .If you should happen to come down here don't fail to look me up. I am sure Mrs. M. can put you up somehow, but understand everything is primitive. . .more often than not there is just enough money around to have a meal of rice and beans. And when you come Bodil, you can be sure I'll kiss you until you faint for that letter of yours.

In addition to the correspondence, Rosa Elena showed me photographs of Bodil and Traven taken at the University of Mexico Summer School in 1927. Bodil was tall and blonde and wore a long skirt. Traven wore a suit and tie; his hair was plastered down and neatly combed. He looked more like a business executive than a college student.

"He registered under the name Torsvan," Rosa Elena said. "He studied Spanish, art, geography, modern literature, history, and received very good grades. I'll show you. I have his report card." Indeed she did. I was amazed that Traven had saved his report card from 1927. Dozens of other, more crucial documents and papers had been destroyed, but the record of courses and grades remained. He must have been proud of his status as a college student.

Bodil Christensen lived in that section of town called San Felipe del Aqua. It was the last stop on the city bus, a quiet neighborhood of cobblestone streets, dry dusty fields, and, of course, the inevitable walls. Bodil unlatched the door and smiled. We shook hands, and she led me into the library—the only lending library in Oaxaca. I handed her copies of *The Bridge in the Jungle*, *The White Rose*, and *Macario*—gifts from Rosa Elena.

"Traven's books are popular here," Bodil said. "He used to

bring me copies of his books. Of course, he never admitted that they were *his* books. He'd say 'Here's Traven's new book. I thought you'd like to read it.' Three weeks before he died he visited me in Mexico City. I was living on Cinco de Mayo then. He stood in the hall and handed me a copy of *The Creation of the Sun and the Moon* and said 'This is Traven's last book.' There was a special way that he looked at me, a special way he said the words 'last book.' At first I thought that he meant Traven's most recent book, but then I realized that he meant that this was the end, that there would be no more books. I wanted to say 'You mean *your* last book,' but I never did. I knew he was Traven and he knew that I knew he was Traven, but neither of us ever said so."

"What's your favorite Traven book?" I asked. I took out my notebook and pencil. For a moment Bodil looked at me suspiciously. "He had so many problems with journalists," she said. "He hated Spota, but I suppose what you're doing won't hurt, and you're a friend of Marianne Yampolsky's, you say."

"Yes, I live at her mother's house in Tlalpan, and I've been working with Mrs. Luján."

"I don't want to do anything to upset him," Bodil said.

"But he's been dead six years!" I exclaimed.

"I know," Bodil said. "You have to appreciate that for forty years I kept his secret. I could have gone to the papers in 1927 or 1928 and told them that Torsvan was Traven but I didn't. I kept my mouth shut. I could have gone again in '48 and explained that Torsvan was Croves and Croves was Traven, but I didn't then either. Even now it's not easy to talk about him because he was such a strange man. My sister Helga and I met Torsvan in the summer of 1927 when we were studying Spanish together. Torsvan had so much trouble pronouncing the *o* in Spanish. Helga drilled him over and over again hour after hour, until finally he could pronounce it correctly. He would come to our apartment on Calle López and we'd go out to eat, always to the cheapest restaurants. There was a place in Tacubaya you could get enchiladas for a peso and a Chinese place that served a *comida corrida,* a three-course meal, for one peso fifty centavos. Torsvan always knew the cheapest restaurants with the best food. We used to call him 'The Funny Man.' "

"You mean he made you laugh."

"Yes, but mostly I mean he was *strange*. One second he was walking on the street with us and the next second he had vanished into thin air. We wouldn't see or hear from him for weeks or months, and then suddenly he would knock on the door, loaded down with his cameras, and his photographic equipment. Neither Helga nor I ever questioned him about his disappearances, and we had no idea where he lived or how to reach him in an emergency."

Listening to Bodil I had the feeling that she had been in love with Torsvan, maybe *still* was in love with him, or at least with her memories of him. She spoke of him tenderly, affectionately, yet she wasn't nostalgic or sentimental.

"What language did you speak with Torsvan?" I asked.

"We always spoke in English," Bodil said.

"Didn't he have a German accent?"

"No, Norwegian," Bodil said.

"How could that be? He lived in Germany before he came to Mexico?"

"I was born in Denmark," Bodil said. "I've heard German, and the Scandinavian languages since I was a little girl, and I tell you that Torsvan spoke English with a Norwegian accent. He told us he was Norwegian, and of course Torsvan is a Norwegian name."

"Maybe you thought that you heard a Norwegian accent because he said that he was Norwegian," I suggested.

"Maybe he was from a town in Sweden along the Norwegian border, or one of the islands in the North Sea, but he definitely did not speak English with a German accent. Helga and I were both positive about that."

"O.K., I believe you," I said reluctantly. "If he was really born in the United States as he always claimed, he may have grown up in an immigrant community where Norwegian was spoken more than English."

"That's very possible," Bodil said. "But we don't know for sure."

"What's your favorite Traven book?" I asked.

"The Bridge in the Jungle," Bodil said. *"The Death Ship* and *The Rebellion of the Hanged* are too depressing for me. I know that the boy Carlosito drowns in the river, but it's not a bleak, depressing picture. No one is whipped, tortured, devoured by rats. I remember one afternoon I met Torsvan by accident on the street and I asked him if he had written *The Bridge in the Jungle.* I hadn't read the book yet myself, and I didn't know what it was about, but I knew that the author's name was B. Traven and the name Traven made me think of the name Torsvan. They're really quite similar, aren't they? You see, Torsvan told Helga and me that he had crossed a bridge in Chiapas on horseback and it collapsed. The Indians looked at him as though he was an evil demon, accused him of coming to destroy their village. It was terrifying! He wanted to be friendly with the Indians, and yet by accident he destroyed their bridge. Later I read the book and found that the plot was quite different."

"Was there an Indian boy who fell from a bridge and drowned in a river?" I asked.

"There was a boy," Bodil said. "But I don't think that he fell from a bridge. Anyway, after I met him by accident on the street he disappeared for years, probably because he was afraid I had guessed his identity and wouldn't keep it a secret. He didn't know me! I never said a word to anyone, except Helga."

"You visited him in Acapulco?"

"Yes, in '48 after Spota had written his articles about Traven."

"Then you must have known Maria de la Luz Martínez."

"Yes, of course," Bodil said.

"Rosa Elena told me I shouldn't visit her," I said.

"I don't see why not," Bodil said. "There was nothing between the Martínez woman and Torsvan."

"How do you know?"

"Because I stayed with him," Bodil said. "You can tell those things about a man and a woman and there was absolutely nothing between Torsvan and her."

"Then how do you explain. . .," I began, but Bodil interrupted. "It may be that Mrs. Luján is being mysterious. You know, *he* loved to be mysterious. It was a game with him. It was fun. He took so much delight in life, the funny man, playing those roles, taking all those different names. He was a wonderful man. Strange that he waited so long before he married."

"What was the Martinez woman like?" I asked.

"An ordinary middle-class woman," Bodil said. "Preoccupied with herself. She had no idea he was B. Traven." Bodil paused a moment and reflected. "But come to think about it, there *was* something strange about Maria de la Luz. The day of his funeral she came to visit me in Mexico City. I wasn't home, but the cook said that she was very upset, sobbing miserably. I never did speak to her; she was gone by the time I came back, didn't even leave a note. I wonder! What did she want to talk about on the day of Traven's funeral?"

28

"*Senor*, you are under arrest."

The cop hadn't drawn his gun, or raised his club; that wasn't necessary. His words were spoken with enough authority to make Lafcadio freeze in his tracks. He was standing in the plaza, surrounded by about fifty Mexicans; even had he succeeded in breaking through their encirclement he would soon be caught. Cocoa, his girlfriend, was sitting at the edge of the fountain.

"I didn't break no law," Lafcadio shouted.

"Arrest him," a woman cried. She was a young mother and she rocked her baby gently in her arms.

"Hell, she's no better than me," Lafcadio said.

"Well, I didn't wash my stinking feet in the fountain," the woman shouted.

"You understand, *senor*, it is against the law," the cop said. "Our people drink the water from the fountain."

"Shit, I didn't know," Lafcadio said. "I'm sorry. I love Oaxaca."

I pushed my way through the crowd until I was standing next to Lafcadio. At first I had been afraid to show my face. Maybe I too would be arrested simply because I was a gringo. Moreover, I felt ashamed of Lafcadio, and angry at him for washing his dirty feet in the public fountain. Maybe he should be arrested and sent to prison. That would teach him a lesson! But then I remembered Bodil Christensen's story about Torsvan and the bridge in the jungle. Wasn't destroying an Indian bridge as awful as washing your feet in an Indian fountain? Torsvan hadn't meant to level the bridge, and Lafcadio didn't mean to pollute the water—but surely the Indians had been as angry at Torsvan as they were now angry at Lafcadio. The accusing finger *had been* pointed at Traven. Now it was pointed at Lafcadio. If this was 1926 and I was standing next to Traven, wouldn't I defend him? It was that thought that prompted me to push my way through the crowd.

"*Senor,* I'm sure that my friend meant no harm," I said. "You see his poor woman crying there. She is three months pregnant." The mother with the baby in her arms let out a little cry of sadness mixed with pleasure. She sat down at the edge of the fountain, took a white handkerchief from under the folds of her dress, and wiped the tears from Cocoa's face. The cop cleared his throat and looked genuinely embarrassed. I was embarrassed too.

Maybe you remember the scene in *The Cotton Pickers* where Gerard Gales watches a barefoot and ragged Indian laborer asleep on a park bench in Tampico. A policeman circles him, raises his leather whip and beats him. But Gales comes to his rescue. He has no white horse, but he has his white skin and that's more valuable, more powerful. He intimidates the cop and forces him to drop his whip. The Indian disappears into the night and Traven observes:

> Woe to the satiated when the welts of lashes eat into the hearts of the hungry and turn the minds of the long-suffering! I was forced to become a rebel and a revolutionary, a revolutionary out of love of justice, out of a desire to help the wretched and the ragged. The sight of injustice and cruelty makes as many revolutionaries as do privation and hunger.

In *The Cotton Pickers* Traven is patronizing. The Indians are meek and passive, and do little to fight for their own liberation. But Gales the noble white man is their champion. Later, in the Jungle Novels, the Indians have no one to defend against tyranny but themselves. They are their own champions.

Injustice, hunger, cruelty—these were not the issues at the fountain in Oaxaca. Unlike Gales or Traven I didn't have the opportunity of helping the "long-suffering." The Indian woman with the child was stroking Cocoa's long, blonde hair. Cocoa stopped sobbing and looked imploringly at Lafcadio.

"We were about to leave Oaxaca," he said.

"O.K., you can go," the cop said. "But remember this is not your country. You are in Mexico now."

We collected our luggage and walked to the bus station. I bought a ticket to Tuxtla Gutierrez, the provincial capital of Chiapas, and picked the seat behind the driver so that I could look out the big front window.

On the highway Lafcadio began a conversation with Pablo, the bus driver.

"I hate the road," Pablo said. "I want a job where I can sit at a desk and go home every night."

"I go wherever I want, whenever I want," Lafcadio said.

"I'm a goddamned slave to the bus schedule," Pablo complained. "When I started driving I thought I was in heaven. I had no shitty boss standing over me and I liked to be on the move, it made me feel I was getting ahead. But now I'm more in debt than when I started. You know, we have to repair the busses as well as drive them; if this bitch of a bus went bust now I'd have to fix her, and I won't be paid extra either. Can't win. Can't even quit the fucking job. Got a wife and five kids, and there's no chance of work in Tapachula now, so I've got to stay on the road. I only see my family when the bus schedule takes me there and I'm already late for Tuxtla. There'll be hell to pay."

After an hour on the road, Lafcadio decided that he liked the scenery and wanted to get off the bus. He was certain that there were Indian ruins in the jungle and fantastic discoveries to be made. Cocoa didn't want to go with him, and he seemed to be relieved to be leaving her. He slung his pack over his shoulder and asked Pablo to let him off. Pablo thought he was crazy; we were in the middle of nowhere. There were no stores, houses, telephone poles, or electricity. But Lafcadio insisted. We watched him disappear into the bush. In a moment we were speeding down the highway. Cocoa stared out the window in a daze. It was hot and humid and the scenery was a lush green. We were in Chiapas now, Traven country, the land in springtime. Traven's initial romanticism seemed real. I could feel it, share it. The vegetation was dense—a living wall of green that climbed higher and higher. Nothing had been polluted or destroyed by man. The bus seemed like a child's toy, the road only a thin pencil line drawn through a sea of infinite greens.

I felt as though I had entered a Traven novel, that Traven's characters—Celso, Andres, Martin Trinidad, and Juan Mendez, "the general from the jungle"—would suddenly board the bus and travel with us through the jungle. I was dreaming again, an incorrigible romantic.

Like my idea of exile, my idea of the jungle had been derived mostly from literature, first from Joseph Conrad's *Heart of Darkness*—where the jungle is wild, evil, chaotic, a symbolic as well as a geographical place—and then from Traven's *The Bridge in the Jungle* and *The General from the Jungle*.

On the bus I had a strange sense of time; the boundaries of past and present crumbled. I was living in history and history was alive. Experience seemed to be heightened. I felt that life in Mexico City was, despite Rosa Elena's melodrama, quite ordinary, and that life in Chiapas was extraordinary. In large measure it was the jungle that gave me this sense of the extraordinary.

At the conclusion of *March to the Monteria,* the third book in the series of Jungle Novels, Traven describes the jungle landscape of Chiapas; at the same time he explores the fantastic terrain of his own inner landscape. It's an intensely sexual, Darwinian universe where only the fittest survive:

It was a wild, nightmarish matting of plants of pre-
historic times. Many of the palm feathers were one
hundred feet high. And there were thousands of
ferns of equal height. One could not see the ground
beside the trail, so heavily was it grown over the matting. Deep in one's mind one perceived the merciless
battle of the plants each fighting the other. All
around, one beheld a ruthless rivalry, a relentless
struggle for space as small as a child's hand. Men's
strife for existence could hardly be waged more in-
flexibly than the battle among the plants in this wide
area. . .Whatever is conceived here, and once conceived grows and survives, has to be of a truly heroic
nature. Softness and timidity are stamped into the
mud to rot. The one that loses the battle serves as
fertilizer for the one of greater beauty, strength and
nobility.

Nightmare, chaos, strife, battle, nobility, creation—these were
the building blocks of B. Traven's universe.

Along the road now were wooden shacks with thatched
roofs. Occasionally a shack had a rusty Coca-Cola sign, a re-
minder not only of the "pause that refreshes," but of the "real
world" beyond this unreal jungle—the real world of television,
and billboards, six-lane highways, radios, soda fountains,
sidewalks, smiling teeth, and smart-looking young executives
on the prowl.

Chiapas had nothing to offer the affluent tourist. (And
everything to offer the hippie.) The scenery was beautiful, but
there were no hotels, and no balconies, not yet, to enjoy the
view. There were miles and miles of coffee plantations, trees
laden with rich, dark beans, but no fresh coffee to drink. The
beans were for export to the capital, while Chiapanecans and
travelers alike spooned out Nescafe from the jar, added hot
water, and stirred.

Chiapas had everything and nothing; she was rich and
poor, dream and nightmare, paradise and hell. Chiapas was

the colony, and not only the colony, but the colony within the colony. Mexico itself is a colony, owned, dominated, controlled by foreign corporations. The Mexican worker, whether his job is south of the Rio Grande, or across the border in Texas, New Mexico, or California, is employed by a North American company. Walk down the Paseo de la Reforma and you see the omnipotence of those companies. In the night sky the neon signs announce the transcendent power and wealth of Ford, Kodak, General Motors, ITT, Westinghouse, IBM, Warner Brothers, CBS.

In Chiapas there are wealthy *haciendas,* and Mexico City has no shortage of peso-less paupers and sub-proletarians eternally out of work. Still, there is a great divide between Mexico City and Chiapas. The center bled the periphery. The people of the jungle were twice robbed, robbed by foreign capital and native capital, by invaders and by their own brothers and sisters.

It was the same when B. Traven arrived here fifty years ago. Then too Chiapas supplied the land, the labor, and the natural resources: oil, timber, coffee, electricity. Then too the Indian was robbed by *mestizos* and by *gringos.* As Traven explained in *March to the Monteria,* the lives of the Indians was determined by a system, not by any single individual or group of individuals. Attack the overseer, kill the president, and you have changed nothing, Traven writes, because the system remains:

> The workers in the monterias, even had they discovered where that power which had such terrible influence on their fate was located, would have been unable to eliminate it or even shake it. This anonymous power was intrinsically interwoven with all other powers in existence. . .The fundamental power was so dispersed, so ramified, so branched out and so interlaced with all the activities of human production and human consumption, that not even God Himself could have pointed a finger at a certain

man and said "This is the one who is holding the original power which determines the fate of the mahogany workers."

As impossible as it would have been to explain to the peons that an office in New York, full of diligent, tireless, typing and calculating men and women, in constant fear of losing their jobs, did not determine the fate of the troop which was marching through the jungle, it would have been less possible still to convince the peons that the fate of a hungry jobless worker is not determined by a person but by a system.

Fifty years later the yoke had not been lifted. The burden was as heavy as it had been in Traven's day.

29

Gazing out the window, watching the jungle race by, I thought of Rosa Elena in Mexico City. The house on the Rio Mississippi seemed like an immense, three-tiered stage, Rosa Elena's own theater. Her performance was brilliant! Equally well she played the roles of widow, mother, aristocratic lady, and the keeper of the Traven cult. The lamp was burning! Each room offered a different setting. Everything was a prop: books, paintings, death masks, clocks, shoes, eyeglasses, beds, papers, and manuscripts. Traven had chosen his leading lady well. She spoke his lines with passion and conviction. She was true, faithful, devoted. She brought B. Traven to life. On the Rio Mississippi one felt that he was alive, that he had stepped out for a short walk, and would return soon with a bouquet of flowers, a bottle of tequila, and a *canasta* of stories. On the road to Tuxtla Gutiérrez, in the world he explored, among the people he portrayed, Traven seemed, at least for the moment, far away. I felt lonely for the house on the Rio Mississippi.

The bus slowed gradually. Ahead, two soldiers with guns stood behind a roadblock. They ordered Pablo to open the door, then one soldier walked down the aisle checking passports and identification papers, while the other soldier stood at the front, his hand on the trigger.

The examination of documents seemed routine and

harmless. The soldiers smiled, commented on the heat and the swarms of mosquitoes that the rain had bred and nourished. I had no trouble and neither did Cocoa. Everyone's papers were in good order—all but one passenger's. He didn't have any, and when the soldiers questioned him he wouldn't talk. He was a sad man with a stubbly, white beard.

The young soldier shoved him off the bus, forced him to lie face down on the pavement and searched him for weapons and drugs. The man didn't resist, didn't protest or complain. He was silent. He acted as though the *Federales* had the inviolable right to remove him from the bus for whatever reason they wanted, whenever they wanted. As for his right to remain on the bus, in the seat he had paid for—that he never demanded.

Not one passenger objected. Pablo didn't say a word, neither did I; and I don't think that Gerard Gales or B. Traven would have opened his mouth in protest either, notwithstanding his white skin. I watched the soldiers and the passengers and noticed that most of the people on the bus looked away; they didn't want to be witnesses. The soldiers handcuffed and blindfolded the man, threw him into the trunk of a blue Ford Falcon and directed Pablo back on the road. Still, no one said a word. We all agreed to pretend that nothing had happened, that the bus hadn't been searched and that no one was missing. Only after we gathered speed and had rounded the curve did Pablo open his mouth.

"Dirty fucking whores," he shouted.

"What happened?" I asked.

"That guy, well, he's been working in Monterrey, made lots of money. They just want to welcome him back home. He's not stupid. He knows. They dragged me off the bus once; now I give them a bottle of brandy, slip them ten pesos, and I haven't had any trouble. It's a tricky business. Sometimes these fucking whores of soldiers are fired and a new man is hired. Shit! That only makes things worse because the greenhorn has nothing and suddenly he wants to get ahead fast. I keep my mouth shut. It's best to shut up and pay up. Then they let you work. Otherwise, it's a shitty life."

When we arrived in Tuxtla Gutiérrez, Pablo took me to a Chinese restaurant. He had two hours to kill before his next departure. After a steady diet of rice, beans, and tortillas, the won ton soup and the sweet-and-sour port were a treat. Then we took a walk. I wanted to see the museum where in 1926 Traven saw photos depicting overseers cutting the ears from disobedient or rebellious Indian slaves. In the Congo during King Leopold's reign they cut off the hands of the blacks. In the American West scalping of Indians was the fashion. In Chiapas in the 1920s it was the ears they removed.

The photographs were a remarkable record of brutality, torture, terror. Strange, isn't it, that the conquerors and invaders—whether they are the Spanish of the sixteenth century or the Nazis of the twentieth century—document their atrocities as though they were proud of them.

Fifty years ago the pictures of the Indians without ears had a profound impact on Traven. The images simmered in his imagination for a decade. Then, while writing *The Rebellion of the Hanged,* he resurrected them in a scene of remarkable power. Candido, an Indian lumberjack, his sister Modesta, and his young sons try to escape by canoe from the infernal mahogany camp. But they are soon caught. As punishment, and as a lesson to the other Indians, Candido's ears, and the ears of his youngest boy, are sliced off. That act of violence inflicted by the overseers sparks the insurrection. The Indian workers refuse to be hacked to pieces, losing an ear, an eye, an arm, a leg, or a life, while they cut and fell the mahogany trees. They turn their machetes and axes against their exploiters and cut them into *trozas.* Blood flows; armies of men and masters clash in the jungles and on the hot plains. But exploitation and oppression continues. As Traven notes sadly, "It never occurred to a single one of the peons to eliminate the *capataces* [overseers] by a combined attack on the system of which a *capataz* was but a tool."

We wandered back to the bus depot. Pablo had a route to Tapachula, so he'd see his wife and boys early in the morning. Cocoa was sitting on a bench, waiting for the next bus to Mex-

ico City. She too wanted to go home. I was still lonely for the
Rio Mississippi, but I bought a ticket for San Cristóbal de las
Casas and barely had time to catch the bus.

It was about midnight when we arrived. San Cristóbal was
like a dream. In Tuxtla we were in the tropics. It was hot and
oppressively humid. But the Tuxtla road had climbed higher
and higher. By the time it arrived in San Cristóbal we were in
the cool, crisp mountain air. For that night anyway, San
Cristóbal had an unworldly appearance. In part, that was due
to the mist and the fog. Buildings and people were blurry, out
of focus, as though the movie projectionist had forgotten to
adjust the lens. The blurry picture added a touch of magic.
Then, too, there was an echoing sound that gave me the sense,
not of hollow open space, but of solidity. This was no dream
world, but a deeper, more profound reality.

The architecture was amazing. I walked down the cobblestone streets, looked at the medieval churches and towers and
felt as though I had stepped back almost five hundred years.
For a moment I thought that I was in Europe, perhaps in the
Swiss Alps, in some remote mountain village. I watched the
Indians and felt that they had not changed much in five hundred years, despite the continuing waves of invaders.

I walked from the bus station to the center of town, stum-
bling along the cobblestones, in awe of everything and everyone I saw. Indians in *sarapes,* their faces hidden by their wide-
brimmed hats, passed through the shadows and into the dim
street lights, talking in a whisper, their words echoing along
the medieval walls of stone. Above me the sky was suddenly
clear. The stars were bright. Now, at last, I felt Traven's
presence.

30

Behind the fence an Indian gardener tended the flowers. He sat on his haunches, swallowed up by the leaves, ferns, and the kaleidoscope of colors. He had patience—all the time in the world—and incredible concentration. Nothing else mattered but the flowers.

I stood a few inches from the wire fence and watched him. He worked with his hands, pulling weeds, loosening the soil, clearing dead leaves and broken stems. He was an artist and he had created a fantastic garden. It wasn't a small, tidy plot with red brick paths and delicate floral patterns, but a lush, wild garden befitting Chiapas. Dr. Marin's parrots were an aberration in Mexico City, but here they would have been at home.

I watched the gardener for about twenty minutes and the whole time he didn't once look at me. I was sure that he knew I was standing outside the fence watching him, but he didn't care, didn't mind. Nothing distracted him from the plants and flowers.

If a stranger from Mexico had stood silently watching me for twenty minutes, while I worked in my garden back home, I'd have become nervous, paranoid, but the Indian remained calm. *I* became impatient, restless. I knew he could easily refrain from looking at me, but I was uneasy about his refusal to acknowledge my presence. It didn't seem like a personal affront, a rejection of my existence, but simply an appeal for us to leave each other in peace, and not encroach on one another's territory.

Watching the gardener, and self-conscious of the fact that I was watching him, I thought of Traven watching the Indians, his eyes following every detail of motion: the flicker of an eyelid, the spin of a finger, the fall of an arm; a woman making tacos, a *carretero* adjusting the yoke of the oxen, an Indian couple dancing in the Zócalo.

Traven had patience. He would watch and watch and watch. Watch, observe, remember—and then record what he had seen in his books. Traven had a deep respect for things as they were. I don't mean he was conservative, or opposed to change. On the contrary, he knew that change was the unchanging law of the universe, that history was a series of upheavals. "In these revolutionary times nothing is safe any longer," he wrote in *The Death Ship*. "Everybody and everything gets restless and wants to change positions and viewpoints." In Traven's world he who is watched today will be the watcher tomorrow. The watched and the watcher. The torturer and the tortured.

B. Traven described things as they were and not as they "should be," and that meant describing changing things and people. Flux flux flux! Traven aimed to tell the truth; that's one reason he didn't want to call his books "novels." In 1936 he explained (using the third person to talk about himself) that he "wanted to present reality, to offer sharp reproduction, even in the smallest detail. He gives us documents. He wants to show us Mexico, the land and its people exactly as they are; he chose the form of the novel only because it's easier to read and offers a more convincing story." Traven's books present photographic reality, but at the same time they are fantastic, surreal. They fuse the real and the symbolic.

Traven would have described the Indian gardener and his garden accurately, but he also would have portrayed the man and his world on a mythic level. The ordinary and the mysterious would flow together.

The Indian gardener was still pulling weeds, and I was becoming more and more anxious and impatient. Traven was right: the Indian is patient, and the white man is in a tremendous hurry to get ahead, bring events to a swift conclusion, find the final solution. Not so the Indian, at least not the Indian gardener I was watching. He wasn't dying for his coffee break, or his lunch break, or the four o'clock whistle. His sense of time didn't seem to have much to do with clocks, alarms, whistles.

Watching the Indian on his haunches I thought of a passage from *Treasure*. The setting is Tampico. Traven describes the oil workers and their women friends bathing in the river. On the cool hills above the port the foreigners enjoy a spectacular view. Traven notes that:

> Ladies coming to a tea-party in this vicinity brought their field-glasses along, for of course they could not go down to the river and join the bathing parties, much as they would have liked to do so. Through their field-glasses they watched the men and girls bathing without swimming-suits. It was so interesting that they never for a moment thought of playing bridge. It might have been just for this reason that this colony was called Colonia Buena Vista, which means "Beautiful View."

But Traven doesn't watch the bathers for very long. He is more interested in the Indian fishermen:

> At this point the river spread out delta-like and it was here the crab-fishers sat. Only the Indians and poorer Mexicans fish for crabs, because it calls for godlike patience. The bait of this meat is fastened on a fish-hook held by a long string and thrown in the

water. The fisherman lets the bait sink down into the mud and rest for a few minutes. Then he begins to draw in the line as slowly as only an Indian can. It takes many minutes before he pulls it up on the low bank. The crab, or *jaiba,* as they call it, grasps the bait with its claws and, eager not to lose the welcome meal, the crab is pulled out of the river and caught. There is no way to tell whether a crab has grasped the bait or not. Often the line has to be pulled in twenty times before a crab is caught. Sometimes the crab outwits the fishermen.

Dobbs, looking for any opportunity to make money, and watching these men fishing, yet knew this was no work for him. Having grown up in a hustling industrial American city, he hadn't a bit of the patience so essential for crab-fishing. He would not have caught one crab in three weeks.

I was as unfit for gardening in Chiapas as Dobbs was unfit for crab-fishing in Tampico. Both jobs took infinite patience. The poor Indians had the patience for it, and Traven had the patience to sit and watch the crab-fishermen bait the hook, toss the line into the water, let it sink, draw it in slowly hoping to hook a crab. Only someone who had watched an Indian crab-fisherman at work would have written the description. It belongs in a guide to fishing in Mexico, a "how-to" book. But there's also the Traven magic in the passage. The poor Indian crab-fisher has "godlike patience." He's an ordinary worker and yet there's the aura of the superhuman about him that hovers about all Traven's humble peasants and proletarians. Watching the Indians, Traven celebrates them and respects their individuality too.

Watchfulness was a key to Traven's character. But he wasn't born a watcher. He had to learn it. As Ret Marut he wanted people to watch him, to be aware of him. He even used anonymity to celebrate and draw attention to himself. Even when he was in the wings, Ret Marut was on stage, inviting the audience to focus their eyes on him. He was a strutting egotist.

It seems to me that Europeans and North Americans tend to view themselves as the watched. We think that we are at the center of the world, that the peoples of Asia, Africa, and Latin America are watching us. (Of course, this is rapidly changing.) When Ret Marut arrived in Mexico he expected to be the center of attention. He wrote about himself, about the adventures of a white man among the Indians. Then, slowly, he changed. Gerard Gales vanished from the stage. Not Traven, or Marut, but the Indians moved to the center of the stage. In the Jungle Novels they are the only actors. There are no Europeans, no North Americans.

Traven asked his readers in Berlin and New York to turn their eyes away from themselves and toward the Indian world. Watch them! Their lives are fascinating, Traven tells us in his books. Even the Indian crab-fisherman; he is extraordinary. Open your eyes! Look!

I was convinced. The Indian gardener had godlike patience; he was incredible. At last I couldn't stand to watch him another moment. I turned, walked up the stone path, and knocked at the front door.

31

"The museum doesn't open until afternoon," the woman said. She was thin and blonde, and as I later learned, a German anthropology student.

"I want to talk to Gertrude Duby," I said. "I'm writing a book about B. Traven and I have some questions to ask."

"I'm afraid she's very busy now—why don't you come back later in the day? I'll give you a tour of the museum and perhaps Frau Duby can see you then. Good day now." She smiled and slammed the door in my face.

I should have known that I couldn't walk into Duby's home and expect an interview immediately. After all, Gertrude Duby was the First Lady of Chiapas, and an honorary citizen of Mexico. Everyone of importance visiting Chiapas stayed at "Na-Balom," Duby's immense house on the outskirts of San Cristóbal. Anyone wanting answers about Chiapas, the land and its people, posed Duby the questions. She was a legendary woman: a refugee from Germany, an anthropologist, author, teacher, and the widow of Franz Blom, the anthropologist who studied the Indians of Chiapas from the mid-1920s until his death in 1963.

"Duby escaped from the Nazis under a fake passport," Mary Belfridge told me in Cuernavaca. "She's a tough character, has a gun and holster strapped round her waist."

"Why does she do that?" I asked naively.

"Oh, it's very wild in Chiapas," Mary said. "You have to be prepared for anything."

Rosa Elena offered another portrait of Gertrude Duby. "She doesn't know anything about Traven," Rosa Elena said. "And she treats the Indians like curios. But by all means go and see her. It can't hurt."

Since Mrs. Duby couldn't see me, I walked back to the center of town, sat down in the plaza and watched the buying and the selling between the Indians and the hippies. The Indians had come down from their villages in the mountains; the hippies had come down from California, Arizona, New Mexico, Texas, and they met in the market place in San Cristóbal. The hippies couldn't speak the Indian dialects, and the Indians couldn't speak English, but they managed to communicate what was necessary—the price of goods.

In the light of day San Cristóbal seemed less magical than it had during the night. But there was a strong sense of history. I saw it in the buildings, especially in the crumbling Catholic churches, and in the symmetrical plan of the city: plazas connected by streets as straight as parallel lines.

Then I climbed to the top of the highest hill, and saw that San Cristóbal was surrounded by mountains, green forests, and meadows. Geographically it was isolated, a European outpost in Indian territory. Here, two cultures, two civilizations approached, clashed, retreated, then approached, clashed, retreated, all over again. It seemed like a deadly ritual.

B. Traven studied the history of San Cristóbal and was haunted by it, especially by one violent incident. In the 1860s, to protest their poverty and lack of civil rights, tens of thousands of Indians seized the roads to San Cristóbal, prevented food supplies from entering and people from leaving. As Traven wrote in *Land in Springtime*, "It was what we today would call a boycott and strike." Then negotiations began between the hostile camps. Six Indians traveled from the mountains under a flag of truce. But once inside the walls of San

Cristóbal they were hanged. The mayor sent word that a peace treaty had been signed, that food could now be admitted to the city. The Indians trusted him. They took his word as the truth and ended their boycott and strike. Later, of course, they learned what had happened to the six negotiators, but by then it was too late to fight. Soldiers occupied the passes and guarded the roads. The Europeans had defeated the Indians; the city vanquished the countryside. Traven couldn't shake that incident from his mind. "The Indians have never forgotten the murder," he wrote. Neither could he.

Traven arrived in Chiapas sixty years after the murder of the six Indian negotiators. Like the Malintzin's betrayal, it was still a heated topic of conversation. I arrived over one hundred years later, and I had the feeling that the Indians had not yet forgotten—not those murders, nor any of the other murders committed over the last five hundred years. Good memories, these Indians. Very good memories.

San Cristóbal was a war zone. I felt the tension bubbling beneath the surface. This was a colonial city. It seemed like something I had seen in a movie, or read in a book (was it George Orwell?) about Africa or Asia. The Indians were the natives and were treated as inferiors; the whites were the occupying foreigners, and with the help of the *mestizos* ruled by force. There were certain customs, certain social laws, that had to be obeyed and respected or else the Indian would find himself with a broken jaw, or in a jail cell.

When Traven arrived fifty years ago the lines between the Indians and the whites had been even more tightly drawn. The colonial hierarchy was rigid, unbending. To go among the Indians, not as a businessman, or an overseer, but as an anthropologist was a revolutionary act. Gertrude Duby's husband Franz Blom went into the jungle as an anthropologist. So did Traven. He broke the social norm. He left European colonial society behind and ventured into *la selva* to see, hear, and live the lives of the Indians. Again and again he returned to Chiapas to explore, to learn from the Indians, and to convey their stories to the outside world.

To the other whites he was strange, peculiar. What was there to study? The overseers didn't see any customs, culture, or rituals, just animals to be worked until they died.

Chiapas was *the* revolution for Traven. Not in Munich, but here his world changed decisively, his imagination grew by leaps and bounds. No longer could he, no longer did he, judge Europe the cultural and historical center of the world, the home of humanity. As he explains in *The Night Visitor,* he came to marvel at the "various cultures and great civilizations that had existed in the Americas when the Romans were still semi-savages and the Britons ate the brains of the bravest of their enemies slain in battle." In Chiapas Traven discovered the "great mysterious civilization which existed and flourished. . .long before Columbus thought of sailing to. . .a new world."

Traveling through the jungles of Chiapas, feeling the power of the Native American tradition, I was persuaded that the questions of Traven's identity, the Kaiser, World War I, the Munich Rebellion, were far less insistent. Not Germany but Mexico seemed to be at the heart of Traven's world. Not the mystery of his birth, but the mystery of his rebirth among the Indians and proletarians seemed crucial.

And yet when I stepped back from the jungle and reflected carefully, I saw that Traven did live simultaneously in two conflicting worlds. Old world and new world, Bavaria and Chiapas, Mexico and Germany, Europe and America, White and Red, *gringo* and *indio,* rags and riches, paradise and hell, tyranny and freedom, life and death—these were the inexorably balanced polarities in Marut/Traven's spectacular universe. The power of the art derived from the author's fusion of two worlds into one world, real yet mysterious, strange yet familiar. It was as if the world had reproduced itself within Traven's heart and soul and then spilled out onto the printed page in book after book after book—a lifetime of labor and love, joy and grief.

It was beginning to drizzle. The sky darkened and it grew

cold. I sat down in a restaurant, ordered a bowl of soup and waited for the shower to end.

It was still raining when I returned to Na-Bolom. I waited for Gertrude Duby in the library, an immense room with a stone fireplace that seemed more appropriate for a baronial mansion in Central Europe than a provincial town in Chiapas. I felt like I was back in the Austro-Hungarian Empire, or on a Hollywood movie set for *The Prisoner of Zenda*. Na-Bolom made the house on the Rio Mississippi seem a crude construction of the *nouveau riche*.

Like Rosa Elena and the Belfridges, Gertrude Duby had an excellent, though idiosyncratic library. All the classical anthropological studies were here, from Franz Boaz to Robert Redfield and Oscar Lewis. And there were magazine reprints and monographs detailing the customs and rituals of every tribe in Chiapas.

The mahogany doors opened and a large, black dog bounded into the library. The young German woman shouted at him, but he didn't obey. The dog jumped at me and almost knocked me down. "Come quick, Frau Duby, please," the young woman shouted. "Macho is wild." Duby charged down the hallway and burst into the library. I looked at her waist; she wasn't wearing a gun or holster, but she was intimidating. The dog collapsed at her feet.

Gertrude Duby was a short, round woman, very handsome and very sensual. She wore a wide skirt and white blouse. She reminded me of Gertrude Stein. I suppose in part it was the name Gertrude, but it was also her physical appearance, her closely cropped hair, large forehead, and broad nose.

"So you're writing the biography of B. Traven, well, good luck to you, young man," she said. "A woman from San Francisco told me that a friend was working with Mrs. Luján on a biography of Traven. I didn't believe her but here you are, so it must be true. Well, I don't imagine that Mrs. Luján is much help to you! More of a hindrance, I'd guess; probably sidetracks you. She doesn't know the first thing about writing a book, and I bet she doesn't know the first thing about Traven either. Am I wrong? No, of course not. Traven didn't tell her anything! Didn't trust her, didn't trust anybody, not like my Franz. We shared everything. I wouldn't like to be a widow in Mrs. Luján's shoes, all alone in that house in Mexico City. Whatever she knows she's picked up from other people, not from him, and what they didn't tell her she's made up. Oh, she's a good storyteller, I won't deny that."

"What can *you* tell me about Traven?" I asked.

"Well, he never worked as a sailor. *The Death Ship* isn't his story but the story of Anton Biglier, a Belgian sailor. Traven and Biglier were lovers—yes, lovers, don't look so shocked."

"How do you know that?" I asked.

"From Gerd Heidemann, the *Stern* reporter. Heidemann came through here a few years ago, came to see me. Heidemann knows everything about Traven. He told me that Traven and Biglier were homosexuals."

"You believe it?" I asked, irritated by Duby's claim.

"Yes, I do. Think about *The Death Ship*. You can't deny that Gales and Stanislav are lovers."

"Comrades, friends," I said.

"Lovers! Lovers! Oh, he doesn't come out and say it, but they're lovers. With a man like Traven you've got to read between the lines, look for the hidden. I've read Traven's novels, young man, and I can see that love between men is the only love that B. Traven understands. It's not only *The Death Ship*, it's between the lumberjacks in the Jungle Novels too. Why do you think he waited until he was over seventy to get married —and then picked a woman who was more of a daughter than a wife? Why? Can you answer me that? Do you think he had a normal, healthy relationship with Mrs. Luján?"

"He always had lovers," I said. "I've read his correspondence. He had women friends in L.A., San Antonio; taxi dancers, prostitutes, lonely widows. In the letters they'd address him as 'Dear Viking' and 'Olaf My Norse Lover.' He had pornography too, pictures of exotic-looking women having sex with tigers and lions."

"He confided in women, relied on women, needed women

to help him write, or translate, but he didn't need them emotionally, sexually, whatever normal healthy men need a woman for," Duby said.

After I recovered from the initial shock of Duby's allegation, I admitted to myself that she had a valid point. Traven thought that his books were frank and honest about sex, passion, and lust. He continually told his German editors that while Europeans were prudish about sexual matters, Americans were uninhibited, that he followed the American way. Rosa Elena disagreed with me strongly, but I felt that Traven's books were puritanical. Sex is usually repressed. He was embarrassed by it.

But Duby was right; Traven did celebrate the beauty, grace, and the power of men—not women. There *is* a sexual attraction between heroes, between Gales and Stanislav, Celso and Andres. (It's almost as if Traven was making love with himself, the optimist copulating with the fatalist, the man of action mating with the man of intellect.)

In *The Carreta* and *The Rebellion of the Hanged* Traven tried to create fuller, more complex women characters in Estrellita and Modesta, but he didn't succeed. I suspect that Traven began to create significant women characters as a result of his relationship with the school teacher, Maria de la Luz Martínez. Probably they didn't have a sexual relationship. Probably Traven respected her, and drew from her character and personality in creating his admirable women characters. I don't have proof, of course, but the time when he was closest to Maria de la Luz coincides with the time his heroines are sharply, sympathetically drawn.

Traven's women are, by and large, the creation of a man who was afraid of, and puzzled by, women—mothers, sisters, daughters, lovers, wives. In Traven's universe women tend to be either pure or damned, virgins or whores. His women are good if they love their proletarian men and provide them with healthy sons; they are bad if they fuck the oppressors and exploiters. For Traven there is no mystery connected with women. The Virgin Mary, the Triple Goddess, sisterhood, mothers

211

and daughters—Traven couldn't care less. Mystery is male. With the exception of the mother in *The Bridge in the Jungle,* Traven devoted his love to men: Gales, Stanislav, Carlosito, Andres, Candido, Juan Mendez, Martin Trinidad, Macario. He wrote about men in groups—sailors, soldiers, prospectors, and the armies of male proletarians who labor far away from the realms of womankind.

Like many Europeans and North Americans who travel in Africa, Asia, Latin America, Traven was aroused by the sexuality of the native, dark-skinned people, and at the same time frightened by it. From his correspondence it appears that Traven did go to Texas and California regularly to meet North American women. He always told them he was a Scandinavian, a Norse wanderer.

In *Land in Springtime* Traven argued that Europeans were sexually repressed, that white European males tended to be sterile and impotent. To attract them, he said, the European woman had to become more and more seductive and erotic. In Traven's eyes the European man was becoming passive and effeminate, while the European woman was becoming aggressive and masculine. The sex roles were reversed and to Traven that was a sure sign of decadence. But Indian sexuality was healthy. The man was potent, strong; the woman made babies. In *The Carreta* Traven wrote:

> There were no dark secrets, no repressed sensuality in their lives. No one taught them to play the hypocrite about natural things and to regard plain facts as sinful. They certainly did not mince words. They spoke as they thought and felt. Problems of sex and psychology had no meaning for them, and so their lives took on no superfluous complexities. Man is man, and woman is woman; and when the two come together they know what they want of each other. That was the sum of their philosophy of sex. They found it a very satisfactory one, and it never played them false.

I felt that B. Traven *was* sexually repressed. Again, Rosa Elena disagreed very strongly with my views, but it seemed to me that he didn't like women and found men more attractive.

"You never met Traven, did you?" I asked.

"No, but Franz did," Duby said. "It took about thirty years for them to get together. In 1926 Traven and Franz were supposed to travel together in the Lacondon jungle, but Traven had an accident. He was riding across an Indian bridge on horseback—stupid of him—and it collapsed. Traven broke his leg. So it wasn't until 1953 that they set eyes on one another. He and Gabriel Figueroa were filming *The Rebellion of the Hanged*. They had to find a mahogany forest and they wanted Franz to help them. It wasn't easy.

"When Traven was in Chiapas in the twenties the mahogany forests were immense. By the Fifties they were decimated. Oh, you can still find mahogany trees but not forests, not like they used to be. The entire film crew, the cameramen, the actors and actresses gathered here in this room. Everyone referred to Traven as Mr. Croves, and for a while Franz went along with the charade. After *Treasure* was filmed everyone in Mexico knew that Croves was Traven, but they were so intimidated by him they didn't dare say so. He was a tyrant. When they were about to leave Franz shook his hand and said, 'Goodbye, Mr. Traven, it's been so nice having you visit Na-Bolom.' Traven was furious. He acted like a spoiled child and stormed out of the library. I was in town shopping, but when I got back Franz was still beaming with delight. 'If only you could have seen his face when I said, Goodbye, Mr. Traven. I won't forget it as long as I live!' "

"Do you think that the Jungle Novels are accurate?" I asked.

Duby paused a moment. "Yes, of course," she said thoughtfully. (I was surprised; after her comments on Traven's personality, I thought she was going to dismiss the books as false, distorted.) "I interviewed an Indian woman who worked in the mahogany camps. They were as hellish as Traven described. It's impossible to exaggerate the brutality."

"Like fascism in a jungle," I said.

"The woman I interviewed was so terrified she traveled through the jungle alone for a month so she could escape. Do you know what that's like? Poisonous snakes, swamps, wild pigs, and the haunting fear of the unknown that is sometimes worse than anything known or visible. Whippings and hangings were common occurrences in the camps, even fifty years ago. The lumberjacks had to fill their quota of two or three tons of cut mahogany, or they'd be lashed mercilessly. The women didn't cut the trees but they cooked and cleaned for the men, and of course some of them were prostitutes for the overseers. They were treated as miserably as the lumberjacks —beaten and whipped into submission, raped and tortured so that they were old hags by the time they were twenty-five or thirty. You see, there were women in the lumber camps, but Traven didn't write about their plight. He wrote as though all proletarians were men. A slight oversight, wouldn't you say? But listen, there's an old lumberjack you could talk to. Pepe Tarrano. He worked in the camps in the twenties, lives in 'El Real' now. There are no roads there, so you'll have to fly in, unless you want to join me on mule back."

"You're going into the jungle by mule?" I asked.

"Yes, of course. I used to go with Franz for months at a time," Duby said. "Now if Mrs. Luján had been with her Traven into the jungle she'd have something interesting to tell you."

"Do the Indians accept you?" I asked.

"They don't scalp, if that's what you mean," Duby said.

"In San Cristóbal there's so much hostility between whites and Indians," I said.

"It was a lot worse," Duby said. "Of course the Indians are still shoved into the gutter and if a *ladino* sees an Indian riding horseback he just might knock him down and take his horse away."

"Steal it?" I asked.

"They don't want Indians above them," Duby said. "Especially not on horseback."

"What about the Indian customs Traven describes? In *Government* the new chief sits on a hot fire until his skin burns. Traven says it was a lesson for the chief not to become dictatorial. In *The Bridge in the Jungle* the Indians float a board with a lighted candle down the river. It stops at the exact spot where the Indian boy has drowned. Mysterious, isn't it? The board stops in the middle of the river, against the flow of the current. Impossible!"

"Impossible things happen," Duby said. "I have never seen either ceremony you describe, but maybe I didn't go to the same villages that Traven went to."

"Is it possible Traven made them up?" I asked.

"Frankly, I don't think that any Indian chief sits on a fire. Let's say Traven dreamed that one up. But I like the idea, don't you? It's never good to stay in one place too long. You stagnate." And with that Duby sprang to her feet and led me to the door. "Do send me a copy of the biography of Traven," she said. "I'd like to read it so very much."

32

Early one morning I walked the fifteen miles to Chamula, a small village in the mountains above San Cristobal—a village Traven had visited in 1926, and described in his books. Then it was a remote Indian village, largely untouched by outside influences. I crossed the valley and climbed the road that moved higher and higher toward the blue sky. The Indians raced down the mountain, down the road and toward the market, their backs bent with heavy loads. They seemed to be impelled by an unseen force—hunger, fear, or death. One after another they descended the mountain, swept past me like a whirlwind, their eyes glancing at mine only for a moment; and then they were behind me.

I had seen them before. Their bodies and their faces were familiar. Before I left Mexico City I examined Traven's photographs of the land and the people of Chamula. They were not as artistic as Edward Weston's photographs. Traven's pictures didn't have the composition, balance, or contrast between light and dark. "I don't go in for 'artistic photography,' just for the sake of compositions; most of my material is documentary from an ethnographical viewpoint," Traven wrote. "But of course I try to get as good a composition in my pictures as possible."

Traven's pictures were a documentary record of the lives of

the Chamula Indians. In 1926 Traven traveled to Chamula, photographing the men and the women he met on the road. I didn't have a camera with me. Marianne Yampolsky had warned me against taking photos of the Chamulas. Marianne was a photographer and described unfortunate experiences taking the pictures of Indians in Oaxaca and Chiapas. Sometimes the Indians were frightened and ran away; sometimes they were angry and smashed the camera.

But Traven didn't meet with hostility from the Indians. From the expressions on the faces in the photographs you can see that they trusted him. Some of the women and children are puzzled by the camera, but no one looks frightened. And many of the men are laughing, clowning, performing.

In the pictures, the men have wide-brimmed hats that come to a sharp point. They carry walking sticks to propel them up, or guide them down, the steep mountainsides. Each Indian wears a leather pouch or sack. A few of the Indians are on horseback; they wear black *serapes* and white turbans around their heads. The Indian women are barefoot. They wear black *rebozos,* and their hair is in long braids. Almost every woman carries a young child in her arms or on her back.

The Indians in Traven's photographs were in black and white, while the Indians I saw were in bright color. And, of course, the Indians in the photographs were frozen in time. Traven caught them as they paused on the road, leaning on a stick, resting for a moment to catch their breath for the steep climb.

I was high above San Cristobal. The air was thin and I was having difficulty filling my lungs with oxygen. I felt dizzy and I sat down on a large boulder. A white man was climbing the mountain a hundred yards behind. He raised his arm and signaled me to wait. Out of breath and legs shaking, he staggered toward me.

"Let's travel together," he suggested, wiping the perspiration from his high cheekbones.

"I don't mind company," I said ambiguously.

"I've been alone for weeks and it's getting to me," he said.

"My name is Paul. I'm from Portland, been taking pictures in San Cristobal." Paul sat down on the large boulder opposite me.

The mountain path ran between us. In the distance I heard the sound of gravel crunching under Indian feet. I watched and waited. The sound grew louder and louder. Then an old man appeared. He wore a cone-shaped hat and carried a walking stick—like the Indians in Traven's pictures. Before he reached the immense boulders where Paul and I were sitting he stopped, removed his hat, and asked, *"Con su permiso?"* His question seemed odd but I answered, *"Pase usted."* The old man put his hat back on his head, peered up at the sun, and passed between the two rocks. When he got to the other side he paused again, looked at Paul and at me and said, *"Vaya con Dios."* Then he continued his march down the mountain.

Every Indian coming down the mountain stopped and asked permission to pass between the two rocks. Paul thought that we were perched on top of two magic rocks, two sacred landmarks, and because we sat on the holy rocks the Indians assumed that we were holy men. That could be. I was struck more by the irony of the situation. There we were, North Americans, thousands of miles from home, lost in the heart of the Chamula nation, and the Indians asked *us* permission. It was crazy. The rocks weren't our rocks, the trail wasn't our trail. Who were we to grant permission? Of course, neither Paul nor I had asked permission from the Indians to walk their road or sit on their rocks. We had crossed their frontiers, had entered their nation, and assumed that we could travel through it, stay as long as we wanted. It never occurred to me to ask permission from the Chamulas to travel to their village.

Perhaps the Indians were superstitious about the rocks. And maybe they were being their normal polite selves. The Chamulas have a formal code of behavior; they have manners, and their manners are a token of their respect for other people. But maybe the crucial factor was race and power. In San Cristobal I had watched the play of manners between the Indians and the *mestizos*. The Indians were courteous and polite, sometimes meek and deferential. But some poor whites received from the *mestizos* the same impolite treatment (or almost) that the Indians received. The play of manners reflected the social and racial hierarchy.

Traven explores this subject in the Jungle Novels. He portrays the Indians as a people with a highly developed sense of ritual, custom, manners. According to Traven, the European colonizers and exploiters used the Indian sense of manners, their ancient rituals and customs, against them. The Indian's sense of honor, dignity, and honesty were his finest qualities, but the whites turned them inside out, and used them to enslave the Indian. Thus, paradoxically, Indian society was an unwilling accomplice in its own destruction. Traven had seen that happen in history: the Indians had trusted the mayor of San Cristobal in the 1860s; they had sent their six negotiators to town, never suspecting that they would be murdered. Much the same sort of thing happens in the Jungle Novels. In *The Carreta*, Andres's *love* for his father enables the whites to trap both father and son. In *March to the Monteria*, Celso's *respect* for both his father and his betrothed enables the overseers in the mahogany camps to work him mercilessly. Every decent, humane feeling the Indians have becomes a yoke. But the yoke is eventually thrown off. Traven showed the European destruction of traditional Indian society, and the creation of Indian proletarians and Indian guerrillas—Indians without manners, *without respect* for their oppressors. The Indians are marched into the jungle as slaves. They march out as disciplined warriors, led by their own "general from the jungle." The manners of slavery are transformed into the manners of liberation.

If Paul and I were Traven villains, like El Camaron and El Zorro, the sadistic slave drivers who appear in *March*, we'd take advantage of the Indian sense of mystery, honesty, and respect. We'd seize the two magic boulders and charge each Indian a peso every time he passed through our territory. We'd turn mystery to profit. Anyone who didn't pay would have the option of going to jail for five years (because he had broken the law), or working for us for a year without pay. Of course, we'd have to use whips and chains, but we'd put things in order. Then, one day, like El Camaron and El Zorro, we'd wake up dead—killed by our own whips and chains. The vultures would pick at our flesh, our bones would disintegrate on the mountainside, and once again the Indians would pass freely between the two rocks of mystery and power.

Sitting on the rock I heard the sound of gravel underfoot. I looked up the path but no one was coming down. An Indian was climbing up toward us. He looked like all the other Indians we had seen; he was short and stout. He too had a conical hat and he carried a thick walking stick. But this Indian didn't stop to ask *"Con su permiso." "Hola"* was all he said as he raced through the rocks and continued his march up the mountain.

Paul was still catching his breath; I didn't want to wait any longer. I was curious about this Indian who didn't ask permission. I jumped to the ground and dashed after him. When I finally caught up with him he kept on going, full speed ahead, and puffing on a cigarette too.

I never found out his name but I learned that he worked for the Mexican government. He was a Chamula who had studied at the National School of Agriculture at Chapingo, and then returned home to help his family, tribe, nation. He was critical of the Mexican government, but he believed that the present administration was slowly improving the lot of the poorest peasants. In the few short years he had been working in Chamula, starvation had been eliminated, and the Indian diet had been enriched. The infant mortality rate dropped and a school had been built. But the task wasn't easy. The government provided seeds, but no machinery, no tools, and no fertilizer. The soil was poor and there was no irrigation. Moreover, the Indians needed to be educated about farming.

The Chamula agricultural advisor showed Paul (who had caught up with us by now) and me how the Indians farmed. The walking stick was also a planting stick. He thrust the stick into the hard ground, drilled a small hole, then dropped a bean seed and covered it with a thin layer of earth. The Indians had used this same method of planting for thousands of years, and it wasn't adequate to the needs of the tribe.

When we arrived in Chamula the agricultural advisor shook our hands and went into the fields to examine the corn. The village was sad, disappointing—in a word, poor. Traven's photos hadn't prepared me for this kind of grim, stark poverty. There were a few well-tended gardens, but most of the land was bleak and stony. In the central plaza the Indians sold mangoes, dolls, tourist souvenirs. The ground was covered with garbage and scrawny dogs searched for scraps of food. The barefoot Chamula children held out their hands and begged *"unpesounpesounpeso."*

Middle-class Mexicans arrived in modern, air-conditioned buses. (Traven's 1926 photos showed no tourist buses.) They had come to see the natives. Even before the buses came to a halt the Mexican tourists opened the windows and threw candies and chiclets to the Indian boys and girls. The young Chamulas reached up their hands, opened their mouths, and cried, *"Un peso un peso un peso."* (This time I could understand the words.) The chewing gum and candy fell in the dust, was recovered and eaten.

Finally, the drivers parked the buses and the tourists descended. Now I realized how skinny the Indians were. The tourists were well-fed, well-dressed, and they were anxious to do well by the Chamulas. They lined up the boys and girls, made them hold out their hands, and then gave each one a bright, shiny coin. Traven's pictures showed no begging, either. I assume it hadn't existed in 1926.

The North American doesn't have a monopoly when it comes to patronizing the Indian. His Mexican counterpart does an excellent job without any help from us. Of course, he thinks he is being generous, kind, loving. But he regards the Chamula as an animal, a small creature who scurries after buses, holds out his pretty little hand, and wails *unpesounpeso-unpesounpeso* until it drives you crazy.

Once the well-fed, well-dressed tourists had given out their coins, they filled the church to kneel, pray, light a candle, leave a few pesos for the priest. They were good Christians; traveling all the way to Chamula made them feel like saints. Now surely their sins would be forgiven them and they would be allowed to enter heaven.

The Chamula elders watched the Mexican tourists carefully. They stood silently, holding their weavy wooden sticks, wearing their ceremonial garb, looking as though they had stepped out of a B. Traven photograph. Not one father rebuked his child, and yet there was sadness in each father's eye. They were the tribal council, the Chamula government. They saw their own crazy children running from one tourist to another begging, *"Un peso un peso un peso."* Those bitter pesos enabled them to eat and they knew it. The Chamulas were valuable because they were living museum pieces, because they enabled the middle-class Mexicans to express their sense of charity. The children begged from me but I wouldn't give them a peso. I remembered Rosa Elena's words about charity. "Before I met Traven I was a very charitable person," she said. "I gave to the poor, the blind, the lame. It made me feel better. I used to think that charity would end the world's problems. Then I met Traven. He told me that charity only perpetuated the problem of rich and poor, starvation and injustice. But it was hard to stop giving. They hold out their hand to beg for a peso and you feel like a criminal if you don't give."

Slowly we walked down the mountain. Now the Indians were climbing up. They nodded greetings, stretched their legs and pulled themselves higher and higher. At one point along the path we stopped to watch a group of Indian men. They were making the special tortillas that are used for the Fiesta de San Juan. No women were visible. Two men sat on the ground, cross-legged, and mixed the finely ground charcoal with the fresh corn meal. While they worked, three Indian men played harp, flute, and drum. No Christian priest had taught them this music; it wouldn't be allowed in church on

San Juan's day. It was the ancient music of the Chamulas, both sad and beautiful, appropriate for a birth, a wedding, a death.

The Indian men didn't want us to watch their ceremony, they resented our very presence; still, we couldn't leave. We were entranced by the sound of flute, drum, harp. The music was gentle yet powerful; it had endured unchanged for thousands of years. Church hymns had not silenced it, nor had the melodies of Bing Crosby or Elvis Presley.

While we were listening, a young Indian woman emerged from behind a small thatched hut that displayed a Coca-Cola sign. She had long black hair and a rich coffee complexion. She looked at Paul and at me curiously. Paul walked toward her, lifted his camera, and using his best sign language asked if he could take her picture. She was an extraordinarily beautiful woman and I could understand why Paul wanted to look at her again and again when he was back home. The woman seemed to understand. She smiled and nodded her head. I squatted on my haunches, listened to the music and looked at the woman's face. She had very fine features, almond-shaped eyes, and smooth, round nostrils. Suddenly the music stopped and the woman became frightened. She shook her head, then dashed behind the hut. It was quiet for a moment, then the sound of flute, drum, and harp began again, and the Indian men continued to mix the corn meal and the charcoal for the coming Fiesta de San Juan. Paul slung the camera over his shoulder and walked slowly down the mountain.

33

By the time I reached Ocosingo the sun had already set. I left the bus and showed a young boy a picture of Vitorino Trinidad, Traven's guide in Chiapas fifty years earlier. The boy didn't recognize Vitorino's face, but when I asked, *"Dónde está el maestro?"* he led me to the end of town and pointed up the hill. Ocosingo was only two blocks long; there were no sidewalks, no paved streets, no neon signs, and no movie theater. The town was a stereotype: sleepy, quiet, slow-moving.

The path up the hill was wide enough for only one person. It followed the river bed, then merged with the river bed, and I had no choice but to wade through the water.

When I arrived at Trinidad's farm it was dusk. Trinidad was asleep, but his wife Emilia was sitting by the fire. "He's an old man," she said. "Eighty-five years old. His memory isn't very good any more. Sometimes he doesn't even recognize me. I don't know what you'll find out about Traven. Vitorino has already told the reporters everything he knows."

"What reporters?" I asked, suddenly afraid that I had been scooped.

"Oh, there have been so many. They come to ask about Traven. I don't understand. What's so special about *him?*" The darkness gathered about Emilia's face, but her voice re-

224

mained clear and strong. "No one ever asks Vitorino about *his* life."

"Did you know Traven?" I asked.

"No, never met him," Emilia said. "That was before my time."

"Does he talk about Traven?" I asked.

"No. Should he?" Emilia asked. "There are more important things in this world, young man. I don't care how far you've come, you'll have to come back in the morning. It's too late to wake Vitorino, poor man. I don't know why you reporters don't leave him in peace. What can he tell you about Traven? Nothing! Absolutely nothing, I assure you. But if you insist. He's awake early. Be here by eight."

"Where can I stay?" I asked.

"There's no hotel, but the priest will let you sleep in the church," Emilia said. "It's a fine place; all the hippies sleep there." To Emilia I was just another hippie, a young gringo wandering in search of something or someone.

I walked back to Ocosingo, trusting my feet to find the path and the river bed. A crescent moon dangled above the horizon and the stars were—as they say—like diamonds. Dogs barked, crickets chirped, kids laughed, and the mosquitoes were deadly.

The Ocosingo church was an immense, roughly constructed building that could easily have held a thousand worshipers. Behind the church was a small house, a school, and a barn. The priest was eating when I knocked on his door. He was tall and balding with a few wisps of white hair. His nose was bright red, and suggested a well-developed taste for alcohol.

"Puede dormir en la iglesia?" I asked.

"Sí," he said. *"Pero recuerda de apagar la luz."* His accent sounded peculiar so I asked him in English, "Where are you from, Father?"

"Boston," he said, munching on a tortilla.

"What are you doing here?"

"Bringing the teachings of Christ to the Indians," he said, with complete sincerity. He was a true believer. "First mass is at five A.M. You can sleep in the church, but don't expect to sleep late. There'll be music early, and I'm hearing confessions, too."

In the courtyard Indian lumberjacks ("jacks," Traven called them) were cooking black beans over an open fire. The coals were white hot, and illuminated their faces and torsos. They were short, dark men, the color of mahogany, their arms and shoulders hard as mahogany. One jack reached into the fire, filled his plate with beans, and sat down on the stone floor. I asked him if he knew B. Traven's novels. No, he didn't; moreover, he was surprised that someone had actually written a book about jacks.

"What's there to write about?" he asked. "We work all day. It's worse than hell, believe me. Besides, I can't read. If I could I wouldn't want to read about the lumber camps. I'd want something more peaceful."

By 7:30 the jacks were ready for bed. Each man slept on a thin strip of canvas covered by an equally thin blanket. I slept on the hard wood floor behind the altar, and was woken at sunrise by the noise of the birds. There were thousands of mud nests in the church; the birds flew in and flew out, their black wings fluttering ceaselessly.

I folded my blanket and went into the courtyard. The jacks were climbing aboard the flat bed of a truck that would carry them into the forest. The foreman was sharpening their big double-bladed axes on a grindstone. The bells of the church struck five. The bus clattered up the muddy street.

I hunted for a restaurant. All I found was a place with a dirt floor and swarms of flies. They buzzed my ears, landed on my nose, invaded my hair. Breakfast was disappointing. I ordered orange juice but was told that only Orange Crush was available, and without ice too. There was instant coffee, but no tortillas, just Pan Bimbo, the Mexican Wonder Bread.

There was no breeze. The sun was only beginning its slow climb up the sky but it was already hot. I took off my shoes and socks and walked barefoot. It was the first time I had walked barefoot in Mexico. Everyone had warned me against

226

it. "Worms will bury themselves in your skin," Mrs. Yampolsky said. "The doctor will have to cut them out with a knife." But I didn't care. I liked the feel of the smooth ground under my feet, and the cool stream flowing through my toes. I walked up the hill, a crowd of young kids following behind me, and I felt like the Pied Piper.

Vitorino came out of the house to greet me. His arms and legs were shaky, and he walked with the aid of a cane. Emilia brought us chairs, then returned to their crude, one-room shack, built of poles and straw. There was a dirt floor and a fire for cooking that was dug into the earth.

Vitorino proudly showed me photographs that were taken the last time he was in Mexico City. He had posed with Rosa Elena at the dining room table, and with the bust of Traven that stood in the backyard. Then he pointed to the jungle behind us and said, "Airplane came, Traven Torsvan's ashes there."

"Why there?" I asked.

"Don't know," he said, rubbing his chin. "I don't, I, I, I, I don't want, it's too hot, no don't scatter me over there, over that that jungle. I know I I I can just bury me grave. Emilia knows."

"You call him Traven Torsvan, not B. Traven," I said.

"Emilia knows," he said. His lips quivered. He was obviously having great difficulty speaking. His grammar and syntax slowly collapsed and died.

"Where did you meet Traven Torsvan?" I shouted.

"San Cristóbal. An advertisement in the paper. He was looking for a. . .a. . .guide. I am I am teaching school school then, but they let me go Traven Torsvan pay, good money. Emilia knows. Because I knew I know I know better than anyone else. His guide. Traven Torsvan's guide. An advertisement. Books. You read. You read? You read??" At first I didn't realize he was asking me a question.

"Yes," I said.

"You know what I mean. Don Quixote, Sancho Panza.

Quixote Torsvan. It doesn't mean anything to them, doesn't mean to, to."

"To who?" I asked.

"The first Torsvan was if I knew revolutionaries. The right man. Captured by counter-revolutionaries Veracruz, wanted information Villa." Vitorino lifted his shirt and pointed to a scar. "Shot me, shot me. . .*pozole? pozole?* Yes?" He stood up and using his cane to navigate, walked slowly toward the house. Emilia handed him a bottle of *pozole* (an alcoholic drink made from red corn and sugar) and he took a swig.

"Bitter stays too long," Vitorino said. "Must finish, finish, I, I, I, the bottle bitter too long." Vitorino had lost interest in Traven Torsvan. He wanted to drink his *pozole* and stare at the jungle, Traven's jungle, the jungle with a million stories, "each story beginning with the last line of the story just ended." His mind wandered, he drooled, then wiped the spittle from his lips.

"What was Traven Torsvan like?" I asked, making one last attempt at communication.

"What?" Vitorino asked.

"What was Traven Torsvan like?" I shouted. For a moment I thought that Vitorino was going to fall asleep. His eyelids closed, and his head nodded, but then his lips began to move. "Traven Torsvan. Traven Torsvan was a man customed, customed, accustomed to be among all kinds, all kinds, peoples races taking things in his strides," Vitorino said. So my journey was worthwhile, after all. That one sentence gave me a sense of triumph. And in the next sentence I was robbed. "Traven Torsvan chewed raw tobacco," Vitorino said, as though it was a piece of vital information, a gem.

Tears streamed down his face. He was whimpering and he cried out, "Emilia. Emilia!" He clutched a white handkerchief in his right hand and the bottle of *pozole* in his left hand. Emilia stood not more than two feet from him, but he didn't see her, or else didn't recognize her. "Emilia, Emilia," he shouted.

"I think you should go," Emilia said. "He's very upset."
The tears streamed down Vitorino's face. He was crying like
a baby.

"Tell, tell Rosa Elena tell her I, I, I'm alive, I'm alive and
and and I'm kick, kick, kicking," Vitorino said. He squeezed
my hand tightly. Emilia lifted him from the chair, and together we carried him inside the hut. Then I put on my shoes and
socks and walked back to town.

34

From Ocosingo to Palenque, one of the capitals of the ancient Mayan empire, was only forty miles, but there were no
connecting roads. Dense jungle stretched between the two villages. I could have hired an Indian guide to lead me there, but
I chose the easier way. B. Traven, of course, would have gone
on foot, or by horseback, with Vitorino, but the idea of following an Indian guide down jungle paths didn't appeal to me. I
took the bus.

On the way we passed an oil camp. Oil covered everything
and everyone. My eyes smarted from the sting of oil, my
tongue was bitter from the taste of oil. Pipes were piled high
and machinery rusted in the fields. The town had been turned
into a garbage dump; tin cans, paper containers, and beer
bottles were scattered everywhere, and the people of the town
sorted through the debris looking for something of value—
something to eat or drink.

In Villahermosa—the midway point of my journey to
Palenque—all the hotels were filled. The oil boom had at-
tracted thousands of workers from all over Mexico. Wages
were high but so were prices. Six men shared a small room
without toilet or running water and paid $200 a month rent.
The oil fields were outside the city so the men commuted by
bus or company truck. Sometimes they worked for a week, a

month, three months, but the jobs never lasted. Some of the men remained in town, found work washing dishes or cars, loading and unloading at warehouses, or they turned to pickpocketing and stickups.

After a long evening's search I finally found a room. I wanted a comfortable tourist hotel with air conditioning and a shower, but all I got was a boarding house. It was the bottom. The lodgers were old, broken-down workers who would die there without families. In my room there was no window and no bed, just a straw mat on the floor; it was worse than a prison cell. It was incredibly hot and humid day and night, and impossible for sleeping. The whole time I felt like I was in a hot bath; my lungs were choking. I could never cool down or keep my skin dry.

Oil was King in Traven's day. It was still King; it was the master of Villahermosa, as it had been the master of Tampico. Oil was manufacturing an army of unemployed and unemployable, but, as the newspapers boasted, it was "modernizing" Villahermosa. *Villa hermosa*, the beautiful village, would take its place among the streamlined cities of the western world.

One day I was walking down the main street; eight young women with clean, scrubbed faces surrounded me and asked if I had some free time. I did. So they invited me to follow them. We walked a few blocks, then entered a drab doorway, and climbed a long, dark flight of steps. At the top we entered an enormous room. The activity was intense. Telephones were ringing, electric typewriters whirring. Only one man was present and he was in charge of the operation.

"We're going to be opening a new tourist hotel," he said. "These girls will be maids and waitresses. They need to know English; maybe you can teach them."

I became an English teacher in Villahermosa. I taught the girls what they wanted to know: how to say "Shall I change the sheets," "Would you like ice water," and "I'll call a cab."

One girl had come to Villahermosa from a small jungle village with her parents. Her father worked in the oil fields, and her mother was a maid in a big house. "What are the Americans like?" she asked. Her idea of America had been formed by listening to rock 'n' roll and reading comic books—which is probably how half the world gets its image of our society. "Are you rich?" she asked. "Aren't all Americans rich?" I couldn't begin to explain the United States to her. She just didn't believe me when I said that there was poverty, crime, prisons, hunger. She was certain I was making up stories to tease her.

The girls learned English quickly. Hour after hour they practiced with each other: "Shall I change the sheets, sir?" "Would you like ice water, madame?" "Come again please."

In several of his short stories Traven is a teacher to the Mexican Indians. There is an air of romance and mystery about his language classes in remote, jungle villages. Mine were strictly business. After all, what mystery can there be in teaching chambermaids the appropriate phrases for American tourists?

From Villahermosa I took the bus to Palenque to see the ruins. Thousands of years ago a city had been carved out of the jungle. Palenque had grace, symmetry, harmony. The sun was hot but when you stepped behind the thick stone walls it was cool and fresh: Mayan air conditioning. Clearly superior to our brand.

The ruins were guarded by soldiers with machine guns. I assumed this was to prevent graffiti from being etched on the walls, but an Indian explained that North American treasure hunters had been robbing Mayan stone figures and smuggling them out of the country. The Americans swooped down in helicopters, pulled the two- and three-ton carvings out of the ground and into the sky. In New York they sold for tens of thousands of dollars. Now the soldiers listened for the sound of propellers.

Palenque was packed with French tourists. They were oohing and aahing. *"C'est vraiment magique,"* the tour guide said. His talk was so full of nonsense about magic and the supernatural that I took a stroll in the jungle. And was caught in a sudden downpour. It rained so hard and heavy that I couldn't see my way. I sat under a tree and listened to the rain drops. It was a cold, violent rain and it persuaded me to return to Mexico City. I wanted to see Rosa Elena, Chele, Malu, Mrs. Yampolsky, Pepe, Marie Louise. I felt as though my journey had come to an end. I had followed B. Traven from Mexico City to Cuernavaca, Oaxaca to San Cristóbal, Ocosingo to Villahermosa to Palenque. I was ready to go home to the Rio Mississippi and write.

The bus ride to Mexico City was unexceptional. There were no mysterious passengers, no strange occurrences. All the express buses were filled so I had to take a second-class bus one thousand miles. It must have made at least five hundred monotonous stops.

I stayed several days in Catemaco, a small town near the Gulf of Mexico. There was an old theater—it had no seats so we sat on the cement floor—but it showed good American movies. I saw Burt Lancaster in *Brute Force,* and Jane Fonda in *Klute.* Sometimes the projectionist got the reels confused. The film would start with reel 2, go to reel 3, and then back to reel 1, but no one in the audience complained.

There was a beautiful lake in Catemaco. Every morning the fishermen went out in their boats and cast their nets. Again and again they tossed their nets, pulled them in, gathered the fish, and tossed the nets again. The catch was always small.

In the center of the lake was an island. In the afternoon I asked one of the Indian fisherman if I could rent a boat to get there.

"No, the boats aren't for rent, but I'll take you there," he said.

"How much is it?" I asked.

"I'll take you there for nothing," he said cheerfully.

I climbed into his boat and he shoved off from the shore. There was a stiff breeze, but he was a good oarsman so we made fast time.

The island was uninhabited; there were no houses or shacks and the vegetation was dense. I climbed the hill at the center of the island. At the summit there was a small clearing and a field with flowers. The sun was directly overhead, but partially covered by clouds. I could see the entire lake, the fishing boats on the shore, the nets hung up to dry. It was peaceful, quiet, serene. I felt in harmony with myself and the world around me, but not for long. The sky grew darker and it looked like a storm was coming. I became nervous, edgy; perhaps the fisherman would leave the island without me. Then how would I get back? So I walked down the hill and toward the inlet. The man was sitting on a rock, repairing his fishing net.

"Can we head back," I said.

"What's the rush?" he asked.

"I'd like to go now before the storm."

"Well, then you'll have to pay ten pesos," the fisherman said.

"I thought it was free," I shouted, annoyed.

"Free? What is there free in life? Tell me! It's hard rowing my boat and you want me to work for nothing. You gringos are all alike!"

"I'll pay, I'll pay," I said apologetically. I reached into my pocket and handed him a ten-peso note. "Why don't you let me row back," I suggested. "I don't mind."

"But then I'll have to return the ten pesos," the fisherman said.

"No, you can keep the ten pesos, but I'll row anyway," I said. "I'd like the exercise."

"Exercise! Is that what you'd like? You pay *me* and you want to row? Both? Impossible. No! No! You can't make fun of me like that."

"I'm sorry," I said. "I didn't mean to hurt your feelings." The fisherman rolled up his trousers, waded into the water, and shoved the boat into the current. We sat silently, neither of us looking at the other, both of us watching the clouds. I was annoyed; the fisherman seemed to be exhausted. Then, in the middle of the lake, his mood changed. As the sky got darker and darker he got giddier and giddier. Finally, he was laughing so hard he couldn't row the boat. One of the oars slipped away and he reached into the water to grab it. But a gust of wind carried across the lake and the oar was soon out of reach. The air was brisk and the waves were choppy. The sky was purple now and rain clouds raced toward the boat. First one, then a second and a third wave crashed over the bow. We were tipping precariously; the fisherman moved to the center of the boat to reestablish our balance and for a moment it seemed that we would ride the storm. I could feel myself stepping onto dry land again. But the elusive oar was still floating on the water. The fisherman made another lunge for it, and almost had it. Unaware of what he was doing I reached for the oar at the same time, and that was too much motion. The boat tilted dangerously on its side. The wind whipped us around, and then a large wave finished us. The boat turned upside down, and I was drenched. I was afraid that the fishman would murder me; he reached out his hand and pulled me violently into the boat. "Hold on," he said, the white spray striking his face and mine. And then he started to laugh again. He was delirious.

"You'd better laugh," he said, with more than a touch of menace in his voice. "You've paid for this, *gringo.*" The fisherman had touched the right nerve. The thought of the money made me relax, and I started to laugh. We held onto the boat, shivering, ducking the waves and laughing.

35

Mexico City had been invaded by ten thousand women. They had come from all over the world, but mostly from California, to attend the events of International Women's Year. There were two separate gatherings: one official, the other unofficial. The official gathering was headed by a man—the Mexican Attorney General—and was addressed by such notables as the Empress of Iran.

I went to the unofficial gathering to hear Laura Allende talk about the Chilean dictatorship, the torture and the concentration camps. "Men and women must work together to defeat fascism on our continent," she said. "Or else we will all be defeated by it."

In the lobby I met Cocoa. At first I didn't recognize her. She wasn't wearing braids or a long dress. Her hair was cut short, and she was wearing shoes. Moreover, she wasn't calling herself Cocoa but Peggy.

"I've been in a woman's group all morning," she said. "We looked at our own cervixes." Peggy reached for her handbag and pulled out a plastic speculum and a small mirror. "It's so exciting. I never knew I had a cervix before."

"Have you heard from Lafcadio?" I asked.

"He's in Peru," Peggy said, uninterested.

"What's he doing?"

"Living with an Indian tribe," Peggy said. "He's a hopeless case. I don't mind if I never see Lafcadio again."

Mary Belfridge was also attending the sessions, but not Mrs. Yampolsky or Rosa Elena and not their daughters either. Mrs. Yampolsky wanted to go, was excited by the meeting, but she had been confined to bed with a bad cold, and was taking Dr. Perralta's medicine. She listened to television and radio broadcasts of the events, and read the newspaper accounts, but that wasn't the same as attending, because the Mexican government was censoring the media coverage of International Women's Year.

At the United Nations the Mexican government wanted to appear enlightened on the subject of women's liberation, but at home it didn't want women's liberation to become a reality. That would be too uncomfortable. The police had even prevented Mexican women from attending events at the unofficial session. The excluded women were joined on a picket line by women from all over the world. They demanded that the sessions be open to everyone.

It was one of the few moments of unity. Otherwise, there was continual disagreement between the women of color and the women of the white world, between the women of the capitalist nations and the women of the socialist nations, between the "official" and the "unofficial" women. The Mexican government came out on top. It kept each group divided, censored the news, and publicized itself as the glorious defender of women's liberation.

Most of the Mexican women I knew didn't want to attend the meetings. Maybe they wanted to go, but their husbands wouldn't allow them. Rosa Elena was curious, but too preoccupied with a Swedish television crew that was doing a special program on B. Traven. For a few days we rehearsed what she was going to say, and what she would show the interviewer. Then, with the camera rolling, she stood in the backyard, next to the bust of "my late husband" and droned on and on about how the Indians had loved him and how he had loved the Indians. She had said it a dozen times before and she would say it again, but the television crew loved it. "Now, if we could only get Hollywood to make a film about Traven," Rosa Elena said. "We wouldn't have to have very much money. His ideas and his values are what we want to communicate."

Chele was helping to organize a demonstration against Franco. Spain was in turmoil again and she felt that it was the strategic moment to concentrate political efforts to weaken the dictatorship. Malu was preoccupied with an Arab oil minister who was in Mexico to negotiate terms of international trade. She took him to lunch, introduced him to friends, made his stay comfortable. "He's invited me to go to Saudi Arabia," she told us at lunch. "Maybe I should divorce Miguel. What do you think, mother?" Rosa Elena hardly listened. Malu talked about divorce every other day. "Do whatever you want," Rosa Elena said.

Chele argued that women's liberation was divisive. "Perhaps it's appropriate for New York or Paris, but not here," she said. "We can't tell the peasant woman from Chiapas that she's oppressed by her husband, that she ought to burn her bra and live with her sisters. We all have to work together to end oppression, don't you think so?"

"I was thinking what Traven would be thinking," I said. "He'd probably say that we're all divided against one another. We're all making war on each other, and yet we're all part of the same family. I don't want to belong to any group, any organization. I only want power over my own life."

"Sounds like you've become an anarchist," Chele said.

"I'm just me," I said.

"You've become spiritual too," Chele said.

"Spiritual? Have I? I suppose so. You can't live and travel in Chiapas among the Indians and not feel spiritual," I said.

"What about the exploited and the oppressed?" Chele asked.

"What about them? You know I'll be marching side by side with you against Franco and against any other dictator, big or small, you name him—but no slogans or banners and no party rules, please."

"You really have adopted Traven's ideas," Chele said.

"Well, I dressed like him, wore his clothes, his glasses, dreamed I was him, hallucinated I was him, saw him on buses, so I guess I could learn from him too. But I won't let him be my god or my hero. He's no saint. He's your step-father, a strange, funny old man. The Funny Man. Sometimes I just can't help but laugh at him."

36

I climbed the steps, unlocked the door, and opened the blinds.
The room was still dusty. The clock read 5:40, the calendar
March 1969. I looked at the death mask again; the face looked
like dry mud and the teeth appeared to be rotting.

I sat down on the edge of the bed and listened to the roar of
the cars, and I thought of B. Traven's last moments, wondered
what he was thinking, what images haunted him, what shapes
appeared on that last stage. His imagination must have been
on fire, his mind like Macario's evading the Bone Man with
tricks, disguises, and never-ending stories. He must have been
planning new ways to fool us, con us, lie to us.

His own death he surely made into a fantastic drama to
entertain himself, but unfortunately never had the time,
energy, or life to put it down on paper for us to read. Probably
didn't want to share it with us, wanted to enjoy it himself. He
alone saw the last act, without Rosa Elena, Malu, or Chele. So
Traven's death, like his birth, had the elements of mystery.
There was no last word, no final message uttered before he
breathed his last—and appropriately so. Hadn't Ret Marut
written in his "Death Song" in March 1918:

No one has yet understood or heard the last word of
a dying man. . .Guard yourself against people whom

240

you hope to hear their last word. They can reject, with one last syllable, their entire experience of life, and you stand there helplessly. The last word of a dying man is less important than that of a man who is senselessly drunk.

I wanted to tear the old calendar from the wall, wind the clock and adjust the hands. That's what Marut would have wanted me to do, eradicate all facts about his death, destroy the records of time and place, and thereby make his death symmetrical with his birth.

Oh, what a colossal error Rosa Elena had made! If I had been with Traven when he died I would never have told friends and family the time and place. I'd have created a mystery about his death. But Rosa Elena had insisted on the hard facts, 5:40, March 26, 1969, the tyrannies of time and place that all his life he had tried to escape. Traven insisted that we love the living. Rosa Elena was in love with the image of the dead. Maybe it was her way of getting back at him. Surely B. Traven would have wanted the clock to go on ticking. Surely he knew that time would continue to tick after death. To stop the clock at 5:40 was to indulge the grandest of illusions. Who cares that he died at 5:40!

Now, the house on the Rio Mississippi seemed like a mausoleum, and Rosa Elena was the keeper of the tomb. She encouraged me to begin writing the biography. "You know enough, and what you don't know I'll fill in," she said. I certainly knew more now than when I started, but I knew too much and too little. While I was traveling in Chiapas, Heidemann returned by mail Traven's manuscript *Art of the Indians* that he had taken from Rosa Elena. There were hundreds of sketches of people and places in Mexico. Traven wasn't a great artist, but his sense of color was exciting, and his portraits were sensitive.

In addition, Traven's dossiers arrived from the States. I got a kick out of his FBI files. One agent had written: "The name 'B. Traven' is a pseudonym which has been utilized over a period of years by an individual whose true identity has not been publicly revealed." Another agent noted, "B. Traven is an author resident in Mexico for many years and wrote *The Treasure of the Sierra Madre,* which later was made into a prize-winning movie. An air of mystery surrounds his identity." B. Traven would have been delighted to know that the FBI hadn't solved the mystery. And if J. Edgar Hoover couldn't, who could?

The State Department files were especially interesting. They showed that early in 1917, when the United States declared war on Germany, Ret Marut went to several American consulates in Europe, claimed that he was a United States citizen, and demanded a passport. His application was denied again and again. For example, the American Charge d'Affaires in Holland noted on April 23, 1917 that Ret Marut:

> alleges that he was born at San Francisco, California, on February 25, 1882, and has been residing in France, Spain and Germany since 1901. Mr. Marut states that his reasons for his protracted foreign residence are as follows: "Travelling in Europe and the study of philosophy and political economy."

The State Department papers "prove" that *The Death Ship* is based on Marut/Traven's own experiences. Gales's encounters with the American consulates that are described in the first part of the book are directly inspired by Marut's experiences. There was more information. On January 11, 1924, the American consul general in London wired the Secretary of State in Washington:

> I have the honor to report that I have received information from the Home Office to the effect that one Ret Marut was convicted at the Thames Police Court on December 17th of an offense against the Aliens' Order and was recommended for deportation. This man claims to be an American citizen and

holds a document issued by the German police at Munich wherein it is stated that he was born at San Francisco on February 25, 1882.

I wrote to the Home Office in Whitehall, London, and received more information:

An alien named Ret and Rex Marut, alias Albert Otto Wienecke, or Adolf Rudolf Feige or Barker or Arnolds, was convicted at Thames Magistrates' Court on 17 December, 1923 of failing to register with the police, an offence under Article (18) (1) (a) of the Aliens Order 1920 (Statutory Rules and Orders 1920, No. 448), and the Court recommended the S of S to make a deportation order. A deportation order was made on 28 December 1923 but extant records do not show whether the order was executed. Marut left the United Kingdom in 1924, apparently as a member of a ship's crew (a fireman) but records do not show what ship he sailed on or its destination. We have no further record of Marut's movements and the deportation order was revoked in 1949.*

More mystery. Mystery upon mystery. Why was he using four

---

*In 1977 I made this material available to Will Wyatt, Executive Producer for BBC Television. Mr. Wyatt's investigative team delved further. In a program aired in London on December 19, 1978, and entitled *B. Traven: A Mystery Solved,* the BBC claimed that Traven's true identity was "Albert Otto Maksymilian Feige, the son of a brickmaker from Swiebodzin" (in the 1880s a German, but today a Polish, village). The BBC also claimed that they had found Traven's brother and sister, Ernst, 83, and Margareta, 86. They showed them a photo of Traven taken on the set of *The Treasure of the Sierra Madre,* and Ernst and Margareta said, "Yes, that's him."

In my view, the BBC program deepens rather than solves the mystery. I believe that Marut was using the names Wienecke and Feige while in England in 1923 and 1924, but it seems unlikely that they were his "real names." Why should Marut have told the truth to the London police after lying to police officials all across Europe? The BBC doesn't say.

It seems unlikely that Ernst and Margareta would recognize their "brother" from a photo taken in 1946, and after they had not seen him in more than sixty years. In my search for Traven I found that there were too many people who were too anxious different aliases, in addition to Marut? The names Wienecke and Feige suggested that he was trying to pass for German, the names Barker and Arnolds that he was trying to pass for English. And what of Rex? Could he really have been calling himself Rex Marut? King Marut? Why the phrase "extant records"? Were some records lost or destroyed, and why was the deportation order revoked in 1949, twenty-five years later? Mystery upon mystery! If only I knew the name of the ship he sailed on and its destination! What could be more mysterious than an unknown ship with an unknown destination. For a few days I suspected the Home Office of complicity in the mystery. Surely they really knew the name of the ship and the destination—but didn't want to tell us? The Home Office was perpetuating the mystery of B. Traven.

Collecting evidence, building my own dossier on Traven made me feel good. I had "proven" that he actually was a fireman who had shoveled coal aboard a steamer. So Gales's adventures aboard the *Yorikke* were autobiographical. I thought of myself as a detective uncovering clues, interviewing suspects, interrogating the books. I would overturn words, inspect sentences, find the hidden doors. I would solve the crime.

Yet this work was also sadly limiting. Now I knew that Marut was a fireman, that Traven based *The Death Ship* on his own experience. So what! Traven had long insisted that his books were autobiographical, that he hadn't "invented" situ-

---

to say that they had known him, that they recognized him. Almost everyone I met wanted to contribute to the Traven mystery, and to become a part of it.

Even if it is true that Traven was born Albert Otto Maksymilian Feige, it does not explain how or why he was so mysterious about his identity, where he obtained his large sums of money, why he took the name Ret Marut, when and where he learned English, how he became an actor, an anarchist, a pacifist. The BBC program does not explain Traven's preoccupation with princes and paupers, with rags and riches. But it is a fitting addition to the Traven mythology. We now have B. Traven the son of the Kaiser, and B. Traven the son of the town brickmaker. It's a perfect twist to the mystery, but the end of the mystery it's not.

What most recommends this hypothesis, in my view, is that Marut called his magazine *The Brickburner*. It may be only a symbolic coincidence, and yet it may also be a definite link from father to son. One further hypothesis: is it not possible that Marut/Traven was an illegitimate child of an aristocratic German who was given to a poor brickmaker to raise? Then, indeed, Traven could be both prince and pauper.

ations. He was telling the truth. But what was infuriating was that he didn't tell the truth about everything; he didn't tell the whole truth and nothing but the truth. I kept hoping that the one decisive clue would come to light, that the jigsaw puzzle would be complete and the picture would become clear. At the same time I knew that there would always be an unsolved riddle about B. Traven. Even if we knew when and where Traven was born there would still be a mystery. There was too much conflicting evidence.

I told Rosa Elena that I couldn't, wouldn't write the biography of B. Traven. There were too many unknown facts, too many contradictions. How could I write the biography when Rosa Elena herself had piled mystery upon mystery? I suspect that B. Traven knew that she would generate more mystery after his death. And yet Rosa Elena insisted that I write a biography. What I didn't *know* she would "fill in," as she put it. She taunted me with insinuations of impotence and homosexuality. "You will never write again," she said. "It must be very tormenting that you are unable to express your trauma. But I understand. I know what it is like. Perhaps Traven will haunt you the way the Kaiser haunted him."

I continued to work on the Rio Mississippi. On the third floor there were more papers to read. After some hesitation Rosa Elena showed me the letters Traven had written to her in March, April, and May 1955—at a critical period in their relationship. They were at a crossroads. Either the affair had to end immediately, or they would go on living together until the end, his end. Rosa Elena was frightened; Traven was pressing hard for marriage. Rosa Elena wanted to remain single; she had just divorced Carlos Montes de Oca. But Chele pleaded with her to marry "Mr. Croves."

"He feels so very, very lonely," Traven wrote of himself on March 2, 1955. "It seems to be his destiny, or part of his destiny, to feel always lonely and be always lonely. This has been the cause of his many mis-elations in his life, his many mistakes he did and which could have been avoided had he in good time met somebody in whose presence he would not feel so terribly alone." How could Rosa Elena resist? Traven continued his love letters. At the end of April he wrote Rosa Elena again:

> You will become so important you will have to ask permission to speak [to] yourself. . .Esperanza always was only a translator and a very limited representative. You will be far more than just a translator. Haven't I told you that you'll get the biggest surprise of your life once you learn what I did.

Rosa Elena was seduced by the power of mystery. She agreed to marry the man who loved mystery. On May 9, 1955, Traven wrote again:

> I wonder why T[raven]. never thought of writing his memoirs. But he would not be T. if he ever did.

When I showed this letter to Rosa Elena and suggested that I couldn't write a biography just as Traven couldn't write his memoirs, Rosa Elena became nervous.

"I don't know, maybe you're right," she said. "Maybe you'll betray him and what he stood for if you write his biography. I just don't know any more." Rosa Elena suggested another tack. She showed me a notebook Traven kept in 1948. There were dozens of ideas for short stories and novels. Rosa Elena thought that I should take Traven's ideas, develop them into stories, and sell them to magazines under Traven's name *and* mine. Several stories tempted me:

> Six doctors meet in a little village to die there because they don't wish to die where they were known to be great. One cures the other.

> U.S. G.I. killed in action. Cannot be buried in Texas because of his Mexican origin. The corpse goes hitch-hiking.

Story of the man who when down on his heels was
helped by a well-to-do citizen and brought back to
good standing. The man thus helped slowly cultivated a terrific hatred against his benefactor until
he no longer could bear it and so killed him. After
this he felt happy and happily went to the chair.

Let the man who loves the jungle be a Don Quixote.
He sees all things in an unnatural blurred way. Lives
forever under the illusion of what he thinks the
jungle life has to be but is not. Cannot get away from
that illusion. Leads him to all kinds of trouble in life.
Writes the most fantastic jungle adventures liked by
the public, all untrue.

Could B. Traven have been thinking of himself? Vitorino had
called him Quixote. Maybe he did identify with Cervantes's
knight. Traven had written "fantastic jungle adventures"—
but surely they were true. Weren't they documentary records?
Untrue? No, that couldn't be! And yet I suspect that he was
describing himself, that he did realize, at last, that he did have
romantic illusions about jungle life.

I locked the door on the third floor and walked downstairs.
Rosa Elena was in the library talking to an American professor who wanted to write a book about B. Traven. She was
describing Traven's life with the Indians in the jungles of
Chiapas.

"Mrs. Luján has told me that you're writing a biography of
Traven," the professor said. "I guess that I'll bow out of the
picture gracefully."

"Go ahead with your book," I said. "I don't want to stop
you because I'm not writing the biography."

"Then you haven't solved the mystery?" the professor
asked, his face brightening.

"Oh, no, you've got me all wrong," I said. "The mystery,
the mystery, it's really quite simple. You'll see. You'll find out
after a while. It all fits together. It's really quite a mystery."

I embraced mystery, I wrapped myself in its folds, but not as an evasion. My search for Traven had taught me above all to appreciate, to revere, the power of mystery. Mystery expressed my sense of life—its beauty and strangeness. It conveyed my feeling that the universe was always in flux, always changing, yielding surprises, and was never finally or completely knowable. We stood in the light of mystery that quickly shaded into the mysterious darkness.

Mystery expressed the sacredness of life, a spiritual joy that connected me to the universe, to all creation, past present future, to Traven, and to the Indians of Chiapas. We were one and we were whole, even in the moment of disunity and chaos.

Mystery was fear but it was also laughter. It was a prank, a clown's mask, a disguise, a way to mock destiny and escape fate for at least a short time.

Mystery was defiance. It was a rejection of bureaucracy, the State, the power of money and all alien forces that would rob us of our identity and destroy the integrity of the individual. Mystery preserved our freedom in a world of tyranny. It elevated us, conferred upon us a touch of divinity, but at the same time mystery bound us in the rags of our commonality.

I embraced mystery because it gave me energy, renewed my faith, and yet it sobered me, taught me my frailties and my limitations. Mystery connected me to power and paradoxically made me feel powerless.

Mystery was reverence and revolution, permanence and change. It was birth and death, beginning and end, resurrection and rebirth. Traven cultivated the fields of mystery because he was a rebel and a priest, a comedian and a magician. It is his great gift to us, the incorruptible treasure we find in his books.

A NOTE ON
BIBLIOGRAPHY

In 1952, eight years before *Aslan Norval* his last novel ap-.
peared, Traven suggested that the "correct order to publish"
his books was: *The Death Ship, The Cotton Pickers, The Treasure
of the Sierra Madre, The Night Visitor, The Bridge in the Jungle, The
White Rose, The Carreta, Government, Trozas, March to the Monteria, The Rebellion of the Hanged, The General from the Jungle,* and
Macario.

With the exception of *Trozas* these books are all available in
English. While they can certainly be read out of this sequence,
and while each stands on its own, Traven's list is helpful. The
books form one single continuous work. By starting with *The
Death Ship,* and moving through the six Jungle Novels to
Macario, readers can follow the recurring themes of death and
resurrection, paradise and hell, rags and riches, and watch
Traven's own journey from Europe to America, Old World to
New World, from the fraternity of exiles and outcasts to the
family of uprooted Indian peasants and guerrillas.

"My novels are autobiographical," Traven told the editors
at the Gutenberg Book Guild. Reading the books in sequence
one can appreciate the truth of that remark.